D0209744

Constructing School Success

CONSTRUCTING SCHOOL SUCCESS

The Consequences of Untracking Low-Achieving Students

Hugh Mehan   Irene Villanueva
Lea Hubbard   Angela Lintz

University of California, San Diego

with Dina Okamoto and James Adams

CAMBRIDGE
UNIVERSITY PRESS

Published by the Press Syndicate of the University of Cambridge
The Pitt Building, Trumpington Street, Cambridge CB2 1RP
40 West 20th Street, New York, NY 10011-4211, USA
10 Stamford Road, Oakleigh, Melbourne 3166, Australia

First published 1996

Printed in the United States of America

Library of Congress Cataloging-in-Publication Data
Constructing school success : the consequences of untracking low-
achieving students / Hugh Mehan . . . et al.].
p.   cm.
Includes bibliographical references and index.
ISBN 0-521-56076-4 (hardcover). – ISBN 0-521-56826-9 (pbk.)
1. Ability grouping in education – United States. 2. Slow learning
children – Education – United States. 3. Academic achievement – United
States. 4. Track system (Education) – United States.
5. Articulation (Education) – United States. 6. Educational change –
United States. I. Mehan, Hugh, 1941–
LB3061.S316   1996
371.2'5'0973 – dc20   95-36205
                                                                      CIP

A catalog record for this book is available from the British Library.

ISBN 0-521-56076-4 Hardback
ISBN 0-521-56826-9 Paperback

CONTENTS

FIGURES AND TABLES

FIGURES

TABLES

ACKNOWLEDGMENTS

THIS RESEARCH WAS FUNDED BY A GRANT FROM THE LIN-
guistic Minority Research Institute of the University of California
and the Office of Educational Research and Improvement of the
U.S. Department of Education. We appreciate the financial and intellectual support of our colleagues of LMRI and OERI. Our thanks
to the San Diego City Schools, especially John Griffith and Peter
Bell, for encouraging this research. We especially appreciate the
support and assistance of Mary Catherine Swanson, Kathy Deering,
and Ron Ottinger of AVID Center at the San Diego County Office of
Education and the cooperation of the teachers, principals, parents,
and students at Bay Meadows, Churchill, Golden Gate, Keeneland,
Monrovia, Nassau, Pimlico, and Saratoga High Schools. Claude
Goldenberg, Ronald Gallimore, Annette Lareau, Nick Maroules,
Richard J. Shavelson, and Randall Souviney gave us helpful advice
on earlier drafts. Daryl Stermon gave us invaluable statistical ser-
vice. Elizabeth Bratton, Amanda Datnow, Diane Friedlaender, and
Claudia Tellez ably conducted observations at school sites.

1

INTRODUCTION

I am the youngest of a family of three – my mother and one sister twenty-two years older than I. My sister never lived with us. My mother, being a single parent, and working two jobs just to keep a roof over us, had little or no time to spend with me. I remember feeling an extreme sense of insecurity as I was growing up. Later, my mother remarried a wonderful man who I would grow to love and respect. He filled my life with all the love and warmth of a family.

After eight years of having a secure family, the effects of my parents' separation nearly destroyed my life. The world of love and security which they had built came tumbling down. I remembered in years back how it had felt to be homeless and I was terrified. I kept asking my mother, "Where are we going to live?"

All those feelings of insecurity and loneliness I had felt while growing up slowly started to come back. I then started eating large amounts of food. Although I did not know it at the time, my struggle with bulimia had begun. At fifteen my life was a disaster, and my grades during that time reflect it. My next regrettable move was dropping out of school. My mother, being too preoccupied with her problems, found it difficult to deal with mine. The strong sense of belonging to someone or something led me to associate with a bad group of people, which in turn resulted in my short stay at Juvenile Hall. My mother then decided we were going to move from Sacramento to San Diego.

Things slowly started changing when we moved. I enrolled at Saratoga for the second semester of my tenth-grade. With the fresh start God had given me, I was determined to change my life and put all my energy in school. My GPA when I began at Saratoga was a 1.3. Now with the help of AVID (a program designed to help students have a greater chance of going on to college) it is a 3.7. I am taking two AP classes which I had never dreamed possible. I know the joy of learning and the sense of accomplishment that comes with doing the best I can. Learning beyond the book has been one of the most rewarding experiences in my high school career. One of my philosophies is if at first you don't succeed, keep trying until you do, which is one of the reasons I have taken the ACT once and the SAT twice. One of the most important things I've learned is how to manage my time more wisely. Knowing that to be accepted into a prestigious college I would need to improve my previous grades, I decided to take two classes in summer school, and to keep my two jobs.

Two things I enjoy doing when I'm not in school or working are volunteering to work with inner-city kids and working at "Casa de Cuna" (House of the Crib). The inner-city kids are at high risk of dropping out of school. I personally try to instill in them the belief that higher levels of education can be their ticket to success and that in turn will be the road out of the ghetto. "Casa de Cuna" is a Catholic orphanage in Mexico, a project I became involved with shortly after I arrived at Saratoga. Each student that is involved does his or her part in raising money, helping out with garage sales, car washes, and helping out with the cleanup of the orphanage. I am also an officer of "Los Hispanos Unidos" (United Hispanics), a club at Saratoga. The goal of this club is to raise the percentage of Hispanic students graduating from Saratoga, and also to have a higher number of those who graduate go on to college.

I plan to apply the strength and determination that have enabled me to be successful in high school throughout my college career. My battle with bulimia, growing up in a dysfunctional family, and working with children who have no family at all played a key role in my decision to pursue psychology as a major. My family's education has never extended beyond elementary school. I plan to change that if I am given the opportunity.

THE LIFE HISTORY TOLD BY LILIA ORTIZ IN HER COLLEGE application essay is gripping. Here we have a young Latina who grew up in a single-parent family, suffered the pain of her parents' divorce, had bulimia, and served time in Juvenile Hall. She is presently living in a mobile home park with her mother, who speaks only Spanish. Given the severity of these circumstances, we might expect that she is destined for a miserable life. Although her mother supported Lilia's college plans, she didn't know the details about required courses and tests, application forms and deadlines, scholarship possibilities and procedures. Lilia acquired vital information about colleges and established an academic record sufficient to be accepted with a Martin Luther King, Jr., Scholarship at the University of California, Santa Barbara, and San Diego State University.

By all accounts, Lilia is academically successful, at least to this point. This story runs counter to the trends being reported nationally – that Latino students are not successful in high school, they are dropping out in record numbers, they are not enrolling in college. But this story is not unusual for the Latino and African American students who are completing an "untracking" program called "Advancement Via Individual Determination" (better known by its acronym, AVID) in San Diego, California. The AVID approach to untracking places previously low-achieving students (who are primarily from low-income and ethnic or linguistic minority backgrounds) in the same "college prep" academic program as high-achieving students (who are primarily from middle- or upper-middle-income and "majority" backgrounds).

THE ROLE OF TRACKING IN EDUCATIONAL ACHIEVEMENT

Untracking stands in stark contrast to prevailing educational policy concerning the education of students. Historically, educators in the United States have responded to differences among individuals and groups by separating students and altering the content of the curriculum to which they are exposed. Since the 1920s, most high schools have offered a "tracked" curriculum – sequences of academic classes that range from slow-paced remedial courses to rigorous academic ones.

The Rationale for Tracking: Matching Talent to Jobs

Tracking starts as early as elementary school. Students who have similar skills are placed in small working groups, often called "ability groups," for the purposes of instruction. Students who have less measured ability are placed in low-ability groups. Students with greater amounts of measured ability are placed into high-ability groups. The curriculum in low-ability groups is reduced in scope, content, and pace relative to high-ability group classes. Often an informal arrangement in elementary school, tracking becomes institutionalized in middle schools and high schools. Students who have been assigned to the "college prep" track receive a distinct curriculum and are separated from students who have been assigned to the "vocational" track.

Tracking rests on assumptions about the nature of the occupational structure and the role of schooling in an industrial society. Tracking was justified at the height of industrialization because it supported a long-standing belief in the United States and Great Britain that a crucial function of schools is to prepare students for jobs (Davis & Moore, 1945). The industrial revolution divided labor into jobs and occupations that require different kinds of skills. As a result, workers who have different kinds of knowledge were needed to fill those different kinds of jobs. The function of the school was to serve as a rational sorting device, matching students' talents to the demands of the workplace (Turner, 1960). Thus, rigorous academic classes could prepare students heading for jobs that require college degrees, whereas vocational programs could prepare students for less skilled jobs or for technical training after high school.

Tracking students for different work lives was thought to be fair because students were thought to possess different intellectual abil-

4

ities, motivations, and aspirations and jobs demand different skills and talents. Thus, a tracked curriculum with its ability-grouped classes was viewed as both functional and democratic. Tracking was functional because it matches students to the appropriate slots in the work force, thereby providing the nation with the range of workers it needs. Tracking was democratric because schools sort students based on their talent, effort, and hard work, thereby providing students with the education that best meets their abilities (Davis & Moore, 1945; Parsons, 1959; Turner, 1960)

The Critique of Tracking: Neither Functional nor Democratic

Recent research and public commentary have shown that the schools' practice of tracking does not fulfill either of its promises. It neither provides students with equal educational opportunities nor serves the needs of employers for a well-educated albeit compliant work force. Students from low-income and ethnic or linguistic minority backgrounds are disproportionately represented in low-track classes and they seldom move up to high-track classes. Students placed in low-track classes seldom receive the educational resources that are equivalent to students who are placed in high-track classes. They often suffer the stigmatizing consequences of negative labeling. They are not prepared well for the workplace.

Accounts of the *differential distribution* of students to ability groups and tracks have been summarized comprehensively by Oakes, Gamoran, and Page (1992). The distribution of students to high-, middle-, and low-ability groups or academic and general tracks seems to be related to ethnicity and socioeconomic status. Children from low-income or one-parent households, or from families with an unemployed worker, or from linguistic and ethnic minority groups, are more liklely to be assigned to low-ability groups or tracks. Furthermore, ethnic and linguistic minority students are consistently underrepresented in programs for the "gifted and talented."

The relationship between students' background factors and track placement is exacerbated by organizational arrangements. Students tend to go to neighborhood schools. Even though high schools in the United States and Great Britain offer comprehensive programs, these schools differ in the curricular opportunities they offer students. Schools serving predominantly poor and minority students offer fewer advanced and more remedial courses in academic subjects than schools serving more affluent and majority students. Even in comprehensive high schools designed to bring students from different backgrounds together under one roof, researchers have found a strong relationship between socioeconomic background, ethnicity, and educational opportunity. The relationships are both simple and direct. The greater the percentage of minorities, the larger the low-track program; the poorer the students, the less rigorous the college prep program (Oakes et al., 1992).

Researchers also report *differential treatment* of students once they have been placed in different tracks. Within elementary school classrooms, ability groups are taught by the same teacher, but they do not receive the same instruction. Low-ability groups are taught less frequently and are subjected to more control by the teacher (McDermott, Godspodinoff, & Aron, 1978; Wilcox, 1982; Collins, 1986). Students in low-ability reading groups spend more reading time on decoding activities, whereas students in high-ability groups spend more time on text comprehension and deriving the meaning of stories. High-group students do more silent reading and, when reading aloud, are less often interrupted (Allington, 1980; Eder, 1981). High-ability groups progress farther in the curriculum over the course of a school year, and this advantage can accumulate over the years. As a result, students with a sustained membership in high-ability groups are likely to have covered considerably more material by the end of elementary school.

In secondary schools, low-track classes consistently offer less exposure to less demanding topics whereas high-track classes typically include more complex material. Lower-track students take fewer math and science courses, and these courses are less demanding. Students in non–college prep curricula take fewer honors or advanced courses. Students in the academic track take three to five times as many advanced courses in math and science (Gamoran, 1987). Students in nonacademic tracks take more courses in the arts and vocational subjects because they have more room in their schedule for elective courses.

Teachers set different goals for students in different groups and tracks. High-group, high-track teachers more often state that they want their students to be competent and autonomous thinkers. In contrast, teachers of low-track classes more often emphasize basic literacy and computation skills and present topics commonly associated with everyday life and work (Gamoran, 1987).

In addition to gaining differential access to curriculum and instruction, students in different tracks get different kinds of teachers. Some schools allow teachers to choose their teaching assignments based on seniority, whereas other schools rotate the teaching of low- and high-ability classes among teachers. In either case, it is not uncommon for class assignments to be used as a reward for teachers judged to be more powerful or successful and as a sanction against teachers judged to be weaker or undeserving. Many teachers covet high-track classes because they find students in these classes more willing to participate in academic work and they pose fewer disciplinary problems. Whether schools assign teachers or teachers choose their assignments, students in low-income and minority neighborhoods are more likely to get less experienced teachers than students in more affluent neighborhoods. For example, teachers of low-track classes at the secondary level in math and science are consistently less experienced, are less likely to be certified in math or science, hold fewer degrees in these subjects, have less training in the use of computers, and are less likely to think of themselves as master teachers (Oakes et al., 1992). A vicious cycle for low tracks is the result. Repeated assignment to the bottom of the school's status hierarchy may demoralize teachers, reducing their competency, which in turn may give students who have the greatest need for the best teachers the least qualified teachers.

Perhaps the most damaging criticism of tracking is that it takes on a castelike character. Once students are placed into low-ability groups, they seldom are promoted to high groups. Ability group membership in elementary school carries into track membership in high school. Students placed in low-ability groups in elementary school are more likely to be placed in general and vocational tracks in high school, wheras students placed in high-ability groups in elementary school are more likely to be placed in college prep tracks in high school. Placement in vocational and nonacademic classes can trap ethnic and linguistic minority students despite their good achievement in school, as this biographical sketch of a Latina high school student illustrates:

> My first day signing up for high school . . . my Dad had been working in the fields, but he came home early this day to take me so I could get registered. . . . there was a counselor . . . and I took my eighth grade diploma which was straight As, and I was valedictorian of my eighth grade . . . and I told him I would like to go to college and could he fit me into college prep classes? And he looked at my grades and everything, and said, well, he wasn't sure I could handle it. My dad didn't understand. He was there with me. And this counselor put me in non–college prep classes. I remember going home and feeling just terrible. (Gándara, 1995: 73–74)

In a word, then, tracking is undemocratic. Although originally justified because schools presumably sorted students on the basis of achievement and not ascription, tracking has carried a racical, ethnic, and social class bias from its inception. At the turn of the past century, low-level academics and vocational training were thought to be more appropriate for immigrant, low-income, and minority youth, whereas rigorous academic preparation was seen as better meeting the needs of more affluent whites.

At the turn of this century, proponents say that tracking is necessary because many students, especially those from low-income linguistic and ethnic minority backgrounds, come to school ill prepared for rigorous academic work and would be better served by a program that prepares them for jobs as soon as they finish high school. But when students are tracked on the basis of class, race, and ethnicity and not on the basis of individual effort and achievement, students in tracked schools are denied equal access to educational and occupational opportunity.

Not only is tracking undemocratic, it is not functional. It has not accomplished its job of matching the talent of the students with the demands of the workplace. Starting with the critique of American schools contained in *A Nation at Risk,* a steady stream of employers, policy makers, national opinion leaders, and educators has expressed dissatisfaction with students' knowledge, skills, and attitudes. The following comments are typical of the complaints that were lodged against America's public schools by business leaders and policy makers in the 1980s:

> We have created an economy that seeks literate, technically trained and committed workers, while simultaneously we produce many young men and women who are semi-literate or functionally illiterate, unable to think critically and untrained in technical skills. (Carnegie Council on Adolescent Development, 1989: 1)

> More than half of our young people leave school without the knowledge or foundation to find and hold a good job. (U.S. Department of Labor's Secretary's Commission on Achieving Necessary Skills, 1992: 1)

> Telephone sales jobs are going begging in Boston because MCI cannot find qualified workers; textile workers are no longer able to operate their computerized machines; and aircraft manufacturers in California have teamed up out of necessity to train employees. Companies such as New York Telephone report hiring frustrations of epic proportions – 57,000 applicants had to be tested to find 2,100 who were qualified to find entry level technical jobs.
>
> The cry from America's boardrooms, education think tanks and government officials is two-fold: America's workers are ill-equipped to meet employers' current needs and ill-prepared for the rapidly approaching high technology, service oriented future. (Commission on the Skills of the American Workforce, 1990: 23)

As the comments from the commission report just quoted show, changes in the nature of work itself contribute to dissatisfaction with the present tracking system. Increasingly, the organization of work has shifted from manufacturing and industrial to service and skilled technology. These jobs require workers to think their way through unfamiliar problems, be more literate, and be able to use sophisticated computers and other technologies. Being literate in skilled technology jobs means something different than it does in industrial and manufacturing jobs. Whereas assembly-line workers needed only enough literacy skills to sign their paychecks, workers in skilled technology jobs must interpret, compare, and analyze all manner of printed information, including graphs, charts, and tables.

UNTRACKING: ALTERNATIVES TO TRACKING

Recognizing that tracked schools are both inequitable and ineffective, educators have been exploring alternatives to tracking practices since the 1980s (Wheelock, 1992). Some of the reform efforts focus on restructuring the manner in which decisions about personnel, curriculum, and instruction are made at the school site level wheras others focus more sharply on the tracking system. We review some of these reform efforts briefly in order to give a flavor of some current reform efforts and to contextualize the AVID untracking effort. Although not all of the reform programs we review explicitly frame their activities as untracking, the end result of their efforts is a school that mixes students heterogeneously and provides them with academically rigorous curricula.

School-Based Untracking Efforts

The Accelerated Schools Project (Levin, 1987) is an example of an approach to school change that provides an enriched, challenging environment rather than a remedial one for underachieving students. The Accelerated Schools Project is as much a way of thinking about academic excellence for all students as it is a concrete process for dismantling the tracking system. Project schools do not follow a prescribed checklist for change. They do engage in a systematic process that involves all parents, teachers, and students at a school reaching an agreement to improve the academic performance of low-achieving students. From this unified purpose, participants develop an action plan, pilot-test modifications in curriculum and instruction, and evaluate their effectiveness. Although each Accelerated Schools Project school has formulated strategies that are relevant for its local circumstances, heterogeneous grouping, and instructional strategies that do not water down the curriculum have been a consistent feature across Accelerated Schools.

The School Development Program (Comer, 1980, 1988), like the Accelerated Schools Project, focuses on organizational change at the school-site level. It uses a process model in which administrators, parents, teachers, and support staff collaborate to address the problem of student underachievement. Reflecting Comer's psychiatric orientation, students' psychological development is seen as the key to promote students' academic achievement. Comer (1988: 48) believes that students' academic and behavior problems result from unmet psychological needs rather than willful badness. Because educators are not often prepared to foster the positive environment that is necessary for students' psychological development, Comer's model establishes a school governance and management team composed of parents and teachers supplemented by a team of psychologists and social workers. These teams decide how to rearrange the academic, social, and disciplinary programs of the school in order to meet the psychological and academic needs of students.

These rearrangements have been effective. Comer's project started at two inner-city schools in New Haven in 1969. By 1980, academic performance at the two New Haven schools had surpassed the national average, and truancy and disciplinary problems had declined markedly. Comer's model with its distinctive features of mental health teams, crisis rooms that provide refuge for students who are out of control, and discovery rooms that enable turned-off students to form trusting relationships with adults is now being implemented in more than 50 elementary, middle, and high schools around the country.

The Coalition for Essential Schools (Sizer, 1984, 1992) is one of the more notable reform efforts that shift the education policy for underachieving students away from the watered-down, compensatory, or remedial instruction associated with low-track classes. Formed in 1984, the coalition is an association of school people and their colleagues at Brown University who agree on a set of ideas that they believe should inform all good schools. They also agree on the proposition that each school must craft these ideas into practices that draw on the strengths of its particular faculty.

The coalition expresses a number of common principles (Sizer, 1992: 207–213). The school should focus on helping adolescents learn to use their minds well. Each student should master a number of essential skills and be competent in certain areas of knowledge. The school's goal of excellence should apply to all students but the means to achieve those goals will vary because the students themselves differ. Teaching and learning should be individualized as much as possible. The student is viewed as a worker and not the recipient of information transmitted by a teacher. The diploma is awarded based on the successful final demonstration of mastery that takes the form of an exhibition. The principal and the teachers should perceive of themselves as generalists first and specialists second.

These principles are directed inward, at managing and developing the local school site. By 1991, more than 200 schools in 23 states had joined the coalition. Most of the schools are public; 18 are private. The coalition also works with the Education Commission of the States to encourage the reform effort "from the schoolhouse to the statehouse" (Sizer, 1992: 209).

What has been learned about students' academic achievement and school change from the coalition's reform effort? Sizer (1992: 210) says that coalition schools report improved academic performance, attendance, morale, and college enrollment rates. In addition, coalition schools admit that the changes they envisioned had been difficult to achieve. Beyond those general observations, however, very little more has been said with authority. Because most coalition schools are in the early stages of their design, comparative and comprehensive assessments of success or failure have not yet been produced.

Reforming Classroom Grouping Practices

Cooperative learning (Slavin, Kaweit, & Madden, 1989; Kagan, 1986) is another example of a reform effort that is explicitly oriented toward dismantling tracking and ability grouping. It focuses on the social organization of the classroom. When cooperative learning is implemented, classrooms are organized so that students work together in small, interdependent, heterogeneous teams. The condition of interdependence is created by making the achievement of any team member contribute to the rewards of all. The condition of heterogeneity is created by either random or matched assignment. In either case, students are not segregated by gender, ethnicity, or measured ability.

Students, especially those from minority backgrounds, educated in cooperative learning environments have improved academically, changed their attitudes toward different ethnic groups, and become more "prosocial" (Slavin et al., 1989; Kagan, 1986). In three different studies, Kagan (1986) found that Anglos showed equal or somewhat greater academic gain in cooperative classrooms compared with that in traditional classrooms and minority students showed far greater gain in cooperative compared with that in traditional classrooms.

Kagan and Slavin both believe that the structure of rewards to students, the transformed role that teachers play in cooperative learning, and the cultural compatibility of cooperative lessons all contribute to the improved academic performance and prosocial development among low-income and ethnic minority students. The structure of student rewards is most crucial. When group rewards are based on individual achievement, students make the greatest achievement gains. In contrast, when group rewards are based on a group product with no individual accountability, students' achievement is no different than that of students in regular classrooms.

The AVID Untracking Program

The AVID approach to untracking is similar in some respects to these reform efforts and different in other respects. AVID is similar to the Coalition for Essential Schools and Accelerated Schools in that it does not simplify instruction or reduce the curriculum for underachieving students. Instead, AVID attempts to maintain a rigorous curriculum for all students while adding increased support for low-achieving students. Its expressed goals are to motivate and prepare underachieving students from underrepresented linguistic and ethnic minority groups or low-income students of any ethnicity to perform well in high school and to seek a college education. The AVID untracking program employs many of the principles of cooperative learning in its curriculum. Its most significant difference is from the Coalition for Essential Schools. AVID attempts to remove the distinctions between college prep, general, and vocational education tracks incrementally wheras coalition schools attempt to dismantle tracked classes all at once.

The idea of untracking low-achieving students was introduced to San Diego in 1980 at Clairemont High, a predominantly white school, by Mary Catherine Swanson, a member of the English department. Untracking became a way to educate minority students bussed to Clairemont from predominantly ethnic minority schools in Southeast San Diego under a court ordered desegregation decree. Unwilling to segregate African American and Latino students into a separate, compensatory curriculum, Swanson and the Clairemont faculty placed the bussed students in regular college prep classes.

AVID soon spread beyond Clairemont High School. One of Swanson's colleagues went to Madison High School; she helped introduce AVID there in 1984. In 1986, Swanson was called to the San Diego County Office of Education to implement the AVID untracking model countywide. Four other schools within the San Diego Unified School District adopted the AVID model of untracking low-achieving students in 1986. The SDCS School Board mandated the adoption of AVID in every high school in the spring semester of 1987. By 1991, 17 City Schools, 50 high schools in San Diego County, and 4 high schools outside the county had introduced AVID programs.

AVID coordinators select students for the program. Low-income, ethnic and linguistic minority students who have average to high achievement test scores, and C-level junior high school grades are eligible for AVID. After these high-potential, low-performance students are identified, parents are advised. Those parents who agree to support their children's participation in the academic program sign contracts to have their children participate in AVID in high school.

AVID advocates a distinctive approach to curriculum and instruction. The acronym for this approach is WIC, which stands for writing, inquiry, and collaboration (Swanson, no date).

Writing is seen as a tool of learning. In the AVID classroom, students are taught a special form of note taking. Students are instructed to jot detailed notes from their academic classes in a wide right-hand margin of a notebook; and as homework, to develop questions based on the notes in a narrow left-hand column of the same notebook page. These questions are to be used the following day in the AVID class. In addition to note taking, the students are to keep "learning logs" and practice "quick writes" (Swanson, no date).

Inquiry refers to the relationship between tutors (students recruited from local colleges) and the students in the elective AVID class. The program provides tutors who work in the AVID classroom to the AVID teacher. Tutors are trained to lead study groups in such subjects as math or English, based on the students' notes and questions. Tutors are trained not to give answers; they are to help the AVID students clarify their thoughts based on their questions. AVID insists on the inquiry method to keep the AVID class from becoming a glorified study hall or homework session (Swanson, no date), and to help students become independent thinkers.

Collaboration is the instructional strategy of having students work together to achieve instructional goals rather than having them work in isolation. Working in ways that are similar to cooperative learning groups, collaborative study teams enable students to serve as sources of information and feedback for each other. Collaboration, AVID asserts, shifts the responsibility for learning from the teacher who directs lessons to the students who participate with the teacher in them.

AVID promotes the integration of methodologies into the academic classes that AVID students take. To facilitate this diffusion of effective teaching strategies, AVID conducts summer institutes. Each school that is implementing AVID is invited to send an interdisciplinary team to the workshop. The team consists of the school principal, the head counselor, the AVID coordinator, and instructional leaders from the English, foreign language, history, science, and mathematics departments. The 1991 San Diego AVID Summer Institute enrolled 720 participants from 68 districts and 169 schools. While at the institute, the interdisciplinary team learns to use the three AVID methods – writing to learn, inquiry, and collaboration – with all students. The interdisciplinary team is invited to return to the institute in subsequent years to learn how to diffuse the AVID methodologies throughout the school. The summer institute is supplemented by monthly workshops, conducted during the subsequent school year, semiannual site team meetings, and semiannual site visitations by AVID Center staff.

The AVID central office suggests a basic plan for the weekly instructional activities within AVID classrooms. Two school days are designated tutorial days. On these days students are to work in small groups with the assistance of a tutor. On the other two days, writing as a tool for learning is emphasized. On these days, students engage in a variety of activities, including essay writing for their academic classes and college applications. One day a week, usually Fridays, are "motivational days." Guest speakers are invited to address the class, and field trips to colleges are scheduled on these days.

In one sense, then, the AVID approach to untracking is more conservative than the Coalition for Essential Schools approach. It does not directly challenge the existing track distinctions, but instead seeks to place more and more underrepresented students into college prep classes until low-track classes are empty. While not a frontal assault on the tracking system, the AVID approach to untracking is a subversive activity and has the potential to serve as the first step in the transformation of a school from a rigid homogeneously grouped track system to a heterogeneously grouped system.

In order for that transformation to occur, however, untracking can not be limited to a small percentage of students with high potential; it will have to be extended to include all students. The extension of untracking efforts is not simply a matter of opening more doors to more low-achieving students, however. As we will discuss in Chapter 9, extending untracking requires the implementation of more extensive support systems. The quantity and quality of instruction students receive in academic classes would have to be increased and the social supports that students receive would have to be intensified.

OVERVIEW

In this volume, we explore the features of the San Diego untracking experiment that make Lilia Ortiz's story of academic success and others like it possible. This investigation is important because there has not been much systematic research conducted on the efforts to reform the tracking system. There have been many glowing reports and celebrations of plans to untrack schools (Wheelock, 1992), but there have not been as many detailed investigations of actual detracking practices. In that regard, we eagerly await the publication of the research by Jeannie Oakes and Amy Wells (in preparation) on attempts to create alternatives to tracking in racially mixed schools.

Our first order of business is to see whether placing low-achieving students in high-track classes has a positive effect on academic achievement. That is, Does untracking work? Second, we want to understand the processes and practices of untracking. That is, How does untracking work? After we review our research methodology in Chapter 2, we devote Chapter 3 to answering the first question, Does untracking work? We do so by examining the college enrollment of students who have participated in the AVID untracking program and comparing their enrollment with local and national averages.

The major portion of the book is devoted to answering the second question, How does untracking work? In this portion of our investigation, we conceive of classroom, school, and community activities as concentric circles of context surrounding students who are in the center. We start by examining the influence that students' socioeconomic and academic backgrounds have on their college enrollment (Chapter 4). Then we go beyond correlations of students' background characteristics and educational outcomes to examine the classroom processes and organizational practices that constitute the untracking program. In Chapter 5, we examine the institutional arrangements within classrooms that support untracked students. In Chapter 6, we consider the influence that the institutional arrangements between the untracking program and the other organizational units at the school sites have on the untracking effort.

In order to examine the outermost rings of the context surrounding students, we step outside the school. In Chapter 7, we consider the impact that students' peers have on participants in the untracking activity. In Chapter 8, we examine the role that parents' expectations, aspirations, and resources have on their children's educational performance.

We conclude the book by drawing the implications of untracking for educational practice (Chapter 9) and theories of social inequality (Chapter 10). We can not propose a comprehensive recommendation for educational improvement based on our study because the real source of inequality lies in socioeconomic conditions and the culture of the wider society, not in the school. But in Chapter 9 we do suggest that educators consider the importance of providing substantial social scaffolding to students when elevating their educational curricula and use students' knowledge and expertise for classroom instruction until there is a major revamping of our cultural, political, and economic system.

The results of our research invite us to reconsider some of the prevailing sociological explanations of inequality (Chapter 10). The strategies that the untracked students deployed to develop academic identities and the institutional machinery that AVID coordinators constructed to assist untracked students achieve academically especially inspire modifications in the reproduction theory of educational inequality. Students from low-income African American and Latino backgrounds acquired some of the cultural capital that has been thought to be reserved for the sons and daughters of the elite. Their teachers served as institutional agents and helped mediate their relations between high school and college. If the sons and daughters of low-status families can acquire cultural capital from their teachers and if the teachers of low-status students can activate social networks, then we must modify the rigid way in which reproduction theorists think about schools. Schools are not always reproductive systems. Schools can be transformed to increase social mobility by passing on cultural capital and constructing social networks.

A reflexive relationship between social agency, culture, and social constraints is needed in order to understand inequality better so that we can work toward social equality in society. Recent ethnographies show us that the poor and powerless resist the social constraints that the powerful attempt to impose upon them. These ethnographies are important because they modulate the structural determinism found in many theories of inequality by showing the contribution of people's actions to their own circumstances. But social agency is more than resistance. People make sense of their lives in a myriad of expressive, assertive, and goal-directed ways within the constraints imposed on them. Including these complex actions in our theories will give us a more comprehensive sense of social agency.

Socioeconomic conditions and structural constraints do not operate directly upon social actors. Cultural processes, working through the actions of the peer group, the family, and institutional mechanisms such as affirmative action or an untracking program, mediate the relationship between social action and social constraints.

Cultural processes can produce inequality or equality as well as mediate relationships. School sorting processes such as tracking, testing, and ability grouping limit students' educational opportunities by giving them differential access to educational resources. Untracking, which provides all students with access to the same academic curriculum while varying the institutional support that students receive, has the potential to provide students with more equitable access to educational resources.

We must continue to examine educational practices such as untracking closely as a contribution to a larger democratic project. In large part, this entails thinking about, talking about, and acting toward schools in a different way. For too long now, we have been thinking about schools as credentialing agencies that help a privileged few accumulate wealth, power, and status. It is time to re-create our schools as institutions to promote the common good and to prepare all children to participate in a democratic society.

2

TRACKING UNTRACKING

WE ARE ATTRACTED TO UNTRACKING BECAUSE OF ITS potential. Untracking attacks the problem of students with varying educational experiences in a fundamentally different way than prevailing educational policy. Untracking attempts to replace the adulterated, watered-down curricular approaches associated with tracking with a policy that provides all students with a similar curriculum, while varying the amount of institutional support that students receive. Having contributed to the literature that has exposed the inequalities generated by such school sorting practices as tracking, ability grouping, and testing, we now feel it is time to work collaboratively with people who are attempting to achieve the goal of educational equity.

Because the first author's intellectual roots are grounded in ethnomethodology (Mehan & Wood, 1975), and he had to wrestle with the dilemmas and contradictions posed by the realization that one's participation in research transforms it, we are sympathetic to the issues concerning reflexivity in research raised by critical and feminist scholars (e.g., Behar, 1991; Lather, 1991) who entreat us to make the researcher's positionality itself a visible part of the research process. In so doing, Behar, Lather, and others do us a service by making the connections between the subjective and the objective poles of social research explicit.

But while we can wrestle with reflexivity, we cannot defeat it, because it is an essential feature of everyday life and social research. If we focus too intently on the researcher's contributions, emotional state, and ethical dilemmas, then we stand the chance of losing the very phenomenon we set out to investigate. Furthermore, the school people we work with would see the endless discussion of the researchers' subjectivity as boring, elitist, and pedantic. They are much more interested in finding out if certain school reform efforts work than experiencing our angst about the difficulties in conducting social research. Since we must work through reflexivity, we will concentrate more on the object of our research (which is inequality and ways to achieve equity) than our subjectivity.

RESEARCHER–PRACTITIONER RELATIONSHIPS

With that caveat in mind, let us provide some comments on our subjectivity. The relationships in this study are not the usual ones of subject and object of research. Various entanglements have both facilitated and constrained this project. The research team is associated with the Sociology Department and the Teacher Education Program (TEP) at the University of California, San Diego, which makes us participants in the educational community we study and not just outside observers of it. While we conduct participant observation as do other ethnographers, we cannot leave the scene when we are finished, as do researchers who enter the scene from the outside. We live in the community we study, which means we are there the next day, supervising student teachers, consulting with principals, and contributing to school improvement efforts.

Representatives of the Teacher Education Program are often viewed as friends of the family, people who have a long-term commitment to the schools, not a quick in-and-out interest in schools. For example, Daryl Stermon, who provided statistical advice to the project, has taught throughout the school system that we studied and, for a time, was on the evaluation staff in the very office that had the responsibility of granting approval to this project. Peter Bell, who works in the evaluation department of the San Diego City Schools, received his Ph.D. in anthropology from the University of California, San Diego. His study of the career paths of students who graduate from the City Schools (Bell, 1993) provided valuable contrasting data for us and shows his appreciation of ethnographic approaches to school reform. He helped us in our dealings with the central office and school principals and graciously provided us much needed information such as students' report cards and districtwide statistics.

The research assistants on the project also had special relations with the schools. Amanda Datnow, who made the first round of observations at schools, was a teaching assistant in the math/ science internship program of TEP, a role that put her in contact with AVID teachers and classroom teachers at several school sites, including one or two of those which we later chose to study. In her teaching assistant role, she was introduced to educators as a concerned practitioner. Later, when she began to visit schools as a researcher, teachers knew her, and were not threatened by her. Libby Bratton first served as an AVID tutor in one of the schools. The relationship she developed with the AVID coordinator there facilitated her entrée to the school when she became a research assistant on this project. Claudia Tellez, an undergraduate student who worked on this project through the University of California, San Diego, Minority Student Research Project, had attended the school where AVID started; when she interviewed students from that school, she was able to establish a special connection with them.

Relationships with parents that went far beyond gathering data emerged during interviews. When Lea Hubbard and Irene Villanueva visited students' homes, parents often saw them as information sources, not information seekers. Before, during, and after interviews conducted in the summer, they were asked to help solve the financial aid problems that had developed for the children since school finished in June, and they were asked to give advice about dealing with immigration, social security, and welfare agencies.

The AVID director, Mary Catherine Swanson, has often asked one of us to report on our research to gatherings of AVID teachers, representatives of school districts contemplating adopting the AVID untracking model, or school superintendents with AVID programs in their districts. One such talk occurred after we gathered college enrollment data, but before we started the ethnographic phase of the research. The AVID coordinators who heard that talk formed a personal impression of us, which means we were not strangers to them when we asked them for their more extensive cooperation.

These blended roles, although essential for conducting research of this sort, placed us in a delicate position in relation to the educators we were studying. Although the results of our research are generally positive, we have attributed the success of the program to different factors than the program does (i.e., more to social scaffolds and social networks, less to inquiry-based curriculum and collaborative instruction in academic courses). We have raised questions about certain elements of the program (e.g., the selection of students who have extremely high academic records, parent programs that are underdeveloped), and we have discovered unpleasant tensions within it (e.g., counselors and vocational education teachers who challenge the underlying assumptions of untracking and students' who question the utility of some of AVID's instructional approaches).

In the spirit of collaborative research, we shared an earlier draft of this research with AVID Center and the eight AVID coordinators who so kindly worked with us. They gave us their reactions to our representations. Some coordinators identified minor errors that needed correcting; others felt we had characterized the program in negative terms, points we tried to deal with in subsequent interactions and editing. Staff from AVID Center gave us a line-by-line reaction to our draft. We incorporated many of its helpful suggestions in this text. But not all practitioners who read early drafts of the text were happy with it. The educators at one school in particular were incensed at our representation of their untracking program as a school within a school. We could not convince them that we had reported faithfully what the school records reflect, what we heard, and what we saw. The description of that school's practice is included without modification.

Even though reporting negatives to people who have given you their trust is unpleasant, it is our belief that people who conduct research on schools cannot run away with the data. Researchers have an obligation not only to present their findings at the end in a final report, but to participate in a dialogue along the way. Schools are too vulnerable to conduct research in any other way.

Because of these entangled personal relationships and the commitment of our group to educational improvement, we are certain that some will criticize our approach for bias and lack of objectivity.

All that we can do in the face of that criticism is lay as much of our research record as possible on the table and let the reader decide about the efficacy of our interpretations.

METHODS AND DATA

To be consistent with the methodological principles of triangulation, we used materials from many sources in this study. We consulted official school records. We interviewed students, teachers, parents, and school officials. We conducted observations in classrooms.

Gathering Baseline Information

The San Diego City Schools (SDCS) kindly supplied us with the Cumulative School Records (CSRs) of AVID students in the classes of 1990, 1991, and 1992. We used this information to determine students' ethnicity and to calculate students' academic record in high school (AVID classes taken, test scores, college prep courses taken and completed, etc.).

Of the 1,053 San Diego City Schools' students in grades 9–12 enrolled in AVID, we found 353 students in 14 high schools who had completed 3 years of AVID during their high school careers when they graduated in 1990, 1991, and 1992. We also identified 288 City Schools students who had entered AVID in the same academic year as the "untracked group," but who did not complete 3 years of the program. Instead, they left after 1 semester or 1 year. Students who entered the program at the same point in time but left after 1 year make an excellent comparison group because they were selected by AVID coordinators according to the same criteria. Therefore, the academic performance of the AVID students who completed 1 year of AVID compared with the academic performance of students who completed 3 years of AVID helps us determine the relative influence of program and background effects.

In order to determine students' activities since they graduated from high school, we attempted to interview the 353 graduates of the classes of 1990, 1991, and 1992, and the 288 students who started but did not complete AVID. We were able to interview 248 of the program graduates and 146 of those who had left AVID. We asked the students in both groups about their activities since they graduated from high school – whether they had enrolled in 4- or 2-year colleges, were working, or were doing other things. In order to place students' college enrollment and work information in context, we asked students about their family background (e.g., parents' education, languages spoken in the home). We also discussed their high school and AVID experiences with them. This information helped us answer the question, Does untracking work?

In order to measure the socioeconomic background of students, we considered their parents' income and educational attainment. We calculated the parents' median income using census track information from the 1990 census kindly supplied to us by the San Diego Association of Governments. We obtained information about parents' education through our interviews with AVID students.

Case Studies of Schools

In order to answer the question, How does untracking work? we recognized we needed to go beyond correlational data and examine social practices and cultural processes. To do so, we conducted case studies of 8 of the 17 high schools in the San Diego Unified School District that are participating in this untracking experiment (Bay Meadows, Churchill, Golden Gate, Keeneland, Monrovia, Nassau, Pimlico, and Saratoga). We chose high schools in the San Diego district because AVID started there and because the City Schools district was the only one in San Diego County at the time of our study that had a computer system capable of generating student records of graduated students. We chose the eight schools based on their ethnic enrollments, their college enrollment rates, and, of course, their willingness to participate in the study.

AVID has an organizational arrangement with the City Schools district that is different than its relation with other districts in San Diego County. All other districts, AVID Center informs us, have identified a high-ranking administrator to serve as a liaison between the program and the schools. It is the responsibility of the district liaison to meet with AVID coordinators regularly and work with them to solve problems as needed. Although the City Schools district does not allocate any special funding for AVID, district liaison officers in other districts coordinate the funding for AVID. These unique organizational features may limit the generalizability of our findings.

After we worked out details about protecting confidentiality and observation schedules with the AVID coordinators and school principals, we observed in AVID and academic classrooms, and interviewed AVID teachers and students from October 1991 until June 1993. The following are brief descriptions of the eight schools we studied closely.

Bay Meadows High School. Bay Meadows is located in a nonresidential area of a San Diego beach community. It is surrounded by small businesses, gas stations, car dealerships, and vacant lots. Many of Bay Meadows's 1,600 students come from areas outside the immediate community, either because they participate in the San Diego City Schools' voluntary desegregation program, or participate in the school's management and graphics design magnet program. The ethnic distribution of the school during the 1991–1992 school year was approximately 50% white, 34% Latino, and 5% African American; the remaining 11% of the student body represented a number of Asian backgrounds. Twenty-eight percent of the students came from homes where a language other than English is spoken.

There are three regular classes of AVID plus a fourth AVID class that operates differently from the others. Students attracted to Bay Meadows for its management and graphics design magnet school attend the fourth AVID class, which is held during a briefer period during which other students engage in sustained silent reading because they can not fit AVID into their schedule at any other time. Each class has approximately 30 students who are heterogeneously mixed. The AVID classroom is very large, and tables can be moved easily to create study clusters. The room is decorated with college banners and motivational quotes. Ten computers, which students use to compose essays and college application portfolios, and bookcases full of current college catalogs and Scholastic Aptitute Test (SAT) and Pre-SAT (PSAT) preparation books line the walls. Students have tape players and VCRs available for their use, and a phone and a sink are available for the teacher's use.

The coordinator of the program, Lisa Hertz, is a science specialist, who teaches biology and physical science courses in addition to her AVID courses. Hertz is involved in AVID at the county level, having served as a mentor coordinator and as a participant in monthly coordinator meetings and summer institutes.

Churchill High School. Churchill High School is a racially mixed neighborhood school in East San Diego. The socioeconomic makeup of its 1,500-student body spans the spectrum from the very wealthy to those receiving some form of state or federal aid. Most students come from families of moderate income. Within the past 6 years, Churchill has had an influx of Indochinese students, which has changed the ethnic balance of the school. At the present time, 32.5% of the student body is white, 26.8% is Indochinese, 19.2% is African American, 16.7% is Latino, and the balance comprises Asian, Pacific Islander, and Filipino students. The school faces problems of high transience, fairly high dropout rates, and a history of schoolwide low test scores. Churchill has been undergoing major restructuring recently and the results of standardized testing administered in 1990 showed schoolwide improvement, especially in the area of reading skills.

AVID attracts a large number of students at Churchill. During the year, we observed five AVID classes composed of approximately 30 students each and included a mix of students from grades 9 to 12. The AVID classrooms were organized with 1 day devoted to a review of the journal entries that students had made during the previous week and to a review of the textbook notes taken over the same period, 2 days devoted to tutorials, and 1 day devoted to notebook checks. The current AVID coordinator, Lucia Pincay, has been at Churchill for 3 years. Currently, she teaches only AVID classes, although in the past she has taught English and Chapter One Reading at Churchill. A recipient of a B.A. in psychology from San Diego State University, Pincay has been teaching for 20 years.

She takes pride in the fact that she returned to school for her degree when all three of her children were teenagers. The coordinator also has Masters degrees in education for both curriculum and reading from SDSU.

Golden Gate High School. Golden Gate High School is located in a suburban neighborhood. The ethnic composition of its 1,970 students is 54.2% white, 31.9% Latino, 9.6% African American, 1.5% Asian, 1.5% "other," and 1.3% Filipino. School officials are proud that 78% of Golden Gate's graduates enroll in colleges, 34% of whom attend 4-year colleges or universities. Approximately 500 students come to Golden Gate through a variety of "magnet" and special attendance programs.

There are three AVID elective classes at Golden Gate. Students from grades 9 to 12 are mixed in all three classes. The current AVID coordinator, Alex Frankfurter, has been with the program since 1989. In addition to his AVID classes, he teaches two periods of English literature. He is fluent in Spanish and English.

Each AVID class is composed of approximately 35 students, who are mostly Latino. There are approximately 25 African American and no more than 5 Asian students in the entire program. About 25 of the AVID students are considered to be Limited English Proficient (LEP). The three AVID tutors who help Frankfurter are enrolled in local universities. In addition, there are two AVID counselors to whom AVID students are assigned if they need assistance with their schedules or other academic matters.

Keeneland High School. Located in the mid-city area of San Diego, Keeneland's population of approximately 2,000 students is approximately 90% nonwhite. The three largest ethnic groups are Latino (37%), Indochinese (30%), and African American (19%). Located in an economically depressed area, Keeneland faces challenges posed by transience, health, and unemployment. During the course of a school year, as many as one-half of the student body will change. During the course of the 1992–1993 school year, approximately 100 young women notified the school nurse that they were pregnant. The school nurse estimates that 7% of the school population is HIV positive. A school counselor estimated that fewer than 20% of the graduates enroll in college. Although 30% of the students dropped out in 1986–1987, only 4% did in 1992. The faculty's restructuring efforts, modeled after Sizer's (1984, 1992) Coalition for Essential Schools, are given much of the credit for this improvement.

AVID has strong ties to this restructuring effort; 2 of the 4 AVID coordinators are coalition teachers. AVID at Keeneland has distinctive characteristics, with a team of coordinators and a pilot program involving ESL (English as a Second Language) classes. Advanced ESL teachers feel that AVID provides students with the extra support they need to achieve at a higher academic level.

Monrovia High School. Monrovia High School has an enrollment of approximately 2,500 students. During the 1990–1991 school year, the ethnic distribution of the students was approximately 8% Latino, 4% African American, 4% Asian, 21% Filipino, 15% Indochinese, and 48% white. The remaining 2% were Pacific Islanders or Native Americans.

There are approximately 90 AVID students at Monrovia. In conformance with the model advocated by the central office, the three classes mix students from three grade levels. Kim Shoemaker, the AVID coordinator, feels that mixing students from different grades allows older students to help the younger students and to serve as role models for them. Shoemaker has been the AVID coordinator at Monrovia since the program started there 6 years ago. Along with her three AVID classes, she teaches English, including advanced English. She has also taught history and peer counseling. She requested the AVID position because she thought it would broaden her professional perspective and put her in contact with her peers in other schools.

The well-lighted and spacious AVID classroom is located in "temporary" bungalows behind the main school buildings. Several computers line the walls while all student desks face the room's main blackboard. The teacher's desk is next to the classroom door, off to the side of the students' desks. The placement of the teacher's desk is symbolic of the role this teacher has adopted. She seldom has direct academic involvement with the students; instead, students work together at the board or with teaching assistants at their desks.

Nassau High School. Located in a wealthy suburban community, Nassau High School is situated among expensive homes. The community is predominantly white upper-middle class. The demographic profile of the school has been in transition since 1985. The Latino population has steadily increased as the white population has decreased. In the 1985–1986 school year, whites made up over 74% of the student body while Latino students composed less than 18%. Six years later, Latinos compose 31% of the student body and whites 58%. At the same time, the African American representation is also declining. In 1985–1986, the school was 6% African American, while in 1991–1992, the school was less than 4% African American. These trends have occurred in part because Nassau participates in the district's voluntary desegregation plan and because the number of families with school age children in the neighborhood has been declining. At present, those bussed to the school from the urban core of San Diego comprise approximately 40% of the student body.

Despite cuts in the school's operational budget, Nassau is well endowed. Annual fund raising activities, including an antique sale, generate income for the school. Recently, a counselor left his entire estate to the school upon his death. This sort of community support makes it possible for Nassau to offer scholarships to its graduates on the basis of financial need, $600 if they are accepted to a community college, $1,000 if they are accepted to a California State University, and $2,000 if they are accepted to the University of California.

Three teachers offer AVID classes simultaneously. Unlike the model proposed by the central office, students are selected in the second semester of their freshman year and complete AVID at the end of the first semester of their senior year. Students continue with the same teacher from their sophomore to their senior year. Some of the AVID classrooms are adjoining, which enables students to move between them to seek appropriate tutoring.

Pimlico Secondary School. Pimlico Secondary School, also known as the Center for Science, Mathematics and Computer Technology, was formed in 1979 as the first integration magnet program within the San Diego Unified School District. The school has an atypical 7–12 grade structure, enabling students to take up to 6 years of mathematics, science, and computer courses.

As the first integration magnet school in the SDCS, Pimlico pioneered the recruitment of talented students from all ethnic and racial backgrounds. Pimlico currently draws 25% of its students from throughout the district and 75% from the local neighborhood. The ethnic composition of the school in 1992 was 45% African American, 25% Hispanic, 12% Asian (including Lao students from the neighborhood), and 18% white.

School leaders measure the success of the first 10 years of the program by the many awards the school has received, including the California Distinguished School Award in 1990. The school claims that 98% of the students in the magnet portion of the school go to 4-year colleges or universities.

Pimlico is currently undergoing a reorganization in which all students from the heavily minority and immigrant neighborhoods will be integrated into the enriched science, math, and computer curriculum. This move, considered controversial by many faculty (who believe that only "elite" students can succeed in a magnet program), is supported by governmental agencies, public school officials, science education experts, and business leaders who recognize that the future of this country requires all of its citizens to have a high level of skill in science and technology (Bixler, 1991).

Jane Mills, the coordinator of the AVID Program at Pimlico, has had responsibility for AVID and ESL for 4 years. She was asked to be the AVID coordinator by the principal and counselors and worked with one of the counselors to bring AVID to the school. With a B.A. in English, a minor in Spanish, and an M.S. in bilingual/ cross-cultural education, she is bilingual.

There are two AVID classes at Pimlico which meet during the fifth and sixth periods each day. Students from grades 9 to 12 are mixed in both classes. The organization of activities in each class is similar. Students come into the class and take seats in desks arranged to face the middle. A student (apparently a volunteer) asks students which study group they wish to join. Usually five groups are formed. The math study groups are always the largest.

Saratoga High School. Saratoga High School is situated in a neat, suburban neighborhood. Most of the homes immediately around the school are relatively new condominiums or apartments. There are also several shopping centers that include fast-food restaurants, which are frequented by the students at lunch. The student population comes from a socially and economically diverse community. It includes students from a military housing area where residents are mostly low income. There are many exclusive homes, in the $200,000–$400,000 range in the area as well. Saratoga's student population is currently 1,810, 13% of which comes to Saratoga through the San Diego City Schools voluntary desegregation program to take advantage of academic and extracurricular activities. The ethnic distribution of students for the 1991–1992 school year was 15% African American, 3.5% Asian, 9.6% Filipino, 12.4% Latino, and 53.7% white. Pacific Islander, Indochinese, or Native American students constitute the remaining 6%.

The school grounds are well maintained. Recently the students' lockers were fenced off and locked, making them unusable by the students. The students resent this action, because now they must carry all of their books every day. The rationale behind this action was security. Last year, there were several fights around the locker area. This year, with the lockers not in use, there are no apparent signs of gang graffiti or violence. For the most part, Saratoga seems to be an orderly school and very security conscious. The police are on campus about 3 times a week and are available on short notice if the school administration calls them. Saratoga has a dropout rate of 22% and a suspension rate of 6.48%, which suggests the school population is relatively stable in comparison with other schools in San Diego.

Measuring College Enrollment and Persistence

In order to determine the relative success of this untracking experiment, we compared the college enrollment rates of AVID students with a measure of the college enrollment rates of all students from the San Diego City Schools (Bell, 1993) and an estimate of the national average (Carter & Wilson, 1991). We make these comparisons with some reservations, however, since the national data and local data are not exactly comparable with our AVID data. The local data, from the San Diego City Schools (Bell, 1993), capture the college enrollment of the class of 1991. The national data are from the American Council on Education (Carter & Wilson, 1991). They are based on census data and reports on classes that graduated each year from 1970 to 1990, but do not report on the students who graduated in 1991. The American Council of Education report, furthermore, only presents aggregate data on the college enrollment of Anglos, African Americans, and Latinos; it does not present aggregate data on Filipinos, Japanese, Chinese, Koreans, Native Americans, Vietnamese, or Cambodians.

We define "college enrollment" following Carter and Wilson (1991) as the percentage of high school seniors who attend college upon graduation. It is a more accurate measure than "college participation," which Carter and Wilson define as the percentage of all persons 18–24 who attend college. There are many ways to operationalize college enrollment, including asking students their plans while they are in high school and interviewing them once they have graduated. We have chosen to operationalize college enrollment via postgraduation interviews because it is a more accurate measure, even though it involves a more time-consuming process. As a result, our measures of college enrollment are likely to be more conservative than reports based on students' projected plans, which suffer from idealizations and inflation.

We implemented an elaborate procedure to track students beyond their first year of college. As noted, our initial contact with students was facilitated by school records supplied by the San Diego City Schools. Using information available on school records, we interviewed students by phone the summer after they graduated from high school. We supplied students with prepaid, self-addressed postcards, with instructions to mail the cards to us if they changed address or phone numbers. Very few of these cards were returned to us, however. School records gave us the permanent address of the students. We used this information to mail follow-up information, hoping that the post office would forward our mail. Despite these procedures, and extensive follow-up via phone, we did not get the follow-up sample size we wanted.

Representing Ethnicity

Ethnic designations give headaches to researchers investigating academic achievement. The use of a single word, either "Hispanic" or "Latino" to name a group of people as disparate as Mexicans and Cubans conflates the cultures. The same is true for the "African American" or "black" designation, because it conflates Caribbean and African cultures. And whatever conflates cultures destroys them.

The "Hispanic"/"Latino" group cannot be defined racially because it includes people whose ancestors came from Asia to settle in the Western Hemisphere thousands of years ago, as well as people from Europe, the Iberian Peninsula, and Africa (Garcia, 1992: 71). The category of religion does not work either, because the group comprises Roman Catholics, many Protestants, Jews, and people who have deep connections to Mixtec, Nahua, and other Native American religious rites and beliefs. Economically the group ranges from members of the presidential cabinet to undocumented farm workers who sleep in burrows dug into the ground in the hills east of Del Mar, Encinitas, and Oceanside.

It is important to distinguish among Latinos based on place of birth because there is some evidence to suggest that native-born Latinos have a different educational and economic record than recent immigrants from Mexico and Central America (Villanueva, 1990). When the earnings of native-born Mexican American men are analyzed separately from those of Mexican immigrants, Chavez (1991: 122) claims a different picture emerges than when these two groups are lumped together. On the average, the weekly earnings of Mexican American men is about 83% of those of non-Hispanic white men, while the weekly earnings of Mexican-born immigrants is closer to 60% of non-Hispanic whites. A similar problem arises when recent immigrants are grouped with native-born Mexican Americans when computing educational attainment statistics because recent immigrants have higher high school dropout rates and lower high school completion rates than native-borns. Only one-half of Mexican immigrants have completed 7 or more years of schooling and only 28% have completed 12 or more years of schooling because most of these immigrants came to the United States as young adults, after they had completed their formal education in Mexico (Chavez, 1991: 112). The Latino category becomes more confusing when immigrants from Central America are included, because they have a different psychological profile (Suarez-Orosco, 1989) and more immigrated from the professional than the working classes (Chavez, 1991).

Native-born blacks are not differentiated in national and local data bases from black immigrant children or children of immigrants. The category "African American" includes students who are U.S. descendants of the African diaspora, Panamanian and Haitian immigrants, and children of immigrants from African countries such as Ethiopia and Eritrea, a practice that blurs the historical, linguistic, and cultural differences between these groups.

There is a similar problem with the "Asian" or "Indochinese" designation. In some reports, Pacific Islanders, Koreans, Japanese, Chinese, Vietnamese, Cambodians, Laotians, and Thais are lumped together as "Asians," whereas in others the last four groups are designated "Indochinese." Both of these categories are unfortunate because, like the African American, Latino, or Hispanic designation, they obscure cultural differences and information about peoples' socioeconomic status at the time of their immigration. The Japanese and Chinese who have migrated to the United States have done so at different times and under different circumstances than the Vietnamese, Thais, and Cambodians. The Vietnamese, in turn,

Table 1. *Ethnicity of 3–Year AVID Students*

Latino	102	(41%)
White	29	(12%)
African American	74	(30%)
Asian[a]	7	(3%)
Native American	2	(0.8%)
Pacific Islander	1	(0.4%)
Filipino	17	(7%)
Indochinese[b]	16	(6%)
Total	248	(100%)

[a]Japanese, Korean, Chinese.
[b]Vietnamese, Cambodian, Lao.

have migrated under different circumstances at different times. More arriving on California's shores after the fall of Saigon came from middle-income families than those arriving in the past decade (Rumbaut & Ima, 1988). A failure to take this fact into account reinforces the stereotype of the academically successful, "model minority" Vietnamese, which masks the educational difficulties of recent immigrants.

Even though we are aware of the limitations associated with prevailing ethnic categories, we are constrained in our use of them. We have settled on "Latino," because that is the term preferred in California. We must use "Latino" rather than "native-born Mexican or "Mexican-born Hispanic" because national, state, and local reports do not make these finer distinctions. Partially out of exasperation with this confusing inconsistency, we will use certain expressions interchangeably: "African American" with "black," and "white" with "Anglo."

The ethnicity of the 248 3-year AVID students we have interviewed is shown in Table 1.

Listening to Parents

In order to obtain parents' perspectives on their children's education, we interviewed 40 mothers and fathers of AVID students. The interviews were conducted in the parents' homes, in the language of the parents' choice. Of the 40 parents, 35 are Latino and 5 are African American. Their students attended Keeneland, Bay Meadows, Saratoga, Golden Gate, and Monrovia, which means that we do not have the opportunity to hear the voices of parents whose children attend Churchill, Pimlico, and Nassau. The topics we discussed with parents included their aspirations for their children, their contributions to their children's education, the resources they deployed in support of their children's education, their interactions with the schools, and the AVID untracking program.

3

DOES UNTRACKING WORK?

STUDENTS FROM LINGUISTIC AND ETHNIC MINORITY
backgrounds and low-income families do poorly in school by
comparison with their majority and well-to-do contemporaries.
They drop out at a higher rate. They score lower on tests. Their
grades are lower. And most importantly for the topic of this book,
they do not attend college as often (Carter & Wilson, 1991).

Students from linguistic and ethnic minority backgrounds are
expected to compose an increasing percentage of the United States
population through the early years of the 21st century (Pelavin &
Kane, 1990; Carter & Wilson, 1991). Jobs that require higher education are expected to increase in number (Commission on the Skills
of the American Workforce, 1990). The current census data, however, show that students from linguistic and ethnic minority backgrounds are not enrolling in college in sufficient numbers to qualify
for the increasing number of jobs that will require baccalaureate
degrees.

African American and Latino students have been enrolling in
college more often recently than they have in the past, but they are
not enrolling at the same rate as white students. In 1970, 26% of
African American high school graduates enrolled in college; this
rate reached a high of 34% in 1976, declined to 31% in 1989 and rose
to 33% in 1990. In 1972 (the first year data were available), 26% of
Latino high school graduates enrolled in college, whereas only 29%
enrolled in 1990. Although these college enrollment figures are improving, they are still well below those of white students; 33% of
white high school graduates enrolled in college in 1970, and 39%
enrolled in college in 1989 (Carter & Wilson, 1991: 36–37).

The problem of the underrepresentation of minorities is evident
at the University of California. Students from diverse linguistic and
ethnic backgrounds are underrepresented in our classrooms. The
enrollment of Asian students at the nine campuses of the University

of California is twice their representation in the California high school population. Similarly, a greater percentage of white students attend the University of California than is reflected in their presence in the California high school population. This relationship does not hold for African American and Latino students, however; only one-third of the African American and Latino students who graduate from California high schools attend the University of California.

Not only are ethnic and linguistic minority students underrepresented at the University of California but, once they enroll here, they do not perform as well academically as their middle-income and white peers. The grades of African American, Latino, American Indian, and Filipino students are lower than those of white and Asian students. Furthermore, students who come from low-income families are three times as likely to encounter academic difficulty (e.g., be on probation, drop out, or not progress normally toward their degrees) as students who come from more well-to-do families (Morrell, 1990).

If the enrollment of students from underrepresented backgrounds in colleges and universities does not increase, and if these same students do not attain college degrees, then the nation will not have achieved the educational, economic, and social equity it has sought. Neither will it have the skilled work force it needs to ensure a healthy and competitive economy. Nor will it have the well-educated and thoughtful citizenry it needs for a vibrant and energetic democracy. Indeed, if the current college enrollment trends continue, then the economic disparities that exist between ethnic and income groups in the United States will widen.

UNTRACKING AND COLLEGE ENROLLMENT

What are the educational consequences of placing low-achieving students in college-bound courses with their high-achieving peers? In order to determine whether untracking works, we will compare the college enrollment of AVID students who graduated in 1990, 1991, and 1992 with that of students who graduated in 1991 from a number of high schools in the San Diego City Schools district; the college enrollment of AVID students who graduated in 1990 through 1992 with that of students who graduated from U.S. high schools in 1990; and the college enrollment of students who participated in the AVID untracking program for 3 years with that of students who left the program after participating for 1 year or less.

These comparisons will provide us insight into the value of organizing schools to emphasize an academic curriculum as an alternative to tracking underrepresented students. The college enrollment records of students who graduated from schools in San Diego and from across the United States, although not matched for socioeconomic status and ethnicity, give us a general point of comparison, whereas the college enrollment records of students who completed 3 years of AVID in contrast to those who completed 1 year will be particularly instructive for determining the effect of untracking students.

Figure 1 shows that 48% (120 of the 248 students reporting) who completed 3 years of AVID reported enrolling in 4-year colleges, 40% (99) enrolled in 2-year or community colleges, and the remaining 12% (29) began working or doing other things, such as engaging in church service, traveling, or doing voluntary work.

Of the 120 students attending 4-year colleges, 52 (43%) are enrolled in colleges within the California State University (CSU) system, 29 (24%) in colleges in the University of California (UC) system, and 39 students (33%) in a variety of private universities in and out of California. Most of the UC and CSU enrollees have stayed close to home; 18 of the 29 (62%) UC enrollees attend the University of California, San Diego, whereas 42 of the 52 (81%) CSU enrollees attend San Diego State University.

Figure 2 allows us to compare the college enrollment of the 248 students who graduated in 1990, 1991, and 1992 after participating in AVID for 3 years with three other groups: (1) those students who graduated in 1991 from a number of high schools in the San Diego district, (2) those students who graduated from U.S. high schools in 1990, and (3) AVID students who started in AVID but left after 1 year. In Figure 2 and all subsequent figures, we will refer to students who completed AVID as "AVID3" and students who left after 1 year as "AVID1."

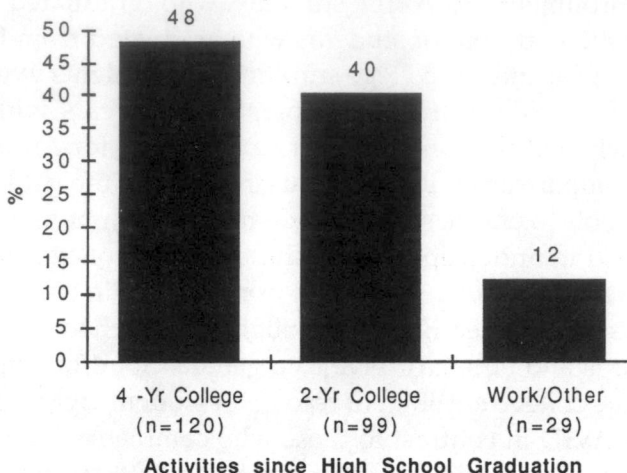

Figure 1. College Enrollment of AVID Students

The AVID 4-year college enrollment rate of 48% compares favorably with the local average and the national average. Bell (1993) surveyed 742 students who graduated from San Diego high schools in 1991. He found that 37% of that class went on to 4-year colleges, 34% attended 2-year colleges, and 29% reported working or doing other things. The American Council of Education reported that 39% of the 20 million students who graduated from high school in 1990 enrolled in 4-year colleges (Carter & Wilson, 1991). This means that the 4-year college enrollment rate of AVID students is higher than the local and national rate.

The 48% 4-year college enrollment rate of students who participated in AVID for 3 years also compares favorably with the 4-year college enrollment rate of students who completed 1 year or less of AVID. Our interviews with the 146 students who left AVID revealed that 34% of them enrolled in college within a year of their graduation from high school. The difference in college enrollment rates between these two groups suggests that the AVID untracking program has an effect on students' career choices after they complete

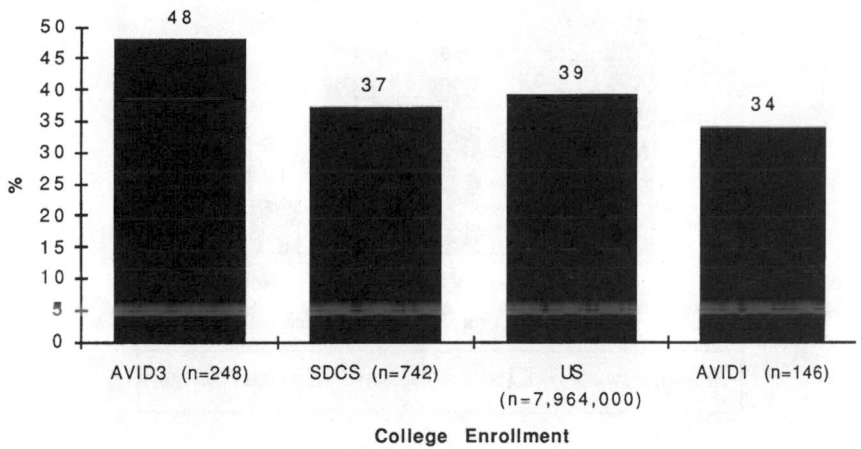

Figure 2. Enrollment of AVID, SDCS, and U.S. Students in 4-Year Colleges

high school. The longer they stay in the program, the better their college enrollment.

The 48% figure for enrollment in 4-year colleges is important because students from underrepresented groups are not going to college at just the time the number of jobs requiring college education is increasing. In fact, students across the nation are enrolling more often in 2-year colleges than they are enrolling in 4-year colleges. From 1978 to 1988, 2-year colleges increased enrollments by 21% while 4-year colleges increased by only 14% (Carter & Wilson, 1991: 4).

In Figure 3 we show both 2-year and 4-year college enrollment figures. AVID sends more students to 2-year colleges than the San Diego City Schools. Forty percent of the students who participate in AVID for 3 years and 40% of the students who participate for 1 year enroll in 2-year colleges. Both groups enroll in 2-year colleges more frequently than do students from the San Diego City Schools district, which sends 34% of its students to 2-year colleges.

If we combine enrollment in these two sectors of higher education, then the AVID college enrollment rate is even more impres-

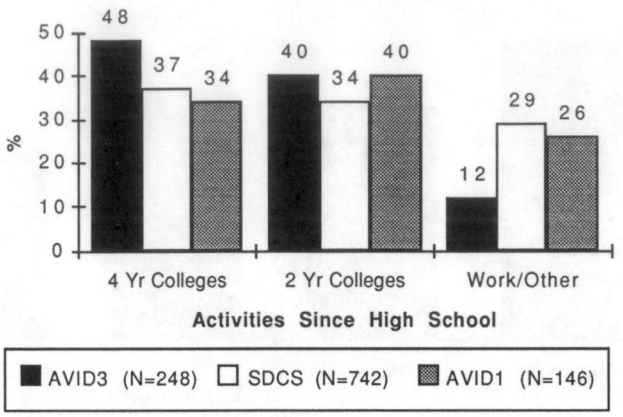

Figure 3. Activities of AVID and SDCS Students after High School

sive: 88% of students who participated in AVID for 3 years report attending some sort of college after they complete high school, while 71% of San Diego City Schools students go on to either a 4-year or a 2-year college. The combined college enrollment rate for San Diego City Schools students and students who participated in AVID for 1 year is comparable; 71% of the former and 74% of the latter go on to some kind of college, which suggests that even minimal participation in the untracking program has some effect on college enrollment.

Entering the work force is the corollary of college enrollment. Whereas only 12% of AVID graduates take a job when they finish high school, 29% of San Diego City Schools graduates and 26% of the AVID comparison group make this career choice after completing high school. These work force data say in another way, then, that this untracking program is influencing students' career choices after high school.

The decline in 4-year college enrollment across the United States is also troubling because few students transfer from 2-year to 4-year colleges, perhaps because community colleges perform a "cooling out" function (Clark, 1960; Karabel, 1972; Erickson & Schultz, 1982), especially for students from minority backgrounds. This untracking experiment, then, provides a model for increasing students' preparation for 4-year college by avoiding the gatekeeping barrier erected at the community college level.

COLLEGE ENROLLMENT BY ETHNICITY

In this section we describe the college enrollment rates of AVID students by ethnic group and compare college enrollment by ethnicity at the local and national levels.

Because both the San Diego City Schools and the American Council on Education report college enrollment for Anglos, African Americans, and Latinos, we can make both local and national comparisons. Because we do not have national data for Filipinos, Vietnamese, Cambodians, and Laotians, we can not analyze the college enrollment patterns of these groups. We also do not include Pacific Islanders, Native Americans, Japanese, and Korean students in the following discussion because there are not enough students from these ethnic groups for systematic analysis. (Each group comprises less than 5% of the sample.) Furthermore, we have been unable to find comparable national data on these ethnic groups.

African American Students

African American students have been enrolling in college more often since the Civil Rights era; 26% of black students who graduated from high school in 1970 enrolled in college, compared with 33% in 1989 (Carter & Wilson, 1991: 36–37). While these figures are improving, they are still below the college enrollment figures of white students; 33% of white high school graduates enrolled in college in 1970, and 39% in college in 1989 (Carter & Wilson, 1991: 36–37).

Figure 4 shows that 55% of African American students who participated in AVID for 3 years attend 4-year colleges, 50% who participated in AVID for 1 year attend 4-year colleges, while 38% of African American students who attended high schools in the San Diego school system go on to 4-year colleges. The national average (33%) is slightly lower than the San Diego average (38%). These

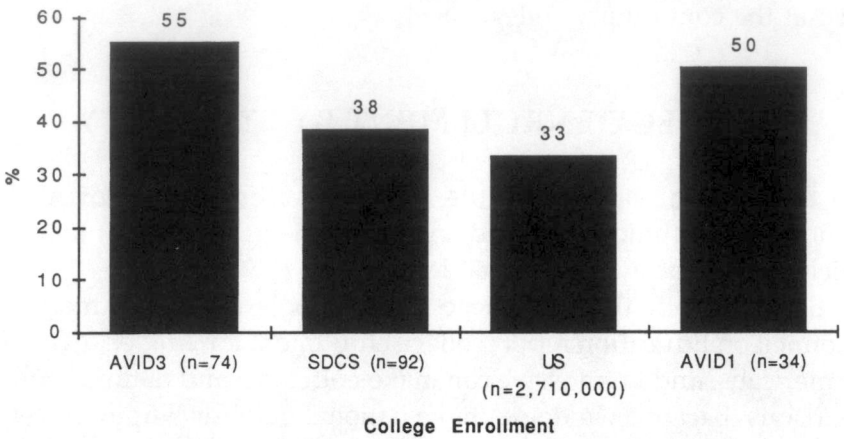

Figure 4. Enrollment of African American Students in 4-Year Colleges

data indicate that African American AVID students, whether they participate in AVID for 1 or 3 years, are enrolling in college at rates that are considerably higher than the local and national averages.

Many students are enrolling in the nation's Historically Black Colleges and Universities (HBCUs). In 1990, approximately 17% of African Americans in college were enrolled in HBCUs (Carter & Wilson, 1991). Based on our interviews with AVID graduates, we are seeing a similar trend among African American students in San Diego; 21% of African American graduates from the classes of 1990, 1991, and 1992 enrolled in Historically Black Colleges and Universities. Likewise, 26% of the African American students who began in AVID but left after 1 year, enrolled in HBCUs the fall after they graduated from high school.

The college enrollment of African American students who participate in AVID is important because the college enrollment gap between whites and African Americans has been fairly constant during the past decade. In 1990, 33% of all African American high school graduates were enrolled in college, while 39% of whites were enrolled in college. This 6% difference indicates that African Americans have made relatively little progress in achieving parity in college participation in the latter half of the 1980s. In fact, the gap

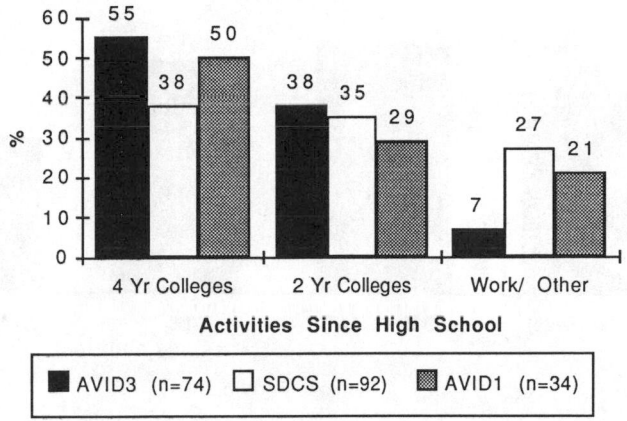

Figure 5. Activities of African American Students after High School

between African American and white college enrollment has widened since the 1970s (Carter & Wilson, 1991: 36–37).

The college enrollment rate for black AVID students is even more impressive when we add 2-year colleges into the equation (Figure 5). Of the African American students who participated in AVID for 3 years, 93% enrolled at either a 4-year or a 2-year college. Only 7% went to work after graduation from high school. By comparison, 73% of African American students who graduated from San Diego high schools in 1984 went to 2- or 4-year colleges while 27% of these students went directly to work after completing high school. Of the African American students who participated in AVID for 1 year, 50% went to 4-year colleges (26% to HBCUs, 24% to CSUs or UCs) and 29% went to 2-year colleges, mostly in the San Diego area.

Anglo Students

As a result of the decline in the number of white high school students in the population, the number of white students completing high school has been shrinking steadily since 1980. In that year, 20,214,000 white students completed high school; 32% of those high school graduates went on to college. By 1990, the number of white students completing high school had shrunk to 16,823,000, but the

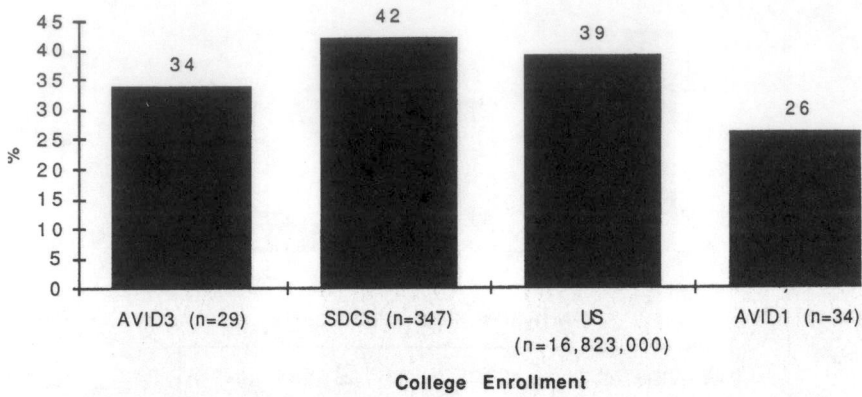

Figure 6. Enrollment of White Students in 4-Year Colleges

percentage of them enrolling in college increased to 39% (Carter & Wilson, 1991: 36).

Figure 6 shows that 34% of the Anglo students who participated in AVID for 3 years went to 4-year colleges. This rate is less than the 1991 San Diego City Schools' average of 42% and the 1990 national average of 39%. White students who participated in AVID for 1 year or less had the lowest 4-year college enrollment rate; 26% of this group enrolled in college. The white college enrollment figure of 34% is also the lowest of the 3 major ethnic groups served by this program. African Americans have a 55% college enrollment record and Latinos have a 43% rate.

This picture changes somewhat when we take 2-year colleges into account (Figure 7). Seventy-nine percent of white students who participated in AVID for 3 years attend either a 4- or a 2-year college after completing high school, which is the same rate as the white students who participated in AVID for 1 year. Both groups attend college more often than students from the San Diego City Schools, 73% of whom go to either a 4-year or a 2-year college after graduation. These data, then, suggest that untracking students has an effect on college enrollment. Students who participate in AVID enroll in college more often than students who do not participate, and the longer students enroll in AVID, the better is their college enrollment record.

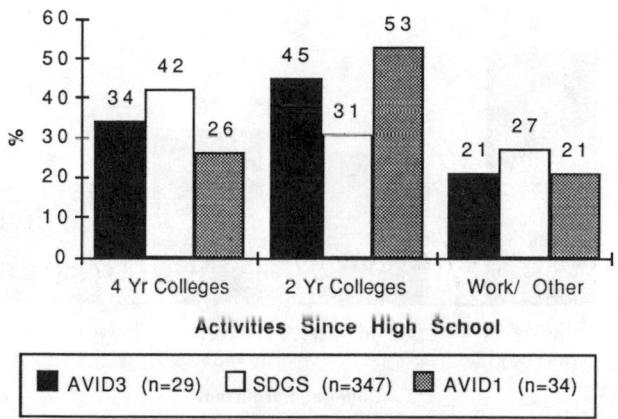

Figure 7. Activities of White Students after High School

As we discuss in Chapter 5, financial considerations seem to play a significant role in depressing the college enrollment of white students. Their parents have enough resources to invest in the preparation of their children for college, but they become trapped in the middle of college aid rules. They have too much money to qualify for student grants and no-pay scholarships, but not enough money to pay for their children's college education outright. In addition, there are not as many scholarships for poor white students as there are for poor students from underrepresented groups. As a result, students from this group enroll more often in 2-year colleges than they do 4-year colleges.

Latino Students

Latinos have made only modest gains in college enrollment in the past decade. Whereas the overall *number* of Latinos enrolled in the nation's colleges and universities has increased since the 1970s, their college enrollment *rate* may be declining. Between 1988 and 1990, the total *number* of Latino students enrolled in college rose by 11% from 680,000 to 758,000 students (Carter & Wilson, 1991: 43). The *rate* of enrollment, however is declining. In 1972, 25.8% of the Latinos who graduated from high school went on to college. For 2

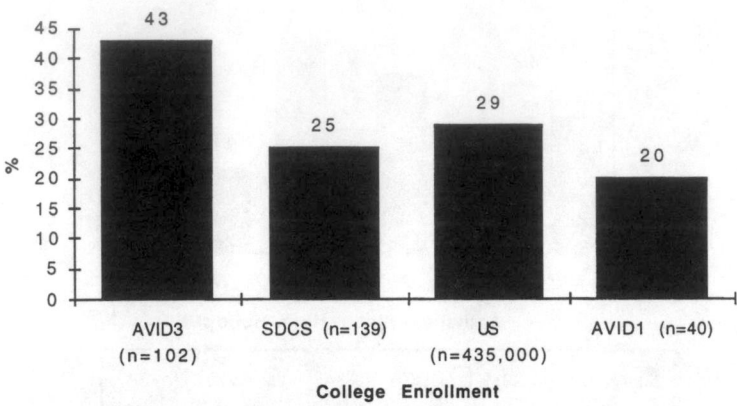

Figure 8. Enrollment of Latino Students in 4-Year Colleges

years, 1975 and 1976, this figure increased to 36%, but declined then, reaching 29% in 1990 (Carter & Wilson, 1991: 37). Furthermore, more Latino students attend 2-year colleges than 4-year colleges. As of 1988 (the last year for which this information is available), 56% of Latino students enrolling in college went to 2-year colleges (Carter & Wilson, 1991: 26).

By contrast, the Latino students who participated in AVID for 3 years almost double the proportion of San Diego City Schools students who attend 4-year colleges; they are also enrolling in college in numbers greater than the national average: 43% of Latino AVID students enroll in 4-year colleges, whereas the San Diego City Schools average is 25% and the national average is 29%. Furthermore, there is a considerable difference in the college enrollment rates of students who participate in AVID for different amounts of time. Those Latino students who participate in AVID for 3 years enroll in 4-year colleges at a 43% rate, whereas those who left the program after 1 year enroll in 4-year colleges at a 20% rate. This finding is especially impressive because the national Latino college enrollment rate is not increasing. In 1972, 26% of the high school graduating class enrolled in 4-year colleges. This figure rose to an all time high of 36% in 1976, but dropped to 29% by 1990 (Carter & Wilson, 1992: 37). See Figure 8.

The college enrollment rate of Latino students is even more im-

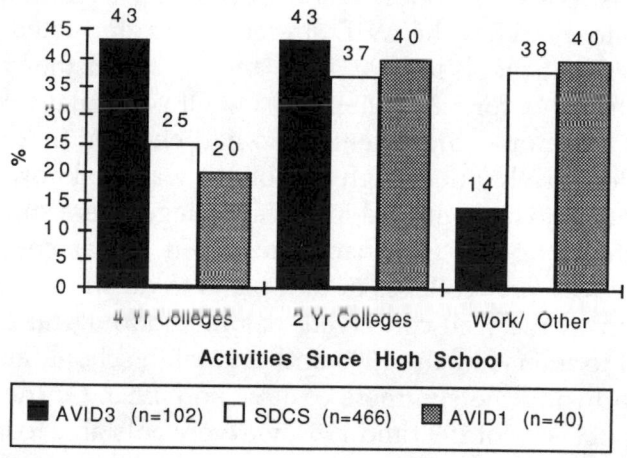

Figure 9. Activities of Latino Students after High School

pressive when we take 2-year colleges into account. Eighty-six percent of the Latino students who participated in AVID for 3 years enroll in either a 4- or a 2-year college. This means that only 14% go to work directly after completing high school. These college enrollment rates compare favorably with those from the San Diego City Schools; 62% of Latino students who graduated from high schools in the San Diego district in 1991 reported going on to either a 4-year or a 2-year college (Bell, 1993), whereas 38% of Latino students from the City Schools go directly to work after they complete high school.

The 2- and 4-year college enrollment rates of 3-year AVID students also surpass those of 1-year AVID students; 60% of 1-year AVID students enroll in some kind of college after graduation from high school, which is considerably less than the enrollment rate of students who participate in AVID for 3 years (Figure 9).

Persistence in College

Increasing the college enrollment of African American and Latino students is an important component in closing the achievement gap between "majority" and "minority" students. But students must complete college if they are to enter managerial and professional occupations. With this concern for college completion in mind, we attempted to interview the AVID students who graduated from the San Diego City Schools in 1990, 1991, and 1992 after they had been out of high school for 1 and then 2 years. Of particular interest are the career trajectories of students who had enrolled in 2-year and 4-year colleges right out of high school. We want to know whether the students who had enrolled in 4-year colleges were still enrolled and whether students who had enrolled in 2-year colleges had transferred to 4-year colleges or had plans to do so.

Our plan, while well conceived, has methodological flaws. We attempted to interview the 1990 and 1991 high school (and AVID) graduates during the summers of 1992 and 1993. Of the 144 students in the classes of 1990 and 1991, we were only able to interview 91 (which is 63% of the original sample) in the summer of 1992. Of the 104 students in the class of 1992, we were able to interview 77 (which is 75% of the original sample) in the summer of 1993. Those interview rates are reasonable, but we were able to interview far fewer students after they had been out of high school for 2 years – 46 of 144 – which is 32% of the original 1990–1991 cohort. This serious decline in cohort size prohibits us from attaching any statistical significance to our statements, but a few descriptive observations are still informative because longitudinal data of any quality on the topic of persistence in college are difficult to obtain.

With that caveat in mind, let us proceed. Of the 168 students we were able to interview after they had been out of high school for 1 year, 54 (or 32%) were enrolled in 4-year colleges, 74 (or 44%) were enrolled in 2-year colleges and 40 (or 24%) were working or "doing other things" (such as church missionary work). All the students enrolled in 4-year colleges had been in college the year before; that is, there were no students who moved up from 2-year colleges to 4-year colleges, which is not surprising, because students seldom transfer from community college until they complete 2 years. In addition, no students stopped working to enroll in 4-year colleges. Of the 74 students in 2-year colleges after 1 year of high school, 54 had started in 2-year colleges and continue there, 12 began in 4-year colleges but are now enrolled in 2-year colleges, and 8 who had begun their career after high school by working now attend 2-year colleges. In short, there was little upward mobility; only 5% (8 of 168 students) went from work to 2-year colleges. More troubling is the downward mobility in this cohort; 7% (12 of 168) left 4-year colleges to attend 2-year colleges.

These trends persist after students have been enrolled in college for 2 years. Of the 46 students we were able to interview in 1993, 16 (35%) were enrolled in 4-year colleges; 18 (39%) were enrolled in 2-year colleges, and 12 (26%) were working, or doing "other things." Of the 35 students enrolled in community colleges, 14 had attended them the year before, 2 transferred from 2-year colleges to 4-year colleges, and 3 had attended 4-year colleges the previous year.

That is, there is not much mobility from 2-year to 4-year colleges; only 11% (2 of 18) transferred after 2 years of community college. That figure is not very encouraging and suggests that policies and procedures, such as "tag" programs (which direct students from an untracking program like AVID to community college with the idea that they will transfer to 4-year colleges after 2 years) need to be examined closely. Likewise, the fact that 3 students dropped out of 4-year colleges during the 1992–1993 school year (which is 11% of the 27 students who were enrolled in 4-year colleges in 1992) gives pause for concern.

SUMMARY: UNTRACKING WORKS

Students from underrepresented ethnic and linguistic backgrounds who participated in the San Diego untracking experiment are enrolling in college in numbers that exceed local and national averages. Of the "untracked" students who graduated in the classes of 1990, 1991, and 1992 , 48% enrolled in 4-year colleges. This figure compares favorably with the local average of 37% and the national average of 39%.

The college enrollment rate for students who participated in AVID for 3 years is also superior to the enrollment rate of students who participated in AVID for 1 year or less (48% vs. 34%). This difference implies that the untracking program has an effect over time; the longer students stay in the untracking program, the greater its impact on students' college enrollment.

The untracking experiment works well for students from the two major underrepresented ethnic groups. African Americans and Latinos enroll in college in numbers that exceed local and national averages. Of the Latino students who have participated in AVID for 3 years, 43% enroll in 4-year colleges. This figure compares favorably with the San Diego City Schools average of 25% and the national average of 29%. African American students who participate in AVID for 3 years also enroll in college at rates higher than the local and national averages; 55% of African American students in AVID enroll in 4-year colleges, compared with 38% from the San Diego City Schools, and the national average of 33%. Here, then, we have an example of what Cummins (1986) has called a "threatening example" to conventional wisdom. AVID pulls the rug out from the assumption lurking in American education that suggests ethnic and linguistic minority kids cannot do well in college bound classes.

Although our database is not very large, we can comment on students' persistence in college. AVID students are staying in college once they enroll; 89% of those who started are in college 2 years later. A troubling pattern may be emerging, however: Students who enroll in community colleges upon graduation from high school are not transferring to 4-year colleges.

4

BACKGROUND CHARACTERISTICS AND COLLEGE ENROLLMENT

HAVING ANSWERED THE FIRST QUESTION OF OUR STUDY (Does untracking work?) in the affirmative, our next step is to determine the reasons for the success of this untracking experiment. How does untracking help students improve their academic performance? Our first point of departure is an investigation into the background characteristics of the students. In this chapter we consider the influence of two sets of background characteristics: one, parents' socioeconomic status (including their income and education), and two, the academic record of students when they enter the untracking program. In both cases, we want to see if the capital that students bring with them into the program has a greater influence than the capital that the students acquire while they are in the program.

PARENTS' SOCIOECONOMIC STATUS AND STUDENTS' COLLEGE ENROLLMENT

Socioeconomic status (SES) has been found to be one of the most influential factors in student success. Minority students do not do as well in school as white students and low-income students do not do as well as more economically advantaged students. Because the connection between SES and school performance is so strong (Coleman et al., 1966; Jencks et al., 1972; Center for Education Statistics, 1986; Haycock & Navarro, 1988), it is important to see if this factor is influential in our data before we move on to consider more subtle social and cultural factors.

Socioeconomic status is normally measured using some combination of parents' occupation, income, and educational level. Our indicator of parents' income is the median household income as calculated from census track data supplied to us by the San Diego Association of Governments. We obtained information about parents' education from our interviews with AVID graduates. If the students knew both of their parents' educational level, we combined mother's and father's education. If the students knew only one of their parents' education, we (obviously) used only that information.

Parents' Income and Students' College Enrollment

As Table 2 shows, we divided our sample into four income strata: $0–$19,999, $20,000–$39,999, $40,000–$59,999, and $60,000 and more. This table also shows the number of black, white, and Latino families and "1-year" and "3-year" students in these four income groups. AVID selected the majority of its students from low-income groups from 1990 to 1992. Of the AVID families in this cohort, 23% (91 of 393) have an income in the $0–$9,999 range, 42% have an income in the $20,000–$39,000 range, 21% of the AVID families had an income in the $40,000–$59,999, range and only 12 families (which constitute 6% of the total) had an income of more than $60,000.

Black and Latino students especially are selected from low- and middle-income families; 81% of Latino students (114 of 141) and 77% of black students (83 of 108) come from families that earn less than $40,000 a year. Only 1 black student came from a family that earned more than $60,000 and only 7 Latino students came from families in this income bracket. White students come from families that are more well to do; 35% (22 of 63 families) are in the $40,000–$59,999 range, 21% (13 of 63 families) are in the $60,000+ bracket, whereas 44% (28 of 63) are from families that earn less than $40,000 per year. Fifty-seven percent of "all other" students came from families that earn less than $40,000 and 43% come from families that earn more than this figure.

There are differences in family income between students who

Table 2. *Number of Students by Median Income, Years in AVID, and Ethnicity*

	Income Brackets				
Ethnic Group	$0–9K	$20–39K	$40–59K	$60+K	Total
White 1-Year	1	14	13	6	34
White 3-Year	4	9	9	7	29
Total White	5	23	22	13	63
Black 1-Year	4	19	10	1	34
Black 3-Year	14	46	14	0	74
Total Black	18	65	24	1	108
Latino 1-Year	16	15	5	3	39
Latino 3-Year	42	41	15	4	102
Total Latino	58	56	20	7	141
All Other 1-Year	7	19	11	1	38
All Other 3-Year	3	17	23	0	43
Total All Other	10	36	34	1	81
Total 1-Year	28	67	39	11	145
Total 3-Year	63	113	61	11	248
Total	91	180	100	22	393[a]

[a]The total number of students does not add up to 394 because we are missing income data on one Latina 1-year AVID student.

completed 3 years of the program and students who left after 1 year or less. Of the "3-year" students, 25% (63 of 248) came from families whose parents are in the lowest income group and 46% (113 of 248) came from the next income group. This means that 71% of the students who participated in the untracking program for 3 years came from families that earned less than $40,000 and 29% came from families that earned more than $40,000. By contrast, 19% (28 of 145) of the "1-year" students came from families in the lowest income group and 46% (67 of 145) came from families in the next income group. This means that 65% came from families that earned less than $40,000 and 35% came from families that earned more than this figure.

Figure 10 shows the college enrollment of students in the un-

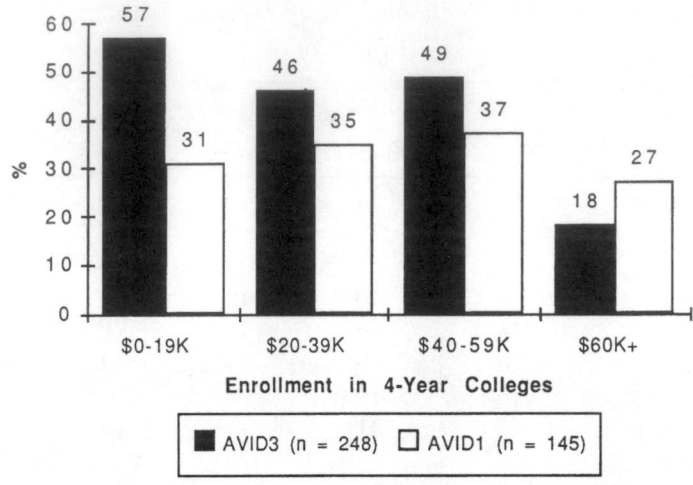

Figure 10. Parents' Income and AVID Students' College Enrollment

tracking experiment according to the median income of their parents and the years they spent in the program. Let us consider the group of students who completed 3 years of AVID first. If we disregard (for the moment) the students from the $60,000+ group, we find that the students who come from the lowest income strata enroll in 4-year colleges in greater proportion than students who come from higher income strata; 57% of 3-year AVID students whose parents earn less than $20,000 enroll in 4-year colleges, which is greater than the college enrollment figure of the 3-year AVID students in the $20,000–$39,000 and the $40,000–$59,000 range. Now, examining the college enrollment records of students who complete 1 year of AVID, we find that 31% of students from the lowest income group and 35% of the students from the $20,000–$39,000 income group enroll in 4-year colleges, compared with 37% of the students in the $40,000–$59,000 income group.

Thus, the college enrollment record of the comparison group is highly correlated with parents' income; the higher the parents' income, the more likely their children are to enroll in college. We do not find this linear correlation among the group of students who have completed 3 years of AVID. Students from low-income families enroll in college at rates that are higher than students who come from more well-to-do families.

When we compare the college enrollment rates of the 2 groups of AVID students at each income level, we find that (with the exception of the $60,000+ group) the students who have completed 3 years of AVID enroll in college at a higher rate than the students who have completed 1 year of AVID. The most striking difference appears in the lowest income group. Three-year AVID students who come from this income group enroll in college at almost twice the rate of 1 year AVID students (57% vs. 31%). In the higher-income brackets, the enrollment gap is not quite as dramatic but is still significant. Three-year AVID students who come from families who earn between $20,000 and $39,999 enroll in college 11% more often than students who have completed 1 year of AVID (46% vs. 35%). Three-year AVID students who come from families who earn between $40,000 and $59,999 enroll in college 12% more often than students who have completed 1 year of AVID (49% vs. 37%).

Let us now turn to the 11 "3-year AVID" students who come from families that earn more than $60,000. Here we encounter a surprising finding. Only 2 of these students enrolled in 4-year colleges and 7 enrolled in 2-year colleges. While that distribution is striking, we cannot find a clear pattern to explain it. Ethnicity is not a determinant. Of the students enrolled in 2-year colleges, 5 are Anglo and 2 are Latino. Of the 4 students who were accepted at 4-year colleges, 2 are Anglo and 2 are Latina. Academic record has some bearing. None of these students had stellar academic records; their grades were in the 2.30–3.00 range and they did not complete the full complement of college prep courses. Two of the students were accepted at 2-year colleges, but did not enroll. Two did not apply to 4-year colleges at all, and 2 applied but were not accepted.

We think that expense might be a factor. One of the Latina students who was accepted at San Diego State said she chose not to enroll there because the campus was "too far away" and she "was not ready to attend a 4-year university." One of the Anglo students echoed the Latina student's concerns about distance. He enrolled in Mesa Community College rather than SDSU because "it was closer to home." Two of the students who did not even apply to 4-year colleges also invoked "distance" as the reason. We think this concern about "distance" is masking the ever increasing cost of higher education. It is possible that students who are coming from higher-income families are caught in the middle. Their parents' $60,000+ income is enough to give them some cultural advantages while in high school and to pump up their college aspirations, but it is not enough money to send them to college without financial support. Given the state of the economy and the educational policies of the Bush administration in effect at the time of this study, students whose families are in this income bracket are not able to garner fellowships and they are afraid that loans will burden them financially. Therefore, they go to 2-year, not 4-year colleges.

In sum, the data we have gathered on parents' income and students' college enrollment suggest that the AVID untracking program is suppressing the well-established effects of parents' income on students' academic achievement. Students who come from the lowest socioeconomic strata and who complete 3 years of the untracking program enroll in 4-year colleges in equal or greater proportion to students from higher socioeconomic levels. Students who complete 3 years of AVID enroll in college in greater proportion than students who complete 1 year of AVID at each income level.

Parents' Education and Students' College Enrollment

The possibility that this untracking program is suppressing the effects of SES gains support when we examine students' college enrollment in relation to parents' education. Recall that 48% of the students who completed 3 years of AVID enrolled in 4-year colleges and 34% of the students who completed 1 year of AVID enrolled in 4-year colleges in the fall after they graduated from high school. Figure 11 arrays the college enrollment of 1-year and 3-year AVID students according to the education that their parents obtained. First, considering 3-year AVID students, we find that those students whose parents have taken college courses or graduated from college do not enroll in college in greater numbers than students whose parents have a high school diploma or less. In fact, students

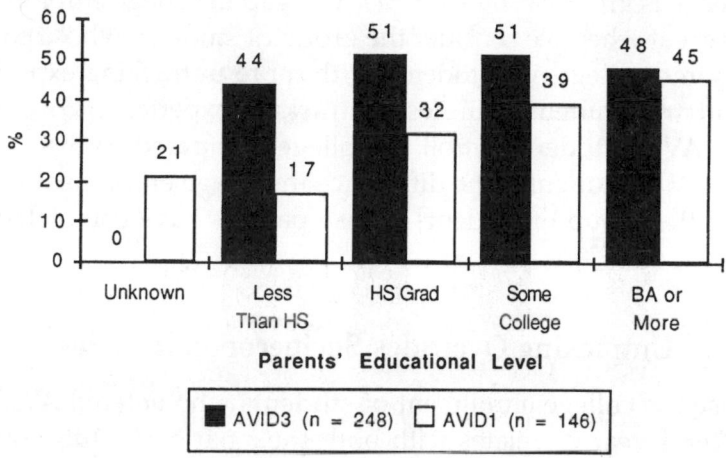

Figure 11. Parents' Education and AVID Students' College Enrollment

who come from families who are high school graduates enroll in college as often as students who come from families whose parents have had college experience; 51% of the former and 51% of the latter go to college.

We find a different, in fact linear, relationship within the comparison group. The higher the educational level of AVID parents, the higher the college enrollment rate of their children. Whereas only 17% of the 1-year AVID students whose parents have less than a high school education and 32% of the 1-year AVID students whose parents have earned a high school diploma enroll in college, 39% of the students whose parents have earned some college credit and 45% of the students whose parents have earned a B.A. enroll in college.

Students who have participated in AVID for 3 years have a better college enrollment record than students who participated in AVID for 1 year at each level of their parents' education. When we consider the group of parents who do not have high school degrees, we find that their children who participate in AVID for 3 years enroll in college almost 3 times more than students who participate in AVID for 1 year (44% vs. 17%). When we consider the group of students whose parents have completed high school, we also find that this difference is greater (51% vs. 32%). The gap in college enrollment is not as great when we consider the group of students whose parents have some college, yet students with more untracking experience still outstrip students with less untracking experience: 51% of the 3-year AVID students enroll in college compared to 39% of the 1-year AVID students. The difference in college enrollment is least among the group of students whose parents have completed college: 48% to 45%.

Untracking Overrides Socioeconomic Status

Because the college enrollment of students who entered AVID but left after 1 year correlates with both their parents' education and their parents' income whereas college enrollment does not correlate with parents' education and parents' income among students who have completed 3 years of AVID, we have some evidence that suggests that the untracking program overrides to some extent the effects of these two important dimensions of SES.

We think this is an important finding, because the so-called "reproduction" school of thought on social class and educational attainment (e.g., Bowles & Gintis, 1976; Bourdieu & Passeron, 1977a; Willis, 1977; MacLeod, 1987; McLaren, 1989) suggests that students from low-income and poorly educated families are hampered by structural constraints relative to the children from middle- and upper-income families. For example, the work of Sewell and Hauser (1975) is often cited to illustrate the reproductive effects that accrue to high-status families. They reported that students from high socioeconomic backgrounds were 2.5 times more likely to continue education beyond high school, 4 times more likely to enter college, 6 times more likely to complete college, and 9 times more likely to receive graduate training. As a result of these constraints, the sons and daughters from low-income and poorly educated families wind up in the same kinds of jobs as their parents. They do not progress upward through the occupational structure; their lowly positions are reproduced, generation after generation.

Our data show that such students are not necessarily trapped by their social circumstances. Students from the lowest income and educational levels are attaining a prestigious and economically important goal, enrollment in college. This means social environments can be rearranged, at least under certain circumstances, in order to facilitate educational opportunities.

STUDENTS' ACADEMIC BACKGROUND AND COLLEGE ENROLLMENT

A different type of background characteristic – students' academic record prior to entering the untracking program – could also influence students' success there, and hence their enrollment in college. In this section, we examine the program's selection practices in order to determine whether this untracking experiment is successful in college placement because it preselects a special group of students.

The recruitment process as described in the AVID manual involves: (1) the nomination of students by seventh- and eighth-grade teachers, (2) a verification of eligibility by the AVID staff, (3) a meeting with potential students to determine their interest, and (4) a contract with parents whose students have been selected. AVID teachers are directed to target students from underrepresented minority groups and students from low-income families who show "academic potential." Ethnicity is determined by teachers who check ethnic identity codes on students' records. Low-income status is determined using free or reduced lunch eligibility when this information is available. Academic potential is measured using a combination of CTBS scores and grades. The AVID coordinators are directed to look for students who have average to high CTBS scores and C grades. A stanine from 4 to 9 is used as an indicator of high potential and C grades are used as an indicator of low performance. Students with grades below 2.0 are considered too great an academic risk and are not to be included in the program unless there are extenuating circumstances. Math scores are weighed more heavily than verbal scores on the CTBS because AVID Center feels verbal scores are unfair to students who do not speak English as a first language and language independent tests are better indicators of students' ability.

Student Selection Profiles

Employing the definitions provided by the AVID program, we divided the group of 394 students in our sample into categories based on their performance on eighth-grade CTBS tests and their grades at the time of their selection into AVID. "High" CTBS scores were a stanine level of 7, 8, or 9, "middle" CTBS scores were at a stanine level of 4, 5, or 6, and "low" CTBS scores were at a level of 1, 2, or 3. "High" grades were those above 3.0, "middle" grades were those in the 2.0–2.99 range and "low" grades were those less than 2.00. This procedure produced 3 categories: (1) a "high" selection group, that contained students who had high CTBS and high GPAs or middle CTBS and high grades, (2) a "middle" selection group that contained students who had high CTBS scores and middle-level grades and those who had middle-level test scores and middle-level grades and (3) a "low selection group" that contained students who had low grades or low scores, or both (see Table 3).

Not all students who graduated in 1990, 1991, and 1992 fit this preferred profile when they were selected into the program; 55% of the students selected into AVID had the recommended combination of grades and test scores – that is, either high test scores and middle grades or middle test scores and middle grades – but 28% had test scores or grades that were higher than the program's definition and 17% were selected into the program with either grades or test scores that were lower than the program recommends.

The selection profile of students who completed 3 years of AVID differs from students who left after 1 year. Whereas 29% of the 3-year AVID students were in the high selection group, 25% of the 1-year AVID students were in this group. Whereas 56% of the 3-year AVID students were in the middle or preferred selection group, 53% of the 1-year students were in this group. The biggest difference appears in the low selection group: 15% of the AVID students who completed 3 years of the program were selected "be-

Table 3. *Students' Selection Profiles*

Selection Group	1-Year AVID	3-Year AVID	Total
High	37 (25%)	72 (29%)	109 (28%)
Middle	77 (53%)	140 (56%)	217 (55%)
Low	32 (22%)	36 (15%)	68 (17%)
Total	146 (100%)	248 (100%)	394 (100%)

low the line," whereas 22% of the students who left after 1 year had grades and test scores below the selection criteria recommended by AVID. The similarity in the profiles suggests that students who completed the program and students who left the program were selected using similar criteria.

Ethnicity and Selection Profiles

When considering the ethnic distribution of students in the high, middle and low selection groups, we followed the practice outlined in the first chapter. While acknowledging the flaws in doing so, we considered Latinos, blacks, and whites as distinct groups. There are 79 students who come from Indochinese, Filipino, Japanese, Korean, Pacific Islander, and Native American backgrounds in our sample. Because there are not enough students in any one of these ethnic groups to treat separately, for the purposes of displaying our data, we place them into the unfortunate "all other" category in Tables 4 and 7.

Latinos compose the largest ethnic group in this sample of AVID students: 36% are Latino, 27% are black, 16% are white, and 21% are from "all other" backgrounds. Latinos also comprise the largest group within each selection category: 38 of 109 (35%) are in the high selection group, 77 of 217 (35%) are in the middle selection group, and 27 of 68 (40%) are in the low selection group.

When we examine the distribution of students within selection groups by their ethnicity, we find an uneven pattern. Most Latino, white, and African American students were selected according to

Table 4. *Ethnic Distribution of Students in Selection Groups*

Selection Group	Latino	White	Black	All Other	Total
High 1-Year	7	7	10	13	37
High 3-Year	31	8	10	23	72
Total High	38	15	20	36	109
Middle 1-Year	19	23	13	22	77
Middle 3-Year	58	19	47	16	140
Total Middle	77	42	60	38	217
Low 1-Year	14	4	11	3	32
Low 3-Year	13	3	17	3	36
Total Low	27	7	28	6	68
Total 1-Year	40	34	34	38	71
Total 3-Year	102	29	74	43	44
Total	142	63	108	81	394

the criteria AVID recommends; 54% (77 of 142) of Latinos, 66% (42 of 63) of whites, and 56% (60 of 108) of blacks were selected using high CTBS scores and middle-range grades, whereas only 47% (38 of 81) of Indochinese, Filipino, Japanese, Korean, and Pacific Islander students were selected according to these preferred criteria. The two Native American students in this sample had high CTBS and high grades when selected.

Latino and African American students are overrepresented in the low selection category: 26% (28 of 108) of black students and 19% (27 of 142) of Latino students had some combination of low grades and low test scores upon admission into AVID. By contrast, only 11% of whites (7 of 63) and 7% (6 of 81) of "all other" students were "below the line" when selected. A disproportionate number of the students in the "all other" category are in the high selection group: 44% (36 of 81) had high grades and test scores upon admission to AVID.

This uneven distribution leads us to ask the following questions at this juncture: Are the selection criteria being applied evenly across ethnic groups? Are African Americans and Latinos being accepted regardless of their academic standing? Are Indochinese,

Filipino, Japanese, Korean, and Pacific Islander students being selected even though they are performing at a standard higher than AVID's cut off point? Or were these students enrolled in lower-level classes where their grades were inflated? Should the 28% (109 of 394) of students who are selected into AVID with high test scores and high grades be accepted at all? We turn our attention to the preparation of students who attempt to qualify for entrance into CSU and UC and their actual college enrollment in order to answer these questions.

Student Selection and College Eligibility

The University of California (UC) and the California State University (CSU) do not admit students exclusively based on their grade point averages. Students must take a specific combination of courses in the arts, humanities, math, natural sciences, and social sciences; this combination of courses is referred to colloquially as the "a–f requirements."

The a–f requirements are practically identical for the CSU and UC systems. Both university systems require a completion of 30 semesters of college preparatory courses with a C or better in each course. Each university requires the following:

a. 4 years of English

b. 1 year of history

c. 3 years of mathematics

d. 1 year of laboratory science

e. 2 years of foreign language

f. 4 years of electives

The CSU and UC systems differ in the f requirement, the electives. The UC system requires that all 4 years of electives come from the a–e areas. The CSU requires 3 years of electives and an additional mandatory year from a new section called "visual and performing arts." This leaves the CSU applicant with 3 years of elec-

Table 5. *Selection Profiles and College Eligibility*

Selection Group	Total Students	UC/CSU a–f Courses	
		Attempted	Completed
High 1-Year	37	29 (78%)	23 (62%)
High 3-Year	72	61 (85%)	48 (67%)
Total High	109	90 (83%)	71 (65%)
Middle 1-Year	77	32 (42%)	11 (14%)
Middle 3-Year	140	95 (68%)	46 (23%)
Total Middle	217	127 (59%)	57 (26%)
Low 1-Year	32	7 (22%)	0 (0%)
Low 3-Year	36	19 (53%)	4 (11%)
Total Low	68	26 (38%)	3 (6%)
All 1-Year	146	68 (47%)	34 (23%)
All 3-Year	248	175 (71%)	98 (40%)
Total	394	243 (62%)	132 (34%)

tives, which may come from a–e areas, or from the visual or performing arts areas.

The University of California imposes an additional requirement: At least 14 of the 30 semester classes must be taken in the last 2 years of study. The university also recommends 1 additional year of mathematics, science, and foreign language. One more fundamental difference between the college systems is the relationship between GPA and college entrance test requirements. The California State University says that no test scores are necessary if a student has a 3.0 GPA or higher. The University of California says no test scores are necessary if a student has a 3.3 GPA or higher.

For the purposes of this study, we employed the CSU definitions of a–f requirements. Table 5 displays the numbers of students who attempted a–f classes at their high schools and the numbers of students who completed these requirements. Because the San Diego City Schools transcripts do not show courses students took at community colleges, we were not able to compute a–f courses that students may have taken there.

This table shows us that 62% of all AVID students attempted to complete the requisite 30 or more courses in the a–f distribution and 34% completed these courses during their high school careers. The greatest percentage of these students came from the high selection group; 83% of this group attempted 30 or more a–f courses and 65% completed them, whereas 59% of the middle (AVID) selection group attempted the requisite combination of a–f courses and 26% actually completed them. Students from the low selection group had the poorest a–f completion record. Whereas 38% of the students who had low CTBS scores and/or low grades when they entered the program attempted the combination of courses that would make them eligible for the California State University or the University of California, only 6% actually completed all the courses in this sequence.

The preparation for college eligibility for students who complete 3 years of the program differs from those students who complete only 1 year. Students who complete 3 years of the program outstrip students who complete 1 year or less. Within the high selection group, 85% of 3-year students attempt the full complement of a–f courses and 67% complete them, whereas 78% of 1-year students attempt and 62% complete this regimen of courses. Within the middle selection group, 68% of 3-year students attempt a–f courses and 23% complete them, whereas 42% of 1-year students attempt and 14% complete them. This disparity is most evident in the low selection group: 53% of 3-year students attempt a–f courses and 11% complete them, whereas 22% of 1-year students attempt a–f courses but none completed this sequence.

These data suggest that the eight AVID coordinators in our study are successful in encouraging students who enter the program with low academic records to attempt academically rigorous classes, but they are less successful in getting them to complete these classes. The disparities in college eligibility also suggest that participation in the untracking activity makes a difference. A group of students who participate in untracking for 3 years accumulates a better college eligibility record than a similar group of students who left this program within 1 year.

Test scores matter. We do not know what the CTBS measures, yet when we compare the college eligibility records of the high, middle, and low selection groups, we find that students who perform well on this test in eighth grade accumulate better academic records than students who do not perform well on it in eighth grade.

Student Selection and College Enrollment

College enrollment is not evenly distributed across selection groups (Table 6). Of the students who entered AVID with grades and test scores in the highest range, 65% enroll in 4-year colleges, while 39% of the students who enter the program with grades and test scores in the middle range, and 21% of the students who entered the program with grades and test scores in the lowest range enroll in 4-year colleges.

College enrollment is related to students' participation in the program. Forty-five percent of the students in the middle selection group who completed 3 years of the program enrolled in college, whereas 27% of the students in this selection category who left after 1 year enrolled in college. There is even a more striking disparity within the low selection group. Twenty-eight percent of the students in the low selection group who completed 3 years of the program enrolled in college, whereas only 13% of the students in the low selection category who left after 1 year enrolled in college.

Only in the high selection group do students who left the program early perform as well as the students who participated for 3 years. Sixty-five percent of the students in the high selection group who left after 1 year enrolled in college, which is the same rate as the students who completed 3 years of the program. We think that these high college enrollment rates are a consequence of students' test scores. Those students who score well on the eighth-grade CTBS and have high grades do well in high school with or without a systemic program of institutional and social supports. Whatever ingredient CTBS is measuring, it seems influential in students' subsequent academic success.

The data in Table 6 send a number of messages. One, AVID's impressive college enrollment rate is influenced somewhat by students whose entrance records are "above the cutoff line" established by AVID. Two, test scores matter. Students who enter the program with the highest CTBS scores have the highest college

Table 6. *Selection Profiles and College Enrollment*

Selection Group	Total Students	4-Year College Enrollment
High 1-Year	37	24 (65%)
High 3-Year	72	47 (65%)
Total High	109	71 (65%)
Middle 1-Year	77	21 (27%)
Middle 3-Year	140	63 (45%)
Total Middle	217	84 (39%)
Low 1-Year	32	4 (13%)
Low 3-Year	36	10 (28%)
Total Low	68	14 (21%)
All 1-Year	146	49 (34%)
All 3-Year	248	120 (48%)
Total	394	169 (43%)

enrollment rate. Three, program participation matters. While an equivalent percentage of 1- and 3-year students in the high selection group enrolls in college, a significantly higher percentage of 3-year students than of 1-year students in the middle selection category (45% vs. 27%) and the low selection category (28% vs. 13%) enrolls in college.

Ethnicity, College Eligibility, and College Enrollment

Table 7 shows college eligibility and college enrollment according to students' ethnicity. There is a significant difference across ethnic groups in the preparation of students for college eligibility. The average "attempt rate" for AVID students in this cohort is 70%. More Japanese, Korean, Filipino, Indochinese, and Native American students (our "all other" category) attempted the full complement of a–f courses (91%) than any other ethnic group. Whites had the next highest "attempt rate" (69%), followed by Latinos (67%) and African Americans (61%).

We see a similar pattern in the a–f "completion rates" for the major ethnic groups. The average completion rate is 40%. "All

Table 7. *Ethnicity, College Eligibility, and College Enrollment*

Ethnicity	Total Students	UC/CSU a–f Courses		4-Yr College Enrollment
		Attempted	Completed	
Latino	102	70 (67%)	39 (38%)	44 (43%)
White	29	20 (69%)	12 (41%)	10 (34%)
Black	74	45 (61%)	20 (27%)	41 (55%)
All Others	43	39 (91%)	27 (63%)	25 (58%)
Total	248	174 (70%)	98 (40%)	120 (48%)

other" students complete more than this average (63%), while Latinos and whites each approximate it. African American students show the biggest drop from a–f courses attempted (61%) to completed (27%).

That is, Asian and Native American students have the best record of attempting and completing the distribution of courses that makes them eligible for entry into UC and CSU schools. Less than one-half of the Latino and white students and less than 30% of African American students in AVID complete these college eligibility requirements.

AVID students' eligibility rates compare very favorably with California eligibility rates. Figure 12 shows that the college eligibility of AVID students in each major ethnic category is equal to or higher than the state average. While AVID prepares 39% of its Latino students for entrance into UC and CSU, the state average is 22%. While AVID prepares 41% of its white students to be eligible for UC and CSU, the state average is 34%. The average for African American students virtually equals the state average, and the average for "all other" students is slightly higher than the California average. So, although a 40% college eligibility rate is not an astronomical figure, it is better than the state of California average.

These eligibility rates, while impressive, are surpassed by the college enrollment rates of AVID students. More African American and Latino students enroll in 4-year colleges than one would predict based on their a–f completion rates. Twice as many African

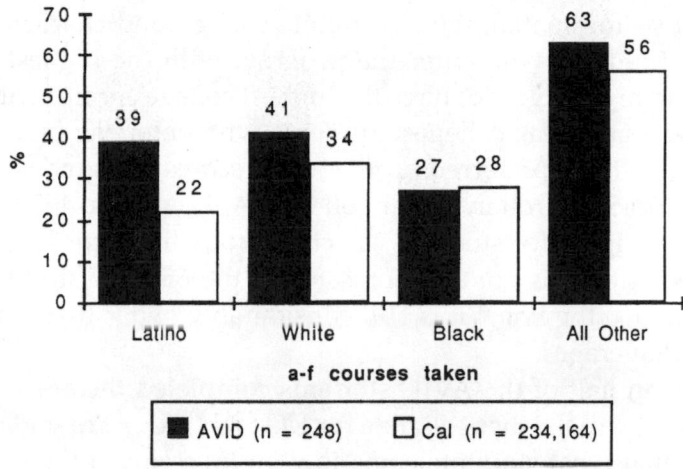

Figure 12. College Eligibility Rates of California and AVID Students (source of California data: CBEDS Data Collection, October 1991)

American students enroll in 4-year colleges (41) than complete UC or CSU eligibility requirements (20). Five more Latino students enroll in 4-year colleges than complete UC or CSU eligibility requirements.

SUMMARY: UNTRACKING SUPPRESSES SOCIOECONOMIC STATUS BUT TEST SCORES MATTER

The factors usually associated with socioeconomic status (parents' income and education) are not responsible for the impressive college enrollment figures of these "untracked" students. Students who come from the lowest income strata enroll in 4-year colleges in equal or higher proportion to students who come from higher income strata. Students who come from families in which their parents have less than a college education enroll in 4-year colleges more than students who come from families who have had a college education.

Although students' socioeconomic background characteristics may not be influential, their academic background characteristics may be. Students who enter the program with the highest CTBS scores and highest grades have the highest college enrollment rates; 65% enroll in 4-year colleges. Students who enter the untracking program with the preferred profile of test scores and grades do not do as well; 45% enroll in 4-year colleges. Although the 45% college enrollment figure for students selected into AVID according to the preferred criteria is not as impressive as the 65% for students selected "above the line," it is still considerably better than national and local averages.

Less than half of the AVID students completed the a–f requirements, which make them eligible for UC and CSU. At first glance, it appears that what students come in with (in terms of their grades and their test scores) is more important in making them eligible for 4-year colleges than what AVID does for students while they are in the program. The students who are most productive in achieving college eligibility are those who enter the program with the highest test scores and GPAs. However, we must not lose sight of the fact that 45% of the students in the middle selection group and 28% in the low selection group completed course requirements and enrolled in 4-year colleges.

The majority of students (55%) were selected into AVID according to the preferred profile of test scores in the high or middle range and grades in the middle range, while 28% were above this line and 17% were below this line when selected into the program. These selection profiles had some influence on the students' high school academic performance. More students from the high selection group attempted and completed a–f courses and enrolled in 4-year colleges than students in the middle ("preferred") and low selection groups. More specifically, 65% of the high selection group enrolled in 4-year colleges, while 45% of the middle selection group and only 28% of the low selection group enrolled in 4-year colleges upon graduation. It looks like the commendable college-going rate is being bolstered, at least in part, by the record of the high selection group.

There does not seem to be an ethnic bias in student selection.

More than 60% of Latino, black, and white students who complete the program were selected according to the preferred AVID criteria. Only "Asian" students were overrepresented in the high selection category, and since there are so few students from any particular ethnic group in this artificial category, it is not possible to draw any specific conclusions. Blacks, with 26% of their total population, and Latinos with 19% of their total population, were overrepresented in the low selection category, which leads us to believe that black and Latino students may be so coveted in some schools that they are selected into the program regardless of their test scores and grades.

A comparison of students who participated in this untracking experiment for 3 years with students who left after 1 year gives us other indicators that untracking, and not the students' prior record, is influential:

1. Students who participate in untracking for 3 years accumulate a better college eligibility record than students who left the untracking program within 1 year (40% vs. 23%).

2. More students who completed 3 years of AVID enrolled in 4-year colleges than the students who completed 1 year of AVID (48% vs. 34%).

3. Students who complete 3 years of AVID enrolled in college in greater proportion than students who complete 1 year of AVID regardless of the family income level: 57% of 3-year AVID students from low-income families enroll in college, versus 31% of 1-year AVID students from low-income families; 46% of 3-year AVID students from families in the $20,000–$39,000 income range enrolled in college versus 35% of 1-year AVID students who come from families in this range; 49% of 3-year AVID students who come from families in the $40,000–$59,000 range and 37% of the 1-year AVID students who come from families in this income range enroll in college.

In short, the capital that students bring with them into the program does not seem to be as important as the capital that students accrue while they are in the program. This fact invites us to look more closely at the educational practices of the untracking program in order to understand the reasons for its success. In the following chapters, we explore the idea that the academic success of "untracked" students is the result of organizational and cultural processes operating within the classroom and between the school and the community.

5

THE SOCIAL SCAFFOLDING SUPPORTING ACADEMIC PLACEMENT

THE INFORMATION WE PRESENTED IN CHAPTER 4 SUGgests that the characteristics associated with students' socioeconomic and academic background are not overwhelmingly responsible for the commendable college enrollment record that the San Diego untracking program enjoys. Because AVID students are enrolling in college more frequently than their early high school records would predict, we are attracted to looking into the inner workings of the program to find the reasons for its success. We take up that task in the next four chapters, starting here with the social organization of the AVID classroom.

IMPLICIT SOCIALIZATION AND THE CULTURE OF THE CLASSROOM

Our discussion of the social processes of untracking rests on two interrelated ideas: One, academic life has implicit or hidden dimensions that students must master in order to be successful in school; and two, a system of institutional supports or "scaffolds" supports AVID students as they traverse this implicit cultural system.

Social Scaffolding

Instead of simplifying instruction or reducing the curriculum for underachieving students, AVID attempts to maintain a rigorous curriculum for all students while adding increased support for low-achieving students. We borrow (and modify) the term "interactional scaffolding" (Wood, Bruner, & Ross, 1976; Bruner, 1986) or "zone of proximal development" (Vygotsky, 1978; LCHC, 1983; Cole & Griffin, 1987) from the cognitive development literature to characterize the practice of combining heterogeneous grouping with a uniform, academically rigorous curriculum enhanced with strong supports.

In the cognitive development literature, scaffolding generally refers to the support that a single learner receives from a more capable peer while engaged in a cognitive task. The idea is to provide extensive guidance to a learner at the beginning of the learning experience and then remove the supports slowly as the learner internalizes the help the guide provided so that the task can be carried out alone.

Social scaffolding entails the engineering of instructional tasks so that students develop their own competencies through their interactions with more capable peers or experts (Vygotsky, 1978). Once students have acquired such competencies, then they can perform in ways that insure their advancement through the system. The role of the expert or more capable peer in social scaffolding is indirect by design, although the support that is provided typically requires planning and installing structured activities and projects without making them appear to be structured, as exemplified by the way that parents teach their young children to read (Ninio & Bruner 1978).

From the beginning, the setting is parent and child and the activity is reading a book. Initially, the child knows very little about the activity of reading and the parent must do much of the work. As the child gains knowledge, as attention shifts from pictures to words, the child begins to recite well-learned pieces of the story. This skill becomes more and more flexible as the support provided by the book and the parent recedes and the child becomes an independent reader. The activity – parent and child sitting together reading the book – remains constant throughout the whole process. What has changed is the degree of the child's participation in the activity.

In the AVID classroom, we have a different organizational arrangement than the one productively described as scaffolding by cognitive psychologists: *Groups* of students are learning about school culture, assisted by *groups* of experts or more capable peers. Nevertheless, the generative idea of scaffolding seems to capture well the processes that occur there. In the AVID classroom, the idea is to provide supports to students at the beginning of their high school experience, and then remove the supports slowly as students internalize the help their guides provided them so they can finally act on their own.

The Hidden Dimensions of Academic Life

Implicit, often unstated dimensions of instruction accompany the more obvious, explicit academic dimensions of instruction. Whether they call it the "hidden curriculum" (Dreeben, 1968; Apple, 1982; Apple & Weis, 1983; Young, 1971) or the "culture of the classroom" (Cazden & Mehan, 1989; Mehan, 1992), commentators are suggesting that certain ways of talking, thinking, and acting are demanded by the conventions of schooling. The imperative to transmit a certain body of knowledge from teacher to students, the concern for factually correct information, the use of "known information questions" in verbal instruction, an insistence on text-based knowledge, the high value attached to naming, labeling, and categorizing information, especially out of context, are part and parcel of this culture. Like other aspects of culture, the unique features of the classroom are tacit, and therefore must be learned implicitly.

The interaction that occurs in the home relates to this culture of the classroom. The discourse patterns and socialization practices of upper-income and middle-income families resemble those of the classroom, whereas the discourse patterns and socialization practices of low-income families, especially those from linguistic and ethnic minority backgrounds, do not resemble those of the classroom. Although coherent and systematic, the discourse patterns and socialization practices of low-income families do not map neatly onto the often implicit demands of the classroom culture (Erickson & Mohatt, 1982; Philips, 1982; Heath, 1982, 1986; Tharp & Gallimore, 1988; Trueba, 1988).

The match between the socialization practices implicitly learned at home and the culture of the classroom appears to give middle-income students advantages over their working-class counterparts. The cultural knowledge or "cultural capital" (Bourdieu, 1977; Bourdieu & Passeron, 1977a) that middle-income and high-income families pass on to their children maps onto the knowledge expected of them in school, whereas the knowledge passed on by low-income families does not match the knowledge expected of students in school. Because the language used by middle-income parents matches the often implicit and tacit demands of the school, their children are being equipped with the very skills and techniques that are rewarded in lessons and on tests. Likewise, because the language used by low-income parents does not match the discourse of the classroom, their children are not being provided with the background knowledge that is so important in lessons and on tests.

Networks of relationships or "social capital" (Bourdieu, 1986) enable resources to accrue to people because they belong to and participate in certain groups. This social capital also enables elite families to assist their children. Because they have been to college themselves, well-to-do parents know what is expected of their own college-bound children concerning what courses to take, how to study, and how to take tests. Because they are more likely to have material and temporal resources, middle-income parents adopt strategies for assisting their students' school careers that are approved and validated by the school (Lareau, 1989). DeMott (1990: 231) shows us how middle-income parents develop class advantages, which become so taken for granted as to appear to be "natural":

> At a school Parents' Night a woman hears a Hispanic father ask a serious but impossibly uninformed question about applying to college. Won't his son be "in trouble with the authorities" if he applies to two places at one time? Again the class response comes swiftly: surprise, vague amusement, condescension – but the woman tries to check it, playing over the question she's just heard in her mind. Because new to the "application process," the man sees duplicity and bad faith in it; she herself sees the same process as practically the law of nature. ("It's just how the system works.")

Kids present themselves over and over . . . get better at it . . . learn how to dope people out, to say things better, to sell themselves. Why would a father flinch at this? *Tonight: dear Princeton, You alone I covet. Tomorrow night: dear Brown, You alone I covet.* . . . But is the questioner a fool? Should his qualm, naïve or not, be mine? What are the costs of institutionalizing duplicity at an early age?

The relationship between implicit socialization and academic success has particular relevance for the students in this study. The linguistic and ethnic minority students who have been "untracked" (i.e., placed in academically rigorous college prep programs) most often come from low-income families. As a result, the untracked students have not been immersed in the implicit socialization process that accrues social and cultural capital to the sons and daughters of well-to-do families.

Based on our observations in schools and interviews with students and teachers, it appears to us that AVID coordinators are engaged in an explicit socialization process in their classrooms that parallels the implicit socialization process that occurs in well-to-do families. AVID coordinators explicitly teach aspects of the implicit culture of the classroom and the hidden curriculum of the school. Furthermore, they serve as mediators between the students and high school educators as well as the students and college educators.

In order to contextualize this discussion, we first turn our attention to the placement of students in academic courses and then we examine the institutional supports that students receive from AVID while they are in college prep courses. Since we established in the previous chapter that student selection practices are not responsible for the impressive college enrollment record of AVID students, we will confine our discussion to the 248 students in our sample who completed 3 years in the program.

THE PLACEMENT OF AVID STUDENTS IN ACADEMIC COURSES

Kids can't go to college if they don't enroll in college prep classes. Nevertheless, Pelavin and Kane (1990: 49) seem surprised to find that students who take geometry in high school are twice as likely to go to college as students who do not take this college prep course. As a means to achieve its main goal of preparing previously low-achieving students for college, AVID works hard to place its students in college prep courses. Students are enrolled as early as their freshman year, usually in an advanced history class, an advanced English class, or an advanced math class. The AVID coordinator at Pimlico High School, in fact, encourages her AVID students to enroll in accelerated courses according to availability and appropriateness in the summer session before their freshman year, so that they will have room in their schedules for the AVID elective course and college prep courses in their sophomore, junior, and senior years. If AVID students are successful in these classes, the course load of academic courses is supposed to be increased in each successive year so that students have the requisite a–f courses upon graduation which enable them to apply to and be accepted into the California State University, the University of California, or other universities that have high academic standards.

You will recall from Tables 5–7 in Chapter 4 that we calculated the number of AVID students who attempted and completed University of California/California State University a–f requirements. Seventy-two percent of AVID students attempted to take the full range of courses that makes them eligible for entrance into the University of California or California State University colleges and 41% completed these courses. AVID students' eligibility rates compare very favorably with California eligibility rates, especially when we remember that students who take the SAT across California are the highest achievers. Whereas AVID prepares 41% of its Latino students for entrance into UC/CSU, the state average is 22%. AVID prepares 41% of its white students to be eligible for UC and CSU and the state average is 34%. The average for African American students equals the state average, and the average for "Asian" students is slightly higher than the California average.

In short, AVID students are preparing for and enrolling in college more often than their local, California, and national counterparts. This record invites us to examine the classroom practices that support the placement of AVID students in academic courses. Scaffolding takes many forms in the AVID classroom. Teachers provide explicit instruction in the often implicit academic culture, serve as advocates of AVID students within the high school, and assist students as they move between high school and college.

SOCIAL SUPPORTS

> The student approached the AVID coordinator in tears. She had just received a failing grade on her biology test. After the AVID coordinator consoled the student, she sat her down and made her practice a speech and set of questions she'd ask the biology teacher about her test, how she could improve her performance, and raise her grades. After one or two rehearsals, the student left to confront her teacher.

This exchange, which is typical of many between AVID coordinators and students, illustrates one of the main ingredients in the success of the San Diego untracking program: the social scaffolding supporting AVID students. Finn (1991) in an otherwise scathing critique of public education, singles out for praise those special teachers (like Jaime Escalante and Marva Collins) who do not confine their definition of education to classroom hours (cf. Goodlad, 1983; Sizer, 1984, 1992).

In the schools we have observed, AVID coordinators define their teaching as a "vocation." They believe teaching is a "calling," not "just a job." These beliefs are manifest in their behavior, as AVID teachers spend many hours before school with parents, long hours after school with students in tutorial programs, and on weekends taking them to colleges and universities. In addition, AVID coordinators bring college recruiters to their high school, obtain college application and scholarship forms, and assist students in filling them out and filing them on time. The net result of this commitment is that AVID students receive explicit socialization into the often hidden curriculum of the school, become beneficiaries of teacher mediators who intervene on their behalf within the high school, and are connected to important social networks that link high school and colleges.

Explicit Socialization into Implicit Academic Culture

An explicit socialization process takes place in the AVID classroom. Students who have been selected into this program devote one academic period per day, 5 days per week for the 180-day school year to a specially designed course, often in lieu of an extracurricular activity or another elective option. Students are assigned to AVID classrooms in one of two ways. The program recommends that students from many classes be heterogeneously grouped (e.g., freshmen, sophomores, juniors, and seniors are in the same AVID class). Some AVID coordinators have elected to place all students of a given class standing in a given AVID class (i.e., all freshmen are in one class period, all sophomores in another, etc.). Teachers who place students of the same class standing together in one class period say such grouping fosters a cohesive cohort. Teachers who mix classes say they like the opportunity for older students to teach younger students and the possibility for younger students to use older, successful students as role models.

Teaching Study Skills. AVID students receive explicit instruction in a special method of note taking that stresses specific techniques for compiling main ideas, abstracting key concepts, and identifying questions that guide analysis. They are required to apply these techniques in notebooks that they keep for their academic courses. Tutors collect and check these notebooks once per week or once every 2 weeks. Students are graded on the completeness and quality of their notes. When asked what helps them the most, the eight Pimlico students we interviewed singled out the importance of learning to organize and manage their time and "learning to take good notes."

Test-taking skills were also taught in all the AVID classrooms we studied, but were differentially emphasized. At a minimum, students were given drill and practice on vocabulary items likely to be found on the Scholastic Aptitude Test (SAT). When a more extensive approach to test preparation was taken, students were provided explicit instruction in ways to eliminate distracting answers on multiple-choice questions and were given strategies for approximating answers and strategies for estimating the probabilities about the success of guessing. One AVID teacher devoted two successive weeks to SAT preparation, including practicing with vocabulary items, administering practice tests, reviewing wrong answers, and teaching strategies for taking tests. This teacher reviewed with her students the kinds of analogies typically found on the SAT so they could practice the kinds of problems found on their tests. This teacher also sent her students to an expert math teacher for assistance on math test items. She justified the time she devoted to test taking by explaining that she was teaching her students the same techniques found in the expensive Princeton Review SAT preparation class. Indeed, her course of study was very similar to those English review classes offered by elite prep schools that are specifically designed to help students prepare for SAT exams (Cookson & Persell, 1985: 75–76).

Teaching Skills for College Entry. Although writing, note-taking, test-taking, and vocabulary-building strategies were taught routinely in the eight AVID programs we studied from 1991 to 1993, by far the most conspicuous and intriguing teacher-led activity revolved around the complicated process of entering college. Seniors were given extra coaching on how to write statements of purpose and how to fill out college applications and financial aid forms. The seniors were reminded about test and application deadlines. At Pimlico, for instance, students must complete an AVID assignment each week in which they perform writing and/or reading tasks in preparation for the total college experience. The junior class at Saratoga was given a handout, "Choosing Your College," containing a checklist of information typically found in college catalogs. Students were instructed to fill in the information for a particular college according to the assigned checklist. This research task was intended to make AVID students more familiar with college catalogs and to help them choose an appropriate college.

Students received very specific counseling information about enrolling in college. Stephanie Lincoln, the AVID coordinator at Saratoga, facilitated this process by use of a packet, "Planning and Preparation for College," a systematic list of instructions that tells students about each step of the college entry process. The process and deadlines were reviewed often. The teacher's vigilance minimized the opportunities that students have to slip up.

Alex Frankfurter, the AVID coordinator at Golden Gate High School, has constructed a particularly elaborate socialization regimen that covers all aspects of the process involved in applying to college. This year-long activity is organized well in advance. Even though application packets are often available to students in counseling offices, to insure that his AVID students are registered for the SAT, Frankfurter personally obtains the application packets from the testing agency and distributes them to the students in his class. To assist his students with application fee waivers, he drives to local colleges to pick up the necessary waiver forms. This extra effort has paid off; Frankfurter's AVID students have been able to get application fees waived by as many as four colleges. In addition, he makes special trips to local colleges to pick up large numbers of application packets so that each of his students will have one. To convince his students that finances should not limit their opportunities to attend college, he distributes information on more than 175 scholarships to his students.

Starting in October of each year, Frankfurter works with seniors as a separate group 4 days per week on all aspects of the college application process. In the first session during the 1992–93 school year, he presented a timeline to the seniors, which marked application deadlines (e.g., CSU due by November 1, UC by Thanksgiving, private colleges by Christmas). From that point on, he checked all students' timelines weekly, to insure that students are on time and on task.

In subsequent sessions, the seniors filled out photocopies of California State University, University of California, and University of San Diego applications line by line. After the draft applications were completed, Frankfurter checked them for accuracy. Only then did students complete the actual applications. Wanting to insure that his students had a college option close to home, he advised every student to apply to San Diego State University, either as a first choice or as a "backup."

Later in October, Frankfurter told the students to start thinking about letters of recommendation. He advised them to ask their junior-year English teacher for a letter of recommendation unless they did not do well in that teacher's class. Frankfurter told the seniors they could ask, in addition to their teachers, religious leaders and employers. Frankfurter himself writes over a hundred letters of recommendation each year for his students.

Many of these special sessions with seniors are devoted to helping students complete their personal statements and essays. Frankfurter reminds each student to include significant aspects of his or her biography. When students have been pressed for time or lacked the skill to type, he has typed final applications for them. Frankfurter's senior students at Golden Gate High School told us this essay writing was easy for them after so many years of practice.

While students were completing financial aid requests in January, Frankfurter passed on information about the intricacies of the financial aid process. To speed up the application process, Frankfurter encouraged students to have their parents file their income tax forms early, so financial information could be included with their applications. He also addressed the interpersonal side of the college application process. Acknowledging that some parents may oppose students leaving home, he advised students to start preparing their parents early, by talking about going to college regularly around the house.

Even students with excellent grades acknowledged that without AVID, they would have missed application deadlines. Students who were not in AVID reinforced this impression: "I missed taking the PSAT because I wasn't in AVID and I didn't know about it. One of my AVID friends asked me if I was going to take the test but it was too late to sign up. You don't know about this stuff unless you are in AVID."

Teaching Conflict Resolution Strategies. In addition to scaffolding the college-going process, AVID teachers explicitly teach conflict resolution strategies as part of their curriculum. Working-class students, both "minority" and white, often have different codes for resolving conflict than their teachers. Alex Frankfurter, the coordinator at Golden Gate High, coaches his students on ways to interact with teachers. If students are not doing well in a class, or do not understand assignments, he encourages them to visit the teacher during lunch or after school to ask for help. This strategy, he explains, gives students confidence and informs teachers that the students are serious and concerned about their work.

Lisa Gonzalez, one of the four AVID coordinators at Keeneland, extends her coaching to the organization of the phrases that students should employ when talking to their teachers. "Don't ask *if* you can make up an exam," she says. "Ask politely *when* the next makeup is. If you miss a class, don't say 'I'll get an excuse,' go to the attendance office, get a copy of the teacher's roll sheet, and say 'I'm sorry I missed your class, but here's my excuse.' " The conversational prompts that Frankfurter and Gonzalez give their students emphasize the importance of polite conversation, not putting teachers on the defensive, and assuming teachers are agreeable people who make honest mistakes.

Gonzalez also utilizes students' knowledge and past experience to teach conflict resolution strategies. When two Latinas told her they were having trouble in their algebra class, Gonzales did not give them advice. Instead, she asked other AVID students in her class to provide suggestions:

TEACHER: What are some of the things they can do?

STUDENT: Study ahead and formulate specific questions.

STUDENT: Go to tutoring after school.

STUDENT: Check out library books on the subject [other math texts].

STUDENT: Talk to someone who understands the teacher.

Gonzalez then praised the class for offering "positive strategies" for doing well in class.

A few days later, the coordinator asked one of the two Latina students to tell the class how she resolved the problem. In eliciting this testimony, the AVID coordinator was encouraging the student to reflect on positive achievements for her own and others' benefit.

Using students to coach students in conflict resolution has the added benefit of encouraging students to be autonomous from instead of dependent on adults when identifying ways to solve problems. In this way, students learn interactive skills that not only work within the high school, but may be helpful in other arenas of their lives when they are separated from their AVID teachers.

Teacher Advocacy

Another role AVID teachers adopt is that of student advocate. When interviewed, students at the several schools we studied consistently reported that AVID teachers intervene in the academic maze on behalf of their students. If students are absent, teachers call them at home in the evening. By talking to their teachers, students obtain missing assignments and make sure they are not penalized by their absence.

The coordinator at Monrovia High School circulated to all teachers a list with the names of the AVID students in their respective classes. She informed the teachers that they would be receiving extra help in their courses, but if the students were having any problems, she was to be contacted. This strategy shifts the burden of failure away from the student and toward a shared responsibility for the student's progress.

We observed several episodes that confirmed student opinion about the importance of teacher advocacy. One incident occurred when a new "tardy sweep" policy was implemented at Saratoga. One of the AVID students was late to a class. According to the new tardiness policy, she should be punished by spending the remainder of the period in a detention room. The AVID student was not going to be allowed to make up missing work, including tests. She was irate. She and her friends complained to Mrs. Lincoln: "I'm just trying to get an education. I just want to learn. They are keeping me from learning, just for being a minute late."

Lincoln arranged for the vice-principal to hear the students' complaints the next day. Many students affirmed that no one would have listened to them had they not been AVID students and if Lincoln had not acted on their behalf. Clearly, this teacher has adopted an advocacy role that extends beyond traditional teaching duties.

Another example of an AVID coordinator acting as a student advocate involved a particular math teacher. Several students at one of the schools we studied were failing their math class, but were doing well in their other academic subjects. They believed their math grades were undeserved and blamed the teacher for their plight. Their AVID teacher spoke with the principal and the teacher on the students' behalf. She arranged for extra tutoring. Although it was difficult to prove the students' assertion, the AVID coordinator insured that both the academic teacher and the principal knew that the situation was being monitored. She was able to help other AVID students by advising them to take math from a different teacher.

Advocacy on behalf of students is not limited to the academic realm; it extends into and blends with the personal realm as well. AVID teachers are described by their students as personal advocates. The following are typical comments:

> The AVID teacher is someone you can talk to. You need to have someone.

> The AVID coordinator is someone who takes time to listen to individual needs. She keeps pushing you and reminding you that you can do well.

Stephanie Lincoln at Saratoga High School confirmed our impression that the AVID coordinator role included duties as a personal advocate. She has intervened in suicide attempts, visited sick students, and called parents if she felt that their child was employed too many hours outside of school or was having difficulty at home. The following episodes exemplify teachers' personal advocacy on behalf of their AVID students.

Holly is a senior at Saratoga who had been missing a lot of school. Lincoln discussed the situation with her. Evidently, Holly had been babysitting a neglected young relative. Holly's grades had fallen drastically. Mrs. Lincoln talked to the head counselor to prevent Holly from being expelled. She then helped Holly continue with her application to San Diego State University and she saw to it that other professionals could relieve Holly of the babysitting responsibility. By the end of the year, Holly's grades had improved.

She had been accepted at San Diego State and both Lincoln and the head counselor were working with Holly's father to insure that personal barriers would not prevent her from going to college.

"Teddy" Borja, a very bright and disciplined Latino student in the AVID program at Keeneland High School confided in Miles Johnson, the AVID coordinator, that he was thinking of dropping out of school. Characterized by Johnson as a "model student" and "definitely college track," Teddy received good grades and participated in sports and student government despite a challenging home environment. His father struggled with seasonal unemployment and had just been laid off from work again. Teddy felt he needed to assume the breadwinner position in his family and could not deal with the additional burden of school. Within hours after listening to the student's heart-wrenching story, Johnson marshaled the resources of the school to assist Teddy to stay in school.

One day, Kristina came to Miles Johnson very troubled, and asked if she could speak to him privately. As they walked out of class, the teacher put his arm around her shoulder. She clung to Johnson, shuddering, and told him she suddenly realized why one of the tutors seemed too disturbingly familiar to her. The tutor had a striking resemblance to the stepfather who had sexually abused her only a few years before, she said. As she began to cry, Johnson asked her if she wanted to get help. When she said yes, he immediately arranged for her to see the school nurse and counselor. Clearly, these teachers' interventions were instrumental in keeping Kristina, Holly, and Teddy on the college track. Although students, especially those from low-income families, continue to labor under heavy academic and social pressures, they receive encouragement and support from dedicated AVID teachers.

Not all interventions, however, are successful. The resources that an innovative school program such as AVID can muster are limited. Sometimes they are not sufficient to overcome the constraints imposed by the overwhelming practical circumstances in the lives of AVID students.

Jamala is one such student. When we interviewed a group of AVID students at Keeneland High School and asked who planned to go on to college, everyone in the group responded in the affirmative. When we asked if they planned to go to college before they started AVID, most, but not all, replied that they had. Jamala was one of the few students who had not had college plans before AVID; she just recently decided to go. When asked what led her to change her mind, she replied: "I didn't want to be like the people in my family. Half haven't even graduated from high school. They stick together but they don't go anywhere together. I found out more specifics about college. AVID showed me that I had a choice."

Jamala's AVID teacher confirmed her story. In her first (freshman) year in AVID, Miles Johnson recalled that Jamala "fought me all the way." She came back from her sophomore year, however, a changed person. In her third year in Keeneland's AVID program, Jamala was much more positive and motivated. Then her life got even more compilicated. Jamala was having trouble in her chemistry class and stopped going. Because Jamala was avoiding school and staying home, her mother, an unemployed high school graduate, suggested that Jamala look after her younger siblings regularly and attend an "alternative" (continuation) school. Jamala decided to do that and left Keeneland. Johnson put Jamala in contact with the AVID coordinator at the continuation school, and Johnson told him that Jamala still has college plans. It will be harder for Jamala to achieve this goal, however, while attending a continuation school, which does not have a comprehensive college prep curriculum. Although Jamala attributed part of her new ambition to the choices that AVID made her see, these high aspirations were not enough. The scaffolding AVID provided Jamala was not sufficient to sustain her ambitions in the face of a weak academic record coupled with overwhelming financial constraints.

Jamala's story is informative beyond the tragedy of her individual life. The existing social resources invested by AVID – a special class that meets once per day for 180 days, a dedicated teacher who serves as an advocate, college tutors who assist with studying and homework – are not sufficient to propel all students down the college track. To reach Jamala and students like her, even more extensive resources are necessary. To be sure, if AVID deployed more extensive institutional resources, then the program could help more low-achieving students. But we have to realize that school reform efforts such as untracking are not a panacea. Until the world of work is reorganized to provide more job opportunities with viable career ladders, then changes in the organization of schooling such as this untracking program will not be able to make a significant difference.

Building Bridges from High School to College

In addition to mediating the life of students within high school, AVID teachers serve as mediators between high school and college. AVID coordinators arrange visits to colleges. Almost all students took day-long field trips to colleges in the local area, most notably San Diego State University and the University of California, San Diego. Most students took trips to schools that are some distance away, UCLA and the University of Southern California most notably. More extensive visits were less frequent, but not exceptional. Of particular note, the AVID coordinator at Pimlico takes her students to northern California schools and also arranges a long trip to include Historically Black Colleges and Universities (HBCUs) every other year. For many students, these field trips provided their first opportunity to see a college campus. While on college campuses, students visit classes, talk to college students, and get a taste of college life.

The following comment underlines the importance these trips play for AVID students: "Field trips were great. I didn't even know what a college looked like until Mrs. Lincoln took us. It's like eating a cookie. It really tempts us to eat another one. You've smelled it and seen it and you want to buy it really bad."

"Career days" are another mediating mechanism that builds bridges between high school and other institutions. Guest speakers are invited to the AVID class to discuss their professions or occupations. Career talks are always geared to those occupations that require a 4-year college degree.

We have already described the elaborate socialization process Alex Frankfurter implemented at Golden Gate High School. His personal involvement in the application process does not end when students complete college application forms, however. He personally mails the applications, sometimes affixing his own stamps if students have forgotten them. He personally delivers the applications to one of the local colleges and goes through each application with the Equal Opportunity Program (EOP) admissions officer there.

In short, AVID teachers first introduced students to the possibility of attending college and then led them through the college application process. In that respect, AVID coordinators act in ways that are similar to college advisors at elite college prep schools (Cookson & Persell, 1985: 167–189), or private "admissions assistance services counselors" (McDonough, 1994). These officials build elaborate personal relationships between college prep schools and colleges. They visit colleges, make numerous phone calls, compile elaborate dossiers, assist students with statements of purpose, counsel the family, and write well-documented letters on behalf of their students.

THE IMPORTANCE OF SCAFFOLDING: LESSONS BY CONTRAST

We learn more about the importance of social scaffolds supporting a rigorous academic program by contrasting AVID to other school programs ostensibly designed to assist students achieve academically and prepare for college. The Educational Development Program (EDP) is also designed to assist students achieve academically and prepare for college. EDP is organized for students having difficulty in school and is designed to offer the same kind of academic assistance as AVID. EDP had approximately 54 students assigned to four classes during the 1991–1992 school year.

EDP students are given a class period each day in which they can study alone or in groups. Tutors are not assigned to the class, but students can go to the school's tutoring center with the EDP teacher's permission. The EDP teacher is available during the class period to assist students with academic and personal matters. Guest speakers visit the EDP class to inform students of career opportunities. Students are free to use the library or visit their designated counselors for curriculum assistance.

Despite the similarities in structure between the two programs, our observations in EDP classes and interviews with 15 of the 54 students in EDP exposed considerable differences in practice between AVID and EDP. Associated with the differences in practices are differences in the actions and consciousness of the students who attended the two programs.

The AVID class is organized to be a mentoring session in which students receive instruction concerning general learning strategies. By contrast, the EDP class period is not academic in orientation. EDP students used their class period chatting with their friends. While a few students tried to work on homework problems, disruptive and abusive behavior was the norm. Students wandered in and out of class with impunity.

The EDP teacher's role was different than the AVID teacher's role. AVID teachers are committed to their students' success; to achieve this goal, they exercised high expectations and spent considerable amounts of time with students inside and outside of class. The EDP teacher admitted he hated his job and felt he was the victim of a system that did not respect his opinions: "I try to get rid of students but they don't listen to me." "There is no professional support" was his complaint.

EDP students said that neither the EDP teacher nor the school counselor offered them any advice about courses required for college or the college application process. They have not been taught the importance of getting good grades in order to attend college.

There were consequences for both students' ideology and their actions. The students were disdainful of the EDP class. Finding it boring and useless, they spent their time socializing with friends. Students did not display an understanding about the correspondence between what they did now and what would happen to them later. Some students acknowledged that they needed good grades to go to college, but they were doing little about that in class each day. They seem to have inculcated only that portion of achievement ideology that says our society provides everyone with an equal opportunity: "Yeah I have the same opportunities as anyone else if I keep my grades up."

While they have the "opportunity" dimension of achievement ideology under control, they have negated or blocked out that part which says opportunity must be accompanied by hard work and effort. Instead they seemed to believe that simply "having opportunities" made the difference, and that they were entitled to the same opportunities as everyone else. The student who vocalized this sentiment to us, like most others in the class, treated EDP as a time to play and socialize.

Students' motivation, acceptance of responsibility and academic effort were absent from the EDP class. By their actions, it was clear that students did not equate academic performance now with occupational success later. One African American junior in EDP stated that she spent "zero time on homework." "I want to be a dental hygienist," she said, but she found "school boring." "This class is boring; it doesn't teach you anything." Another African American student who had good grades and wants to go to college, did not spend his time contributing to his academic record. Instead, EDP gave him an opportunity to be rowdy.

EDP students, unlike AVID students, felt very uncertain about their future, especially the merits of college. When asked about their future plans, many EDP students and virtually all AVID students quickly and uniformly responded "I'm going to college." But there were other differences between the two groups. Most EDP students had only a vague and general idea about their college plans, whereas most students in AVID were much more specific and could name the colleges they plan to attend.

In addition, AVID students clearly state the connection between college and "a good job." EDP students, by contrast, do not make this connection. One 10th grader who had been busy chasing a student around the classroom and stealing her books commented: "My dad is in the Navy, maybe I'll do that for a while. I may go to college but I really want to go into business for myself." Although this student was getting good grades, he admitted he hadn't taken the PSAT. As a result, he hasn't articulated the connection between the need for a college degree and an entrepreneurial career.

Both EDP and AVID kids are placed into an academic environment that is designed to foster academic success. Yet the EDP program is failing and the AVID program is succeeding. Some of
AVID's strengths may lie in the environment it creates. Students are
socialized into an ideology that supports working hard, getting
good grades, and entering the academic world. Then they are provided with a system of social supports that reinforces that ideology.
Both the ideology and the supporting structures are missing from
EDP. EDP, which was designated as an academic environment, has
evolved into a free-for-all. It is not enough, apparently, to have a
program designated as an academically enriching one; active practices, which operate on a daily basis, must be instituted to achieve
the goal of academic enrichment.

SUMMARY: SOCIAL SCAFFOLDING
CONTRIBUTES TO THE SUCCESS OF
UNTRACKING

The placement of low-achieving students in rigorous academic
courses is a fundamentally important ingredient in the success of
this untracking project. It is a simple fact: Kids can't go to college if
they don't take college prep classes. Certainly, placing low-
achieving students in rigorous academic programs is an essential
ingredient in the success of any untracking effort. And AVID is
diligent in placing its students in college prep classes: 70% of all
students attempt the full complement of college eligibility courses,
and 40% complete this arduous sequence.

While it is necessary to place students in college prep classes to
prepare them for college, academic placement in and of itself is not
sufficient. AVID is working with students who have not had previous experience with college prep classes. Institutional supports
must be in place in order to insure that students who have not had
previous experience with academically oriented classes succeed in
them. The social scaffolding supporting student placement in college prep courses is as important as the academic placement itself.

Among the most visible social supports in AVID classrooms are the teaching of test-taking, note-taking, and studying strategies. By dispensing these academic techniques, AVID is giving students explicit instruction in the hidden curriculum of the school. That is, AVID teaches explicitly in school what middle-income students learn implicitly at home. In Bourdieu's (1986) terms, AVID gives low-income students some of the cultural capital at school that is similar to the cultural capital that more economically advantaged parents give to their children at home.

Teacher advocacy (which is what an AVID teacher does to help a student within the high school) and bridging (which is what an AVID teacher does to assist a student move between the high school and a college) complement this explicit socialization process. Rose (1990: 35–43), in explaining his transformation from a voc ed to a college prep student, vividly shows us how important a mediator can be. John McFarland, an iconoclastic English teacher at Rose's Catholic high school, first revitalized Rose's mind by introducing him to English literature, then made phone calls on his behalf, which facilitated Rose's acceptance at Loyola Marymount University.

The success of the San Diego untracking experiment is due in large part to the fact that the academic life of AVID students is supported by dedicated teachers, who, like McFarland in Mike Rose's autobiography, enter the lives of their students and serve as mediators between them, the high school, and the college system. By expanding the definition of their teaching role to include the sponsorship of students, AVID coordinators encourage success and help remove impediments to students' academic achievement.

Let us consider a situation in which an admissions officer is reviewing the records of two students, both with 3.00 GPAs, both African American, both from low-income families. But in addition, one student presents a well organized college application dossier, appears on time, with a compelling personal statement, strong letters, accompanied by a personal appeal from his English teacher (who is also his AVID teacher). Which student will get the nod in a competitive environment? Cookson and Persell (1985: 183) present a real-life case in point that illustrates the power and influence of personal lobbying, especially when backed by the personal involvement of a representative from an elite school:

> A counselor from the Midwest went to an eastern Ivy League college to advocate for a truly outstanding student from his school; the candidate had SATs in the 700s, top grades in his class, class president, star athlete and nevertheless a friendly modest person. An advisor from an elite eastern prep school was also there, lobbying on behalf of his candidate – a nice undistinguished fellow with SATs in the 600s, middle of his class, average athlete and no strong signs of leadership. After hearing both the counselors, the Ivy League college chose the latter candidate.

AVID coordinators who advocate on behalf of their students, like prep school or private counselors who lobby on behalf of their students, help insure that they will get to the college door. In effect, AVID coordinators are placing the hand of an ethnic minority student in the hand of a college admissions officer, an especially effective practice at those colleges that actively recruit students from underrepresented backgrounds.

The teachers' practices of advocacy and bridging seem to operate in the way that Bourdieu (1986) says *social* capital works, but these practices have a different institutional base. In Bourdieu's framework, social capital is rooted in the institution of the family, indeed the elite family. Although his conceptualization does not preclude the location of social capital in other institutions, the thrust of his formulation privileges the family as the basis of social capital. Elite families associate with other elite families. These associations form networks, which can be played to benefit the sons and daughters of the elite. Job opportunities and college placement are only two of the benefits that accrue to the children of the elite because their parents are embedded in a rich set of interlocking directorates, "old boy" networks, trade associations, school ties, and political associations.

In Chapter 4, we discussed the influence that students' academic background had on their subsequent academic achievement. We reported that students who enter the program with the highest

CTBS scores and the highest grades have a higher college enrollment rate than students who enter the untracking program with lower test scores and grades. Now we are in a better position to explain these differences. Explicit instruction in test taking, note taking, and studying has the greatest influence on students who have had little previous experience with these academic activities, whereas teacher advocacy and bridging have their greatest influence on students who have had at least some implicit socialization in the hidden curriculum of the school. On the one hand, students who have already accumulated high grades and test-taking abilities are not helped appreciably by having the hidden curriculum revealed to them. On the other hand, students who have not been exposed to the hidden curriculum are boosted by the AVID teacher who helps them apply to college, complete scholarship forms, and meet test deadlines.

Teacher advocacy and institutional bridge building look like the workings of social capital. Yet these processes are rooted in different soil. They have the school, not the family, as their base. In effect, AVID teachers act like the upper-middle-income parents Lareau (1989) described; they check on their students' work and intervene actively if they are not succeeding in the way they expect. In fact, middle-income parents probably could not play the student advocate role as well as AVID teachers, because they do not have the requisite knowledge of school operations and the social position necessary to effect change. The students' teachers, not the students' families, provide the "backing of the collectivity" that Bourdieu (1986) says is emblematic of social capital. The students' teachers, not the students' families, "provide a credential which generates 'credit' in the educational world," which Bourdieu (1986: 248) says marks the deployment of social capital (cf. Lamont & Lareau, 1988: 156).

If schools, not just well-to-do families, can deploy social capital to form productive social networks, then it means that schools can become transformative institutions, not just reproductive institutions. The sons and daughters of less privileged families can gain access to the often invisible networks of relationships that are often reserved for the sons and daughters of more privileged families.

Lest we seem overly romantic in our formulation of the counter-vailing mechanisms of social mobility here, it is important to remember where AVID sends its students. AVID students enroll in San Diego State University and the University of California, not Yale and Princeton. There is a well-established relationship between the particular colleges people attend and their subsequent career success in a variety of fields. For example, the social prestige and selectivity of one's college is related to the prestige of the graduate or professional school one attends, to a person's professional occupational attainment, and to attaining a high rank in business (Cookson & Persell, 1985: 168).

This means that AVID students may be making it to the first tier of mobility, but those in powerful positions above them are still able to make more subtle distinctions to judge and exclude them. San Diego State University grads may become "players" in the San Diego business or social world, but they do not automatically become "players" in New York or Washington. Members of elite groups can invoke finer distinctions of social knowledge, social connections, and taste to maintain their position and defend the borders against these upwardly mobile intruders.

We close this summary section with a final comment on the social consequences of relying on committed teachers to implement and sustain educational innovation. Although the presence of the committed teacher is vital for the success of this program (and others like it), depending on teacher commitment has its downside. It means that the innovative program, the one trying to implement change, runs on the energy of dedicated people, who commit their personal time and money, while the rest of the educational institution runs on the inertia built up from past practices. What happens if these dedicated people get tired, or suffer from "burnout"? Will the program be able to replace them with other committed teachers? The AVID untracking plan tries to spread the responsibility for students' academic success to school site teams and wider segments of the faculty. It will be necessary to institutionalize these practices in order for the momentum of the program to be sustained.

6

ORGANIZATIONAL PROCESSES INFLUENCING UNTRACKING

WE CONTINUE EXAMINING THE INSTITUTIONAL AR-rangements that influence untracking in this chapter. The loci of the organizational processes we focus upon are outside the classroom. They reside in district offices, in counselors' or principals' offices. Despite the fact that these institutional arrangements operate at some distance from the classroom, they impact the career of untracked students in significant ways. Because untracking represents a significant modification in long-established educational practice, we place this discussion in the context of the history of innovations within large-scale organizations.

ORGANIZATIONAL INNOVATIONS AND LOCAL PRACTICE

The history of innovations in educational and other institutions shows a remarkable and consistent pattern: Organizational innovations undergo changes as they become institutionalized. Attempts to reform or change organizations, especially those introduced from above or from outside them, are modified at the local level. The innovations are absorbed into the culture of the organization and adapted to fit preexisting routines or standard operating procedures. This pattern has been found repeatedly in business, philanthropic, and political organizations.

Michels' s (1949) account of Germany's Social Democratic Party was perhaps the first that identified the adaptability of formal organizations to changing circumstances. Following suit, Selznick (1949) described the Tennessee Valley Authority (TVA) as an organization founded during a reform movement whose original goals have been transformed in order for the institution to survive. According to Zald & Denton (1963) a similar process occurred within the YMCA. As it expanded, its rules rigidified, its mission changed from an evangelical Christian orientation to a more general social service orientation. An ethos of managerial efficiency replaced particularistic leadership.

Public institutions dedicated to social reform have also modified their goals in the face of bureaucratic constraints. For example, in a spirited moment of reform, progressives in the United States attempted to rehabilitate prisons and juvenile courts and reform mental asylums during the early years of the 20th century. Within decades, however, the initial innovations to improve the lot of criminals, delinquents, and the mentally ill were transformed into routine bureaucratic procedures that maintained administrative rather than humanitarian interests (Rothman, 1980).

We see the same process in education. Innovations proposed from outside the school are absorbed into the culture of the school. Public Law 94–142, the "Education for All Handicapped Students Act," changed the education of special students. Instead of being segregated in self-contained programs, they would be placed in the "mainstream" of regular classrooms or in the "least restrictive" educational environments available. In addition, this law mandated expanded decision making, notably including parents as essential partners in the special education placement process. In local schools, however, educators have modified these federal mandates by adapting them to preexisting routines and standard operating procedures (Mehan, Hertweck, & Meihls, 1985; Mehan, Mercer, & Rueda, in press). After an initial impulse of reform, educators at the school site once again routinely place students in available programs, obtain waivers for parental consent, and establish informal procedures that circumvent the formal procedures mandated by federal law.

The history of technological innovations in schools provides another instructive example. Attempts to introduce machine technologies (such as radios, film, instructional television, and computers) have traversed a cycle of exhilaration, scientific credibility, disappointment, and blame (Cuban, 1986). In each case, the cycle began with extravagant claims for the revolutionary power of the machine to transform teacher practice and student learning. Fervent believers in technology readily predicted that computers and radios would replace teachers, and motion pictures would render textbooks obsolete. Reformers, including public officials, foundation executives, school administrators, and machine sales representatives, fastened onto the innovation and promoted it as a solution to school problems. School boards and superintendents adopted policies and allocated funds to secure the machines. Soon after the machines appeared in schools, academic studies reporting that the new technology was as effective as a teacher using conventional practices appeared in journals. Shortly afterward, the pessimistic phase of the cycle replaced the optimistic phase. Teachers started to complain about logistical difficulties in using the machines, reported problems in getting access to machines, and found new machines to be incompatible with existing programs. These scattered complaints marred the mantle of scientific credibility that had begun to settle over the innovation. Later, large-scale surveys conducted by university researchers documented infrequent teacher use of the machines. These results were then used by supporters of technological innovation to criticize both teachers and administrators for blocking the advance of technology and classroom improvement.

The history of the junior high school followed a similar pattern. Although designed to be a fundamental change in schooling, over time it has been revised to become only a modest addition to the high school (Cuban, 1992). A more recent effort to correct the flaws in junior high schools through the middle school movement shows little change in the original design. Reforms of the junior high school curriculum and its tracking practices have been adapted to the "existing social architecture of the school" (Cuban, 1992).

Without doubt, AVID is an educational innovation. The program's untracking philosophy runs counter to the conventional educational wisdom about the education of low-achieving students. For the past 50 years, the prevailing practice has been to separate and segregate students by ability and place them in different, albeit, homogeneous groups. AVID advocates heterogeneous grouping: placing students with different measured abilities in the same academic course of study.

AVID requires educators to conduct their business in different ways. Teachers are encouraged to adopt high expectations for all students (not just high-achieving ones) and use classroom tutors and new teaching techniques (e.g., collaborative groups, inquiry methods) to insure equitable educational opportunity. Counselors are encouraged to take a special interest in low-achieving ethnic and linguistic minority students. Principals are asked to untrack low-achieving students and insure that their staffs achieve the goal of educational equity for all students. AVID Center is to hold schools publicly accountable for their work with underrepresented students.

Although originated by teachers as a grass-roots effort at one high school in San Diego, in successive waves of implementation, this innovation has been introduced into the high school from outside, by the County Office of Education. Perhaps because they are recommended by an authority outside the school, we have found that the innovations encouraged by AVID create a tension at the local level between old and new ways of conducting business.

We could find very few cases in which all of the innovations proposed by AVID have been adopted as prescribed at one school site. In most cases, the recommended innovations have been modified or absorbed into preexisting daily educational routines. In one or two extreme cases, the innovations have caused turf battles, resentments, and jealousy among faculty and staff, or have been rejected outright. The end result is a considerable modification of the practices that AVID recommends.

We start by discussing the examples of the innovative practices recommended by the AVID central office that have been most closely implemented as planned and those modified at the school-site level, and then consider the tensions created when a school attempts to implement two innovations simultaneously.

IMPLEMENTING INNOVATIONS AS DESIGNED

The innovations that have been implemented in ways that conform most closely to the recommendations made by the program planners are concerned with the organization of the AVID classroom itself. The AVID central office suggests a basic plan for the weekly instructional activities within AVID classrooms. Two school days are designated tutorial days. On these days students are to work in small groups with the assistance of a tutor. On the other 2 days, writing as a tool for learning is emphasized. On these days, students are to engage in a variety of writing activities, including essays for their English, social studies, science, and history classes. One day a week, usually Fridays, are "motivational days." Guest speakers are invited to address the class, and field trips to colleges are scheduled on these days.

The eight schools we studied generally conformed to this schedule. At Pimlico, the first 3 weeks of the year were devoted to socializing students into the program and teaching them study skills and note-taking and time-management strategies. For the remainder of the year, 2 days a week were devoted to tutoring and 3 days a week were devoted to writing activities. Notable among the writing activities was the preparation of entries for school-sponsored essay contests. AVID students were encouraged to enter these contests. They were very enthusiastic about them and worked on their essays during the Monday class period. On the 2 tutoring days, the students worked on homework problems with other students who have chosen the same academic area. The most popular collaborative group was math; typically one student worked on a problem at the chalkboard, and the other students assisted. Students worked together while the AVID coordinator and her tutors circulated to help. During this time, the coordinator also engaged students in short conversations about events in their lives or progress in their classes. She did no direct teaching except during the first 5–10 minutes of class, when she gave announcements or explained assignments. On Fridays, students entered their essays into computers and tutors checked notebooks. This day was also used for guest speakers, who told the class about college or work opportunities.

At Churchill, the time and space within the AVID classrooms were organized differently. Mondays were devoted to a review of the journal entries that students had made about their learning over the past week and to a review of the textbook notes students had taken over the past week. Tuesdays and Fridays were devoted to tutorials and Wednesdays were devoted to notebook checks.

Keeneland also has the standard division of the work week. Mondays and Wednesdays are lecture or writing days, Tuesday and Thursdays are tutorial days. The Friday sessions are inspirational days, which sometimes have a quasi-religious overtone. Former AVID students or friends of AVID students who are attending college testify about the exaltations and trials of college. During student testimonies, the coordinator and students interject questions that direct the narrative to emphasize self-reflection and personal progress. For example, an Eritrean immigrant, who had graduated from Keeneland and AVID, relayed her first-quarter nightmare at Berkeley in which she found her admission to classes barred because Keeneland had not forwarded her transcripts on time. Although this bureaucratic problem was eventually solved, it delayed her registration and financial aid. When this testimony was completed, Miles Johnson, the AVID coordinator, sympathized with the student's troubles, and then reminded her (and the other students assembled) about her progress, from immigrant, to high school grad, to Berkeley student:

TEACHER: Tell us about the move to Berkeley, was it hard?

STUDENT: The school work is much harder.

TEACHER: But you're doing great, aren't you?

STUDENT: (smiles sheepishly)

TEACHER: Did you work very hard in high school?

STUDENT: I should have worked more, but now I know I have to do my work, it comes first.

TEACHER: You had to change your study habits to stay afloat at Berkeley?

STUDENT: (nods "yes")

In this exchange, the AVID coordinator encouraged the returning student to reflect on the process of positive change in her life. Her testimony, as interpreted by the coordinator, is intended to benefit her as well as the assembled students.

MODIFYING INNOVATIVE PRACTICES

We see how innovative ideas have been adapted to the "existing social architecture of the school" (Cuban, 1992) in the way in which classroom assistants are utilized in AVID classrooms, in the way in which the AVID program is defined differently at different school sites in response to the challenges presented by their local circumstances, and in the way in which schools resolve conflicts between programs that compete for students' attention.

Using Classroom Tutors

The untracking program provides tutors to AVID teachers. Typically recruited from local colleges and often previous AVID students, tutors' primary responsibility is to serve as mentors to the AVID students in their classrooms. Mentors are to lead collaborative study groups based on students' questions, which are often posed in their notebooks. Mentors are also to assist students gain general academic skills that they can apply to their course work. Other duties assigned to classroom assistants or mentors include helping the AVID teacher with administrative tasks (such as grading, attendance, and notebook checks).

Sometimes tutors acted as mentors, but more often than not they served as homework helpers. They provided detailed assistance on specific homework assignments, not general guidance on problem-solving strategies. To be sure, tutors sometimes taught the way they were supposed to. They gave general advice and helped students to help one another and did not simply help with homework or supply correct answers to problems. In extreme cases, tutors provided little or no help; they sat in the back of the classroom, waiting for students to ask them for help. If no students called upon them, they continued to wait. In these classrooms, students worked on the day's homework assignments independently.

Organizational complexities account in part for the transformation of the tutor's role from mentor to homework helper. AVID tutors are supposed to be trained at the beginning of the school year in teaching methodology. However, some tutors selected for AVID never made the training sessions; others who did subsequently left their AVID jobs for other jobs or quit due to schedule conflicts. Whatever the reason for their diminished preparation, many tutors worked intuitively with tutees instead of applying carefully designed pedagogical techniques.

Our observations were confirmed by students and parents, most of whom defined AVID as a tutoring session and a productive one at that. The students explained to us that they work or play sports after school, which makes completing school work at home a problem: "It takes a lot of pressure out of doing homework. You don't have to cram everything in the evening. My sports take a lot of time. AVID really helps me to get my studying done. Mrs. Lincoln really pushes us."

From some students' point of view, then, AVID provides them with a time and a place to study, a chance to stay on top of their homework and to exchange ideas, thoughts, and feelings with their peers. In addition, they appreciate the academic help from their classmates and the emotional support from the AVID teacher. Danielle, a senior at Saratoga, commented on the importance of having peers to study with: "I use study groups a lot. Tazona and several of the other girls and I spend a lot of time studying together. We also use it as a time to discuss our feelings." Carla, a junior at Saratoga, said that before she entered AVID, she felt as if she was the only one who was having academic trouble. Since she has been in AVID, she feels "everyone is in the same boat" and "I really use my friends a lot to help me with math." Comments such as these suggest that AVID students appreciate the homework help tutors provide and the emotional support peers provide and do not miss the mentoring that tutors are supposed to provide.

Representing the Program

The central office clearly represents AVID as a program to help underrepresented minority and low-income students of any ethnicity achieve admission to 4-year colleges. Not all coordinators describe it in these terms to students, parents, or faculty members, however. These different representations are a response to the different circumstances that the program faces at local school sites.

A Program for "Minority Students" or a Program for Students "with Potential"? Stephanie Lincoln, the AVID coordinator at Saratoga, confided to us that she never says in so many words that her AVID students should be minority students. "Minority" and "low income" become unspoken parts of the definition of AVID at her school. As a consequence of this definition of the situation, Saratoga students have a very specific view of AVID and themselves. They defined AVID as a college prep program for students with potential, a representation consistent with their coordinator's. Rarely did any student mention socioeconomic or minority status as a criterion for selection. Instead, several respondents stated that the main criterion was "being smart."

In stark contrast, Kim Shoemaker at Monrovia High School talked about AVID as a college prep program "first and foremost" for underrepresented minority and low-income students. When Monrovia students and their parents were asked who got into AVID, they reiterated this perspective. In our interview with her, Mrs. Sanchez said that her daughter learned about AVID at her junior high school when "all the Mexicans had to go to a meeting."

Shoemaker asserted that AVID is designed not only to help minority students enroll in 4-year colleges but to keep them there: "There is no point just getting someone into college, they have to be able to stay. I figure if the kid is not going to work here, he will never work there when it gets really tough." These representations influenced practice at the school sites. Shoemaker's curriculum was designed to keep her students on a rigorous academic path. In addition, she selected students with impressive academic records. Of the 10 Monrovia students in AVID in 1990–1991, 8 had high

CTBS scores (those in the 7–9 range) and high GPAs (+3.00) when they were selected into AVID.

A 1-Year or a 3-Year Program? Not all AVID coordinators believe in selecting only 9th and 10th graders and exposing them to a 3-year regimen. They often pick up promising students in the 11th and even the 12th grade and take them through the college application process. To be sure, this practice assists students from underrepresented backgrounds enroll in college. However, it inflates schools' college enrollment records and it shifts the ground out from under the reasons for program success – from program activities to selection practices. The practice of picking up promising students in 11th or 12th grade also explains the disparity in college enrollment rates reported by local school sites and by our research. Many AVID coordinators report the college enrollment of those students who have been in AVID at one time or another, whereas we report the college enrollment of only students who have been in AVID for 3-years.

Preparation for College or Assistance with Life's Challenges?
As we explained in Chapter 2, Keeneland is a port-of-entry school, composed of students from immigrant groups, many of whom do not speak English as a first language. In response to these circumstances, Keeneland is working with AVID Center to pilot-test a special program combining ESL and AVID. For an entire academic year, two teachers and four tutors work with Latino, Indochinese, and African immigrant students to prepare them for more advanced work in ESL classes. Teachers in other advanced ESL classes feel that this special AVID ESL class provides students with the extra support they need to do a higher level of academic work. Students are allowed to try higher-level classes if they are in AVID ESL because teachers feel they have the necessary scaffolding provided by AVID tutoring. This redefinition of the program to accommodate the pressing needs of the school's population has consequences for the composition of the AVID program. Students are selected with lower CTBS and grades; they complete fewer college

prep classes and go to college in lower numbers than at many other schools.

Because of the special circumstances confronting their school, AVID coordinators and counselors at Keeneland define their purpose in different terms. Although AVID at Keeneland is not a prevention program for at-risk students, the program coordinators are just as concerned to help students through their high school careers as they are to prepare them for college. "Latanya," selected by AVID in her ninth grade, became pregnant and went to an alternative school. Although the coordinators thought that college was not likely to be in Latanya's future any time soon, they readmitted her upon her return to Keeneland after she had her child because "she was such a fighter, a single mother from a single-parent home with college aspirations."

The basic AVID classes and the special ESL AVID class at this port-of-entry school face other challenges. Some of the immigrant students in AVID classes are undocumented. They have the same college aspirations as their documented peers but their residency status presents financial obstacles to higher education, especially now that California voters passed Proposition 187, which denies educational and health services to noncitizens.

"Julia," an undocumented Latina immigrant, graduated from Keeneland with a 3.7 GPA. The AVID coordinators who knew her said she was bright and diligent. She applied to SDSU and was admitted as a resident because she had lived in California for years, but she was not eligible for financial aid. She planned to attend a local community college because she could not afford to pay university fees on her own. But Julia could not be admitted to the community college as a resident; therefore, she will be required to pay the higher nonresident tuition. It seems that the California State University system is following a court decision that allows undocumented students to pay the lower entrance fees available to California residents if they can prove they have lived in the state. The University of California and California's community colleges, however, are abiding by a court decision that defines undocumented students as foreigners, no matter how long they have lived in the state; hence, they are subject to higher nonresident fees. Consequently, Julia, and other students like her, may not be able to afford college in any of the three tiers of the California system, and will attend no college in the fall after her graduation despite a commendable high school record.

Altering the College Prep Curriculum

The curriculum and course load for AVID students have also been modified at local school sites. The AVID central office insists that all AVID students take a full complement of a–f courses as soon as they are accepted into the program. As our analysis of students' a–f course completion records in Chapter 3 showed, this goal is not realized in practice; 71% of AVID students attempted to take the full range of courses which makes them eligible for entrance into UC or CSU colleges and 40% completed this regimen.

Part of the reason for this gap is the perception on the part of some AVID coordinators and their colleagues who teach the academic courses that some "AVID students are not ready" for college prep work. These coordinators keep AVID students in regular classes until they think they *are* ready for a more demanding curriculum. This practice can have a detrimental effect on students' academic careers, because their class standing is out of sequence with the a–f courses required for a given grade level. And, as our admittedly skimpy college persistence data (presented in Chapter 2) shows, preparing students for community college and not the university is problematic, because so few students transfer from the former to the latter.

RESISTING INNOVATIVE PRACTICE

Some of the innovative ideas that AVID has developed, such as the organization of the AVID teaching schedule, have been implemented as prescribed and others, such as the use of classroom tutors and placing all AVID students into the college prep curriculum, have been adapted to preexisting daily operating procedures. Still other innovations recommended have been met with resentment and hostility and, in extreme cases, have been rejected.

Debates over Student Schedules

The introduction of AVID into the culture of the school impacts students' schedules. Once students are selected, they require a special academic program. The AVID class is designated as an elective in their schedules. We found that the AVID student recruitment process and the preparation of students' schedules caused tensions between new and old practices at the school sites. As of this writing, many of these tensions have not been resolved, but the argument over the way to resolve the problem speaks to the way in which practical circumstances constrain the implementation of an innovative educational idea.

Out first example concerns a very practical matter: The school calendar constrained the possibility of recruiting students at Pimlico High School during the 1991–1992 school year. After the AVID teachers identified the names of the students who were eligible for AVID, they tried to schedule an assembly with the prospective students. They had difficulty arranging this meeting, however, because of conflicts with other school activities. The dates they wanted to meet with the students coincided with schoolwide testing. The school administration would not, or could not, change testing dates, which slowed the AVID recruitment process because they had to scramble for alternative dates.

Another conflict arose concerning the AVID students' academic plan and the counselors "4-year plan" for every student. All the counselors at Pimlico began meeting with the eighth-grade students to plan their high school schedules before the students were selected into AVID. This meant that prospective AVID students' schedules were formed without taking AVID into account, which, in turn, meant some students were at first precluded from participating in AVID. Once these problems were uncovered, some students' schedules had to be rewritten, which placed an extra burden on the counseling staff, a situation that was not well received.

A similar calendar conflict influenced operations at Saratoga. By the time recruitment was underway in 1992, student schedules had been prepared. Many students had already been committed to other elective programs such as art, drama, or drivers' education.

114

These competing demands made it difficult for students to enter or remain in the AVID program.

The course of study for AVID students, once they are selected, is also an issue. Because Pimlico is a magnet school that requires all of its students to take heavy concentrations of math and science courses, there is limited flexibility in students' schedules for all the courses they must take. Since students need to set aside one period for AVID, it eliminates that period for academic courses. The current solution to this problem is to have the eighth graders who are selected into AVID attend summer school before their freshman year. They can choose to take a compressed world history course or a science course in this mandatory summer program.

The existing solution to the problem of overcrowded schedules poses a problem for new AVID students. They are forced to take an advanced academic course, in a compressed period of time, without the benefit of the academic and social supports that would accompany such a course if they took it during the regular academic year. As a result, newly selected AVID students at Pimlico are placed at an immediate disadvantage in their summer courses because they do not get that all important scaffolding.

It is not surprising, then, that the counselors and some faculty in the Pimlico history department do not like the idea of having AVID students take courses during the summer. They propose adding a seventh period, or moving AVID to an after-school program, or placing the entire school on a block scheduling plan instead of using summer school for AVID students. The AVID teachers are adamant that AVID not be an "after-school add on" because then it would lose its importance in the eyes of the students. Forced to compete against extracurricular activities, such as band, sports, or drivers' education, they fear that the Pimlico AVID program might lose its students.

The school counselor on the AVID Site Team at Pimlico had a more radical solution to the problem of the conflict between AVID courses and academic courses. She wanted to limit the AVID experience to one course, which would be taken only once, probably in the freshman year, instead of a course that is taken every semester for 3 years. She believes that offering AVID for 3 years is not necessary because students can be taught study skills in one semester. The extreme position this counselor takes on scheduling AVID classes reveals her representation of AVID. She sees it as a study skills course or a homework program. She does not see it as an instructional innovation or a scaffolding operation for underrepresented students.

Not all debates over students' schedules dilute the untracking effort. Some produce positive results. For example, the AVID coordinator at Golden Gate High has devised a system that keeps students in AVID and drivers' education at the same time. Since AVID and drivers' ed are offered as electives at Golden Gate (and many other local high schools), students often had to choose between one course or the other. In order to foreclose the loss of students, AVID coordinators and drivers' ed teachers have arranged for AVID students to take drivers' ed as an independent study. Each week, the AVID students in the independent study program pick up their reading assignments and homework packets from the drivers' education teacher. They often work on the assignments on AVID tutorial days or at home. Coordinators give the AVID students their drivers' ed quizzes during the AVID class period or after school. This arrangement generates extra work for AVID coordinators to be sure, but it provides a safeguard against student defections from the program and provides them the scaffolding they need to negotiate one important component of the educational system.

Resentment over "Special Privileges"

AVID is without doubt a program that offers students many additional resources. In addition to a dedicated teacher and increased instructional assistance, the program offers its students opportunities that other students don't have. They go on field trips to colleges, they have guest speakers, they get special counseling. At a time when school budgets are being slashed, some teachers and students are jealous and voice resentment toward AVID, denigrating these innovations as special and unwarranted privileges.

For example, Gary Antelope, a graphics arts teacher, characterized AVID in terms of reverse discrimination, asserting that

AVID is an unfair preferential program. He claims that AVID gives advantage to people who don't really deserve it. Minority students who have not done well, but have been designated as having potential, are given opportunities that are denied to whites. He feels that there are "lots of students who could benefit" but they are not classified as acceptable under the AVID guidelines. Furthermore, Antelope asserts the students AVID chooses are not really getting good grades and wonders, therefore, why these underachieving, mostly minority students should be rewarded with a special program while other more deserving kids don't get the same benefits. It is possible that Antelope holds these beliefs because AVID directly impacts his interests. "They are creaming the best students," he says, those who would normally be tracked into his general education curriculum. He has "the leftovers," which he doesn't think is fair.

Antelope has voiced these complaints loudly at school meetings and has received support from other teachers and some parents. The counselor at his school reported that "it's a real sore spot with the community that their kids can't get into the program." Many white parents feel that their children should be given the same opportunity for a college prep curriculum as minority students are given.

Some members of the counseling staff resent AVID as well. At some schools, AVID enjoys the benefits of having one counselor dedicated to monitoring the academic progress of all AVID students for their high school career. Often counselors who are advising college-bound students have a smaller case load than counselors who are advising general education students. One of the two counselors at Saratoga High School responsible for 11th and 12th grade students who are not in AVID expressed anger toward the counseling system. He doesn't think the AVID kids should be given special treatment: "I feel just as qualified as the head counselor to counsel these kids."

Although there is obviously some resentment among faculty and staff about the legitimacy of the AVID program, most students seemed unaware of any resentment directed toward them as participants in the program. They felt that other teachers and students didn't even know they were AVID students. If their non-AVID friends knew they were in the program, for the most part they were jealous of them. One student commented "My non-AVID friends want into AVID because we find out things before anyone else. They want to go on field trips and be kept abreast of college deadlines, etc."

Rejecting Curricular and Instructional Suggestions

In response to the educational reforms proposed by AVID, innovations have been implemented as planned, have been absorbed into existing operating procedures, and have been resisted. We also have examples of innovations that have simply been rejected.

A case in point concerns the implementation of the AVID instructional methodology, which (as we described in Chapter 1) involves using writing as a tool for learning, inquiry methods, and collaborative learning groups. Writing used as a tool for learning did appear in AVID classrooms, but with a significant modification. Although writing was intended to be used as a learning tool in academic courses such as English, science, social studies, and history, by far the most striking use of writing within AVID classes was related to preparation for college entry. AVID teachers devoted considerable class time to assisting their students write biographical essays and statements of purpose. In addition, they often helped their students fill in each blank of admissions and scholarship forms.

Whereas writing as a tool for learning was used in AVID classrooms, we seldom found writing across the curriculum in the academic classes that AVID students attended. That is, math teachers, social science teachers, foreign language teachers, and history teachers, even those who attended AVID summer workshops, seldom used writing as an instructional tool in their classrooms.

The same can be said of collaborative groups. Whereas all AVID teachers grouped students together for the purposes of instruction or tutorial assistance in their AVID classrooms, the academic teachers did not tend to use this instructional technique. Their classrooms were organized in more traditional patterns, with teachers in the front and students in rows of desks. To be sure, science teachers organized lab demonstrations in which students worked in clusters. But at these times, students tended to work on teacher-directed activities; they did not solve problems collaboratively.

One of the coordinators who had once been very involved in the AVID instructional process gave us insight into this situation. She said she no longer participates in AVID's teacher training activities (monthly meetings and summer workshops) because "the meetings make me angry." She is angry because the central AVID office insists that AVID coordinators try to convert all other teachers into proponents of and practitioners in the AVID methodology. Every school is supposed to have a team of teachers, one from each academic discipline. This school-site team is supposed to attend AVID meetings and teach the AVID methodology. While AVID Center reports that 93% of AVID teachers attend summer institutes, this teacher explained why teachers from her school stopped participating after the first year:

> Initially they did this [attended meetings], but the teachers [at her school] got turned off. They [the meetings] just weren't interesting enough. Some teachers got mad because other teachers were sitting above them making up stuff as they went along with stuff that didn't fit their needs. The trainers were not well prepared and teachers felt they were being talked down to.

Although these comments were voiced by an AVID coordinator critical of a local innovation, they could just as easily have been made by a teacher participating in any number of curriculum reform efforts currently underway in the United States (e.g., those in Sizer's Coalition for Essential Schools, or Levin's Accelerated Schools, or Comer's School Development Program). Prevailing teaching techniques and curricular and instructional methods are deeply ingrained in the culture of the school. Such deeply routinized practices are not easily changed. Indeed, our brief review of the course of AVID's innovations shows that the existing culture of the school is a more powerful force than the package of curricular and instructional innovations advocated by AVID. To counter this resistance, the equitable education of language and ethnic minority students has to become a priority of the entire school, not just a few dedicated teachers.

THE DIFFICULTIES OF IMPLEMENTING TWO INNOVATIONS SIMULTANEOUSLY

To this point in the chapter we have documented the tensions created when innovations directed from the top or outside of a bureaucratically organized institution, such as a high school, interact with routines and standard operating procedures that have had a sustained history at the local level. Although some innovations are implemented as designed, we have suggested that innovations are more likely to be modified, sometimes resisted, or even avoided entirely in this contentious environment. At this point, we want to discuss the consequences for innovation when schools attempt to implement recommendations from two different designs for change simultaneously. To illustrate this point, we first describe a school attempting to desegregate its student body and untrack its students at the same time and then describe a school attempting to restructure and untrack simultaneously.

Desegregating and Untracking

Nassau High School participates in the San Diego City Schools district voluntary integration program. Latino (and a few African American) parents choose to send their children to Nassau, presumably to secure a better education for their children and to escape unsafe conditions in their local neighborhood. Because Nassau is so far away from their neighborhood, the students ride school busses back and forth. The issues and conflicts that arise at Nassau High School as it attempts to implement a voluntary integration program present AVID with a different set of institutional constraints than we have seen at the other schools untracking underrepresented students.

A "school within a school" has emerged at Nassau in which the sons and daughters of the wealthy Nassau residents are separated from the African American and Latino students who ride the bus to school. The separation between the two groups is epitomized by an early morning routine designed to assist the voluntary integration students. Bussed students arrive an hour before school starts to

120

receive a hot meal in the school cafeteria. This humanitarian gesture, while providing sustenance for the students, places them on campus an hour earlier than the local white students and isolates them from the local white students who arrive on campus just in time for their first-period classes. The local students have practically no contact with the early arrivers before school, and even less throughout the school day because the students find themselves in different academic programs or "tracks."

Many members of the Nassau faculty claim that the Latinos and African Americans who ride the bus are "not up to par with their Nassau peers." Off the record, the teachers talk about the bussed students as "troublemakers," "responsible for the drug problem," and as those who "pull the school down academically." These opinions are widely shared by the faculty. Although not quoted for attribution, they can be heard in the teachers' lounge and faculty meetings and help create the conditions for a school within a school.

Differences in the academic programs and the academic records of neighborhood and bussed students attest to the existence of a school within a school. In 1992, approximately 300 students graduated from Nassau. While white students compose 60% of the school population and the graduating class, 78% of them completed a–f requirements. By contrast, Latinos compose 31% of the school population and 29% of the graduating class, yet only 11% completed the a–f regimen. Only a few African Americans attend Nassau (3.8% of the school population) but less than 1 percent complete a–f courses.

Tracking contributes to this uneven distribution. Because a–f courses are organized sequentially, students need to take and pass certain prerequisite courses (notably Algebra 2, first-year chemistry, and first-year physics), in order to enter more advanced courses. In the 1991–1992 school year, 859 of 892 (96%) of white students were enrolled in or had already taken these milestone courses, while this was the case for only 31% (117 of 378) of Latinos.

Here, then, we have a predominantly white school struggling to diversify its student body. But the voluntary integration program has not yet succeeded. Majority and minority students seldom interact socially and they are seldom in the same academic courses. In effect, we have a case of resegregation (Jules-Rosette & Mehan, 1978).

How do these conditions affect AVID's attempt to untrack students? Because the AVID students are drawn from the bussed population, not the local population, a line of antagonism has already been drawn between the AVID students and Nassau faculty before the untracking effort even begins. Many members of the Nassau faculty, especially those in the math and science departments, are not wildly enthusiastic about including AVID students, who are almost exclusively Latino, in their college prep classes.

This line of tension seems to have tacitly affected the AVID selection process. The Latino students who ride the bus to Nassau express a wide range of student cultural styles, from the *"cholo"* look of khaki pants with flannel shirts open to the neck over clean white t-shirts to the "skater" look of oversized trousers and shirts to the "preppy" look of chinos, loafers without socks, and designer polo shirts favored by the local whites. The Latino students within AVID, however, do not display this diversity. The ones selected seldom affirm a *cholo* or skater identity; most, but not all, are drawn from the subset of conservatively dressed Latinos. The resulting uniformity in self-presentation among the Latinos in AVID is striking and is quite different than other schools we have studied, where a wide range of identity displays is visible. This uniformity speaks, we think, to the moves that the AVID program at Nassau has made in response to the tensions created by the implementation of the voluntary integration plan.

Now, we do not know for certain whether AVID self-consciously selects students that match the local population or whether once selected, these students begin to emulate the locals, but we have hints that the program encourages Latinos to assimilate. After the initial screening, Dennis Pease, the AVID coordinator, checks students' school records and invites those students who have high CTBS math scores to a meeting where veteran students provide testimonials about the benefits of AVID. He then asks the prospective students to answer questions about their career goals and interest in college. Pease said he uses the students' answers to these questions to eliminate students who are not serious about college or careers that depend upon college.

Pease confided that most of the students he selects "seem different." They don't have steady boy or girl friends; they talk about school more often than they talk about parties. He also admitted that he may unconsciously select students who already "seem to have strong affinities for school and see their future as college bound" rather than selecting students who have previously unrecognized academic potential.

Our interviews with Latino students at Nassau reinforce our impression that AVID seeks students who assimilate. By any criteria, Alma is an AVID success story. When she migrated to the United States with her mother from Central America, she could not speak English. Her mother worked as a maid for a wealthy Nassau family, who arranged for Alma to attend the middle school that leads to Nassau instead of her neighborhood school. After 2 years of ESL classes, she was placed in regular English classes. Her middle-school teachers wrote letters of recommendation on her behalf to Pease. In addition to accumulating an excellent academic record, Alma was active in school government and the school drill team and volunteered her time to a political campaign. Unlike bussed students, Alma said that most of her friends were Nassau students and that she felt very comfortable there. When asked why she was successful and comfortable at Nassau, Alma attributed her success to, as she termed it, "the difference in Hispanics." She explained that most of the Latinos at Nassau are Mexican American and Catholic, and they have a different culture than she does: "In my country" she clarified, "there is a strong group of Christians and we have a different work ethic than Catholics. I work hard and know that it is up to me. I make my future. I have control." Alma enrolled in SDSU after she graduated.

Victor, who described himself as "just another no-future Hispanic before AVID," credited the academic skills such as note taking for his improvement in grades, but he also acknowledged that the AVID teachers "helped him dress better so that teachers would take him seriously." Victor enrolled in San Diego City College after graduation.

Rafael's brief and unhappy tenure with AVID reinforces by counter-example the idea that the program at Nassau promotes Latino students who conform to Nassau norms and rejects students who try to maintain a home identity. Rafael entered AVID upon the recommendation of an English teacher at Nassau. With distinctively Latino facial characteristics, he dressed in jeans and plain shirts, not in a *cholo* manner. Rafael gained the reputation of a troublemaker for talking out of turn, interrupting, and generally provoking Pease's negative attention in the AVID elective class. His resistance to the AVID ideology is exemplified by his actions on the day Pease introduced prospective students to the veterans. At one point, Pease said to the new recruits, "AVID is a program for students who want to go to a four-year college. This isn't a program for students who want to go to City College" [a community college]. Shortly after Pease said this, the phone rang and he had to leave the room. While he was gone, Rafael said in a loud voice, "I must not belong in AVID. I'm going to a two-year college." His comments resonated throughout the room; five or more of the other seniors shook their head in agreement. On another occasion, Rafael asked Pease where he should list a certain college on his financial aid application. Pease ignored that question and challenged Rafael about the seriousness of his intentions:

MR. PEASE: You haven't even completed the application yet. Is college your goal?

RAFAEL: Yeah.

MR. PEASE: Is it planned?

RAFAEL: Yeah, by Friday.

After this exchange he pointed to the graffiti on the back of the chair in front of him that says "SHUT UP PEASE." Later, Pease said that Rafael "has many problems and just seems to laugh them away." Rafael left AVID in the second semester of his senior year.

Ricky's biography demonstrates this is not an entirely predetermined system. He was the only student in the AVID class who dressed in *cholo* garb. His hair is slicked back. The son of an Anglo mother and Mexican father (who left when Ricky was an infant), Ricky learned Spanish on his own "from the streets." More so than any other Latino, Ricky spoke Spanish in the classroom. From his speech and his dress, he seemed to define himself as *Chicano*. Ricky told us about his mother's alcoholism, her back disability, her smoking habit. He felt a responsibility to care for his mother, a commitment he feared would preclude him from attending college. "How can I leave my Mom? I'm all she's got." Ricky assumed household responsibilities, including working as a cook in a convalescent hospital. Since he had the 4:00–7:30 P.M. shift, public transport didn't get him home until 9:30 or 10:00 P.M. Despite his late hours and added responsibilities, he did well in school. "I do all right, As and Bs, but in eleventh grade I got my first C in history." A competent computer user, other AVID students sought him out to type essays for them. Ricky had adopted a critical stance toward AVID, however:

> I was getting good grades even before AVID. I got kicked out once because I refused to take stupid notes on every fucking thing. My grades have dropped since I've been in AVID. It's a joke. It has only made me more confused. The only good part is getting college information.

When asked about why he bothered to stay in AVID if it wasn't helpful, Ricky said he liked it because his friends are there. His relations with peers were not peaceful, however; he says he didn't fit in with the local Nassau students because of his speech and dress, and he didn't fit in with the students who rode the bus because of his academic aspirations. His relations with teachers were not calm, either. The AVID and the academic teachers alike interpreted his expression of *Chicano* identity as a sign that he was a troublemaker and not a serious student. Yet he resisted the pressure he felt from AVID to dress and act differently. In the final analysis, Ricky realized that the constraints placed on him by his family circumstances impeded his ability to attend college right after high school: "Perhaps I'll be able to take some night classes at City and later go to a four year." Ricky's prediction, made during his senior year, proved accurate. After graduating from Nassau with a 2.88 GPA and 30 of 33 a–f courses completed, Ricky enrolled in a local community college.

Rafael, Victor, Ricky, and the other AVID students at Nassau are being told implicitly that if you don't have money, then at least act like you do. Tacit instructions about identity, speech, and dress tell AVID students who are bussed to Nassau that race and class matter in getting ahead in the world. Injunctions to "pass" as a member of a different, more affluent group rather than project one's own culture-based identity play into and indeed affirms the class-based divisions that exist at Nassau and the broader society.

These instructions to assimilate help place students on the margin. The Latinos in AVID told us they feel isolated and segregated from the white students at Nassau. As Ricky said, "The white students here think they are so superior." Many of these students have ridden buses to the elementary and middle schools which are "feeders" to Nassau; but few have ever developed any friends from these schools. Local students may talk to the AVID students from the barrio in class, but as Wilma, an AVID student who graduated in 1992, said for her classmates, "The white kids act like they don't even know us outside of class."

Rejected by the locals, AVID students from the barrio are also alienated from their families and friends back home. Martha, the oldest of four children whose parents were both born in Mexico, wanted to go to college, and went to Nassau because she thought that would help her achieve her goals. She credits Pease for keeping her motivated, AVID for "helping me to be organized and to take good notes," and her uncle for pressuring her parents to allow her to go to college. But her friends and her younger siblings do not get bussed out of their neighborhood: "They don't want to leave their school because they say they don't want to become a nerd like me. They always tease me when I'm doing my homework. I can't get along with my brothers and now that my sister is in junior high, it's getting hard with her, too."

Martha was desperately trying to fulfill her aspirations, but was feeling the pain of rejection by family and friends for becoming too academic. Relenting to the pressure she felt from her brothers and sisters, she stopped working with AVID tutors and returned home early after school to help her mother with work. She enrolled in a local community college in the fall of 1992.

The lessons we learn from these brief biographical sketches are confirmed by the general academic record of AVID students at Nassau. In 1992, 22 AVID students, all but 2 Latinos, graduated from Nassau. Four of these students enrolled in 4-year colleges. This 36% college enrollment rate is considerably below the AVID average. The students who went to college adopted the locals as their reference group and Alma explicitly rejected her Latino heritage. Ricky and Raoul, who openly resisted the AVID strategy of assimilation, now attend community college. As we will show in the next chapter, these strategies are much different than the strategies adopted by AVID students at other schools.

Why is the AVID program less successful at Nassau than it is at other schools? The circumstances there are much different than elsewhere. In most schools, even magnet schools such as Pimlico and Bay Meadows, AVID students are bussed, but they are also drawn from the local neighborhood. At this school, which is trying to desegregate, we have distinctive class distinctions on top of cultural differences. AVID kids are bussed kids. When they arrive at Nassau, they are tracked by faculty, shunned by local students, and asked to minimize their cultural identities. And to make matters worse, as Martha's poignant story tells us, they have to endure hazing from their neighborhood friends.

No school-based program like AVID can, by itself, break down the institutional barriers that exist in the Nassau community. The social class distinctions that impinge upon this program exist outside the school, are brought into the school by the students, and are reinforced by the faculty's sorting practices. In order to provide an equitable educational environment at Nassau, the entire community will have to be committed to end elitism and classism. The final goal would be the elimination of all vestiges of the tracking system, which effectively minimizes the possibility of a 4-year college education from the careers of the majority of minority students. Intermediary steps that could be taken to help achieve that goal would involve expanding the social support systems for AVID students at Nassau High. At the present time, AVID students at Nassau, like AVID students at other schools, receive 180 hours of tutoring and mentoring in the special AVID elective class. The academic record of the AVID students at Nassau suggests that this regimen is not enough. The quantity and quality of instruction need to be increased at Nassau, perhaps through after-school programs that extend the school day and end-of-year programs that extend the school year. We return to this issue in the concluding chapter.

Restructuring and Untracking

A school attempting to restructure decision making and untrack students at the same time provides us with a second example of the complications that arise when schools attempt to implement innovations simultaneously. As we discussed in Chapter 2, Keeneland High School is redesigning its curriculum, instruction, and governance to implement Sizer's Coalition for Essential Schools (Sizer, 1984, 1992). Attempting to implement the educational changes recommended by two innovative programs simultaneously has caused conflicts at this school.

The Keeneland coalition teachers first introduced the interdisciplinary approach to teaching math, science, social studies, and English with the 9-grade class. In the second year, they continued the interdisciplinary curriculum with the students who became 10th graders and initiated a new group of 9th graders. As it is becoming clear that the entire school will soon be taught in this interdisciplinary manner, teachers in certain subject areas such as studio arts and vocational education have voiced concern that their courses will be forced out of the students' schedules. To reduce this tension among the faculty at Keeneland, coalition teachers are trying to find ways to integrate the academic program with vocational education and art education. These compromises put pressure on AVID. The schedule for the school day is so tight, particularly for those students who are college-bound and have a–f course requirements to fulfill, that a reorganization of AVID has been discussed. Possibilities included holding the program before or after school, or only intermittently, or making it available to all students. Since AVID is designed to be a full 3-year program for a selected group of students that meets every day, if any of the proposed modifications were adopted, then AVID's structure would be changed significantly.

A more general issue emerging from the restructuring effort will influence the AVID untracking effort at all schools. The San Diego City Schools district is attempting to implement an educational plan that decentralizies decision making. Faculty, staff, and parents at the school site level are making more and more personnel and financial decisions. The authority to decide how to spend certain federal and state educational money has been delegated to schools as a part of this decentralizing move. As a result, principals and their "school site councils" are not obligated to spend money on programs that have been organized and directed at the school district level. More specifically, schools are not obligated to use their funds to place tutors in AVID classrooms. The districtwide restructuring effort means AVID must compete for funds with other programs. If tutors are not assigned to AVID classrooms, then the organization of this untracking effort will be changed significantly.

SUMMARY: TENSIONS BETWEEN UNTRACKING INNOVATIONS AND STANDARD PRACTICES

The circumstances we have described illustrate the difficulties in implementing an innovative program such as the AVID untracking effort. We have presented examples of situations in which various combinations of the primary parties concerned – the AVID staff, the school administration, the academic teachers, the counselors – do not agree on certain aspects of the program. When educators at the school-site level were presented with innovations that required them to modify their standard operating procedures, they responded in a variety of ways: They implemented some to be sure, but they also absorbed the innovations into their routine teaching practices, resisted the innovations, or discarded them entirely.

These turf battles substantiate Sarason's (1982, 1991) point about the far-ranging effects of organizational innovation. An innovation that appears only to touch one part of a complex organization such as a school, has impact – often unintended and unanticipated – throughout the whole system. On the surface, it appears that AVID is working with only one segment of the school – underachieving minority and low-income students who can be motivated to go to college. The actions educators direct toward that one segment of the school population, however, influence other aspects of the school.

No one at Pimlico anticipated at the beginning of the school year that planning an assembly at the same time as testing had been scheduled would have deleterious consequences on student selection. Not being able to resolve that conflict had a spillover effect, because a smaller cohort of students was selected at one school in 1992, and this selection process did not occur as efficiently as desired.

So, too, this untracking program makes special resources available for its special group of students: a designated teacher, a separate classroom, tutors, visits to colleges. "Regular" students in "regular" classes (as well as many other types of special students in other special programs) may not have access to these kinds of resources. The availability of these resources for AVID students stirred other parts of the school system, and in some cases has led to animosity toward AVID teachers because their students benefit from these resources while other students do not.

Most of the innovations that were not implemented or were seriously modified at the school site level appeared in the instructional and curricular domains: the use of tutors, writing as a tool of instruction, the inquiry method, the use of collaborative groups in AVID classes. Even though classroom aides serve as homework helpers instead of mentors, even though the inquiry method or collaborative groups do not dominate academic classes, AVID students have a commendable college enrollment record. The success of AVID students even when curricular and instructional innovations have not been widely implemented reinforces the point we made in Chapter 5: The success of untracking is strongly influenced by institutional supports in the form of scaffolding, teacher advocacy, and bridging.

Having made this observation, a point of clarification is in order.

We *are not saying* AVID and schools should abandon their attempt to implement curricular and instructional innovations such as the inquiry method or collaborative grouping. Spreading the use of such teaching techniques will probably enhance the academic environment in classrooms and increase the zest that teachers feel toward their teaching. We *are saying* that the academic and curricular dimensions of an untracking effort can not exist without cultural and institutional supports. As the circumstances at Nassau vividly illustrate, socially organized support systems constitute the possibility of students' academic success.

To illustrate this point better, let us draw an analogy to the social construction of genius. Feldman (1986) convincingly argues that child prodigies develop the expertise of adult masters at a very early age through a complex constitutive process. The child's "raw talent" is one ingredient in this process to be sure, but we must keep in mind what counts as talent is culturally and historically constructed (DeNora & Mehan, 1994). Furthermore, Feldman takes pains to explain that prodigies' talents do not ripen "naturally"; they must be recognized and interpreted by someone who understands their significance. Furthermore, this talent is not general or universal; that is, it can not necessarily be used or applied in a variety of domains or in many contexts. Prodigious achievement seems to require talent to be molded in domains that are highly structured, such as math, music, or chess, because these domains contain discernible patterns with a well-organized history that can be taught systematically. In addition, a knowledgeable teacher or coach must conscientiously train the potentially talented person. Genius, then, is a construction. A highly structured domain of knowledge, someone who identifies the possibility of raw talent being developed, and an expert mentor are ingredients that must co-occur with raw talent in order for prodigious achievement to develop. If these ingredients do not occur together in the same time and space, then prodigious achievement does not develop.

Feldman's careful description of the construction of childhood genius has wider implication. Despite the claims of biological determinists (e.g., Herrnstein & Murray, 1994), that seemingly "natural talent" we call "intelligence" or "giftedness" is socially constructed.

Its forms and contours have been constructed through conventions that have developed through history. Likewise the academic success of untracked students is a construction – not an accident, but the consequence of a confluence of forces, some cognitive, some institutional, and, as we will show in the next two chapters, some peer and family based. Just as the absence of a coach or interpreter can mean that a child genius does not develop, the absence of high expectations or inquiry methods or mentoring or scaffolding or sponsorship or advocacy can mean that an untracked student does not make it to college.

Lurking underneath this discussion of the social construction of academic achievement are ironies created by the individual–collective dichotomy. The tension between the individual and the collective appears in the very way in which the program talks about itself: AVID stands for Advancement Via *Individual* Determination, after all. The program emphasizes achievement ideology, impressing upon students that their personal initiative leads to success. AVID teachers take pains to emphasize that students succeed because they work hard, not because the program works hard. Yet our examination of the daily practices of AVID points out that these individual efforts are sustained by an elaborate system of institutional supports, peer and group and family relations, which are all quintessentially collective enterprises. The program also insists that its success is a function of its academic orientation and curricular approach. Yet our observations show that the writing process was more likely to be used in AVID classrooms for the college entry process than essays in English and college student assistants were more likely to be used as homework helpers than mentors. Collaborative groups were used widely in AVID classrooms but were virtually nonexistent in academic courses such as English, math, or biology. We found that the program was sustained by social mechanisms, most notably exposing the hidden curriculum of the school and sponsoring graduating AVID students at selected colleges than it was by innovative curricular practices.

The fact that students' individual efforts are placed within a context of social support mechanisms is fascinating to us. At the very least, it supports the observations made by writers from George

Herbert Mead to Lev Vygotsky: Social phenomena appear first within the social realm, and then move to the individual realm. It also reinforces an observation made by some ethnomethodologists (Pollner, 1987; Mehan & Wood, 1975): Society (or at least U.S. society) is organized in such a way that the social practices that constitute objects are detached as those objects become reified. The detachment of constitutive practices from the objects they assemble is especially apparent when the individual is inscribed as the locus of action as when talented musicians are said to have "genius," or when special education students are said to possess a disability, or when students who score high on IQ tests are said to be "smart," or when AVID students are said to be empowered to determine their academic success. Given the prevalence of this individualistic bias in U.S. society, privileging the academic and the individual over the social and the collective is probably strategic for the untracking program. The U.S. educational community is more likely to support an enterprise that suggests success is the result of individual effort and is less likely to support one perceived to require massive amounts of institutional resources.

7

PEER GROUP INFLUENCES
SUPPORTING UNTRACKING

To THIS POINT, WE HAVE REFLECTED ON THE CONTRIBU-
tions that academic, social, and institutional processes make to
the success of the San Diego untracking experiment. We have suggested that the cultural capital in the form of academic skills that
AVID students acquire from their mentors and the social capital
they receive in the form of advocacy from their sponsors contribute
substantially to AVID's respectable college placement record.

For the most part, these processes operate within the walls of the
school: between teachers and students, between AVID coordinators
and academic teachers, counselors and administrators. To be sure,
some of these processes reach out beyond the school, as when personnel from the AVID central office and coordinators interact with
college faculty members and university placement officers; but for
the most part, what we have taken up so far operates within the
boundaries of the school.

In the next two chapters, we want to turn our attention to cultural
processes that have their primary locus outside the classroom. One
set of those practices, the topic of this chapter, operates between
AVID students and their peer groups. Another set, the topic of the
next chapter, operates between AVID students and their parents.

IDEOLOGY AND ACADEMIC ACHIEVEMENT
IN U.S. SOCIETY

The poor academic performance of poor white, black, and Latino
youth has recently been blamed on the actions they take that flow

from their critique of the limits of the capitalist system (Willis, 1977; Weis, 1985; MacLeod, 1987; McLaren, 1989; LeCompte & Dworkin, 1991; Solomon, 1992). The sons and daughters of the poor realize that their access to high-paying jobs is limited. As a result, they withdraw from academic pursuits. Their critique is limited and ironic, however, because their unwillingness to play the academic game insures they will stay in lowly economic positions.

We have found that the students who participate in AVID for 3 or 4 years develop a much different ideology and adopt a much different course of action than has been previously attributed to the sons and daughters of the working poor. The African American, Latino, and Asian high school students from low-income families who have participated in AVID express a belief in their own efficacy and a belief in the power of schooling to improve their lives and the lives of others. They translate their beliefs into action by participating actively in school, yet they do not adopt a romantic or naive commitment to achievement ideology. They are all too aware of the barriers erected in front of them by the history and practice of racism and discrimination. To handle the complexities of the world they confront, they adopt strategies that many researchers (Cummins, 1986; Gibson, 1988; Gibson & Ogbu, 1991; Ogbu, 1978, 1987b; Matuti-Bianchi, 1986; Ogbu & Matuti-Bianchi, 1986; Suarez-Orozco, 1989) have associated with recent immigrants to the United States: They maintain their ethnic identity while actively engaging schooling. That is, they accommodate to the norms of school and society without assimilating or compromising their ethnic identity (Gibson, 1988).

In the main body of this chapter, we describe the contours of the accommodationist ideology we have found among Latino and African American youth and describe some of the cultural processes and organizational practices that seem to have nurtured its development. Before doing so, however, we provide a context for this discussion by reminding our readers that "achievement ideology" is the prevailing belief about success in the United States which explains why the collectivist, resistant ideology of the working poor is such a threat to it.

The Conventional Wisdom about Success in American Society: Achievement Ideology

There has long been an egalitarian political and educational ideology in the United States that views people's chances for success in life as primarily the result of personal achievement, individual effort, and hard work. People in the United States like to believe that we are not limited by our background characteristics. "My parents may have been poor; my ancestors may have been slaves; my mother may have been hurt by prejudice, but I can overcome these limitations of the past and succeed on my own."

The school plays an important role or function within this "achievement ideology." It is the responsibility of the school to provide all children with equal opportunity to acquire the general cognitive skills necessary for the pursuit of success. The operation of a "contest mobility system" (Turner, 1960), in which virtually every school child is supposed to have the opportunity to compete for requisite resources, fosters this belief in equality of educational opportunity. Such competition is achieved by delaying and minimizing the selection of students for positions within the occupational structure. Although people will eventually wind up in different positions, the schools give them equivalent training and cognitive skills. In short, the school is supposed to be a vehicle for all people – the children of the poor and the children of the rich – to obtain the cognitive skills and educational preparation necessary to compete in life (Davis & Moore, 1945; Parsons, 1959; Dreeben, 1968).

Note that this conventional wisdom about success and failure in the United States is expressed in personal, individualistic terms. When people speak in what Bellah and his colleagues (1985) have called "the first language of American Society," they say that a person's place in life is a function of the hard work and effort that person invests. This "achievement ideology" makes each individual student responsible for what she achieves or doesn't achieve. If a student is successful in school or work, then it is because of individual effort; if a student fails, it is because he didn't work hard enough.

136

The Antiestablishment Ideology of Low-Income Minority Students

Students from low-income and ethnic and linguistic minority backgrounds have been represented as having a much different belief system. Either they don't buy into, or they have given up on, the belief in hard work and individual effort. If they have beliefs at all, they are said to be antiestablishment. If not antiintellectual, they are at least antiacademic.

Willis (1977), MacLeod (1987), Foley (1991), and Solomon (1992) let us listen to the voices of the antiestablishment ideology of the working class. This ideology includes a critique of the capitalist system that rationalizes their lack of academic and economic success. The "lads" in England, the "Hallway Hangers" in Boston, the "*vatos*" in South Texas, and the "jocks" in "Lumberville" realize that no matter how hard they work, they will still be relegated to low-paying jobs or, worse, no jobs at all. These beliefs are translated into actions; students from the working class withdraw from academic pursuits, act up in class, ignore assignments and homework, cut classes. Their critique is somewhat shortsighted, however, because their ideology leads to actions that contribute to their stagnant position in the status hierarchy.

Ogbu's (1978, 1987a, 1987b) research into the folk models of schooling associated with "non-immigrant minorities" and "immigrant minorities" sharpens the representation of minority and working-class youth as oppositional and resistant. Immigrant minorities (such as the Japanese, the Koreans, the Chinese) accept school norms, work hard, and alternate their academic identity at school with a nonacademic identity with friends, Ogbu says. Blacks, Native Americans, and Latinos have a different folk model of schooling that encourages different patterns of behavior. These "nonimmigrant minorities" tend to equate schooling with assimilation into the dominant group, a course of action they actively detest. As a result, they do not try to achieve academically; instead, they engage in collective actions of resistance against school and societal norms.

Ogbu implies that the ideology that blacks, Latinos, and other encapsulated minority groups have developed contributes to their relatively poor academic and economic success. Because it is collectivist and oppositional, the ideology of involuntary or encapsulated minorities has led them to adopt strategies that scorn the idea of individual achievement that is so important in American society, in favor of collective strategies, which blame failure on racial discrimination and other structural forces.

Labov (1982) reported that low-income black students formed group identity based on in-group linguistic codes. While these communication patterns help maintain group cohesion, they also have alienating effects. The black vernacular, like rap and reggae, distinctive dress, and demeanor are a source of distinction and pride (from the low-income black student's point of view), but are signs of opposition and irritation (from the white teacher's point of view). The folk model within the black peer culture required speech markedly different than the "good English" expected in school. Students who spoke "school English" and did well in school marked themselves as different and risked rejection from their peers. Because they valued peer validation, these students opted out of academic pursuits and into oppositional pursuits, which meant they spent more time resisting authority and being confrontational and much less time and effort in their school work.

Fordham and Ogbu (1986) and Ogbu and Matuti-Bianchi (1986) expanded on Labov's argument. Because involuntary immigrant groups still experience prejudice, they have come to believe that social and economic success can only be achieved by adopting the cultural and linguistic patterns of the majority culture. This puts high-achieving blacks in a bind, because they must choose between maintaining their ethnic identity or striving for high achievement, which their ethnic peers regard as acting superior, or "acting white." To resolve this dilemma, many Latinos and blacks reject academic life in favor of an oppositional life-style:

> To be a Chicano means to hang out by the science wing; it means, *not* eating lunch in the quad where all the gringos, "white folks," and school boys eat; it means cutting classes by faking a call slip so you can be with your friends by the 7–11; it means sitting in the back of a class of *"gabachos"* and *not* participating; it means *not*

carrying books to class or doing your homework; it means doing the minimum to get by. In short, it means not participating in school in ways that promote academic success and achievement. (Matuti-Bianchi, 1986: 253)

When Latino and black high school students rebuke their peers for "acting white," they are actively resisting white structure and domination (Fordham & Ogbu, 1986; Matuti-Bianchi, 1986; Ogbu & Matuti-Bianchi, 1986). Likewise, when black college students go through the routine of schooling but exert little effort in their studies, they are resisting an education that they see as "only second best" to that available to whites (Weis, 1985). So too, when West Indians in Toronto form separatist groups, refuse to follow school rules, and play sports to the exclusion of their school work, they are creating a "lived culture" that contributes to their own school difficulties (Solomon, 1992).

In short, poor black and Latino students are said to have an ideology and a course of action that directly challenges conventional American wisdom about the relationship between academic performance and occupational success. The ideology and practice of resistance contributes to the lowly position of blacks and Latinos in the occupational structure, therefore, because they refuse to develop the skills, the attitudes, the manners, the speech necessary for achieving success in capitalist societies.

Because of the ways in which "encapsulated minorities" and lower-income students have been characterized in the literature, we expected to find a serious tension between the academic demands of the San Diego untracking program (AVID) on the one hand and the more recreational, oppositional demands of peer groups on the other hand. Students selected for AVID would feel pressure from their friends not to achieve academically we reasoned, and would be drawn away by non-academic enticements. Well-known hostilities among blacks and Latinos against "acting white" (which includes doing well in school or speaking standard English) fueled our concerns.

We were wrong for the most part, we didn't find an ideology or practice of resistance. With the exception of Nassau, we didn't find antagonism between AVID and non-AVID students, and we didn't find AVID students being tempted by indulgent, countercultural enticements. Instead of AVID kids being lured away by non-academic peers, we found that AVID kids formed new academically oriented peer groups. From these new voluntary associations, academic identities were formed and new ideologies were developed. While acknowledging the necessity of academic achievement for occupational success, these ideologies displayed a healthy disrespect for the romantic tenets of achievement ideology and a healthy respect for cultural maintenance.

In the next few pages, we present the contours of the reflective ideology we found among the Latino and African American youth in this untracking program. After that we describe some of the cultural processes and organizational practices that seem to have nurtured its development.

THE DEVELOPMENT OF A REFLECTIVE ACHIEVEMENT IDEOLOGY

The "involuntary minority" students in AVID have developed an interesting set of beliefs about the relationship between school and success. They do not believe naively in the connection between academic performance and occupational success. Although they voice enthusiastic support for the power of their own agency, their statements also display a critical awareness of structures of inequality and strategies for overcoming discrimination in society.

Belief in Individual Effort, Motivation, and Opportunity

AVID teaches a version of achievement ideology, telling students they can be successful (which AVID defines as going to college), if they are motivated and study hard. The AVID coordinator at Saratoga High School stated this philosophy succinctly when greeting her incoming freshman class: "The responsibility for your success is with you. AVID is here to help. Your goal should be to go to a 4-year college. There is lots of work to be done, but you will have more help, support, and love than you will ever need."

Interviews with AVID students suggest that they internalize this ideology, articulating success in a way that reflects the message that AVID teaches. Andrew, a freshman at Saratoga, highlighted the value of motivation in providing equal opportunity: "Before AVID I was unsure about college. I was always changing my mind. AVID teaches you that you have the same opportunity to get to college as anybody if you just stay motivated." This sentiment was echoed by Susan, a second-semester freshman at the same school:

> I am more motivated to go to college because AVID made me want to go. Before I got into AVID, I didn't think I had many opportunities. I thought I couldn't afford it and that I couldn't get good enough grades. Mrs. Lincoln says we can get financial aid. And, well, now my grades are really good.

Margaret, like Andrew and Susan, insists that her opportunity to achieve success is the result of her individual effort: "I have a better opportunity than others because I am really striving for it. AVID helps me know what to do. I try hard, so I have to say I have the opportunity because of who I am. I have my own individual identity and not the identity of a group of people."

Students also echo the sentiments of the AVID program when they claim they have the same opportunity to achieve as anyone else, regardless of their racial or ethnic background. Elijah, an African American male, maintains he has an opportunity to succeed because "the key to success is your own body, your own self."

Experience with Prejudice and Discrimination

AVID students believe in individual effort, motivation, and opportunity. But these students also recognize that the world is full of discrimination, prejudice, and racism. Furthermore, many AVID students have personally experienced prejudice. Doug and Ron, two AVID seniors, said they had stopped at a stop light and a white man in the car next to them got out of his car and pulled a gun on them for no apparent reason. They took off "like fast." AVID students have experienced scrutiny and harassment from the police in ways that resonate with the tales retold by Anderson (1991: 190–206). These students rattled off incidents to us that suggest the police define their social control work as keeping middle-income white neighborhoods "safe" from low-income blacks. Ron and two other friends, for example, were walking home from a school dance behind some white guys; a police patrol stopped and harassed them, but never stopped the white guys. According to Kent, he was at home one night when cops just burst into his home without reason and left without explanation. To the comment, "It sounds like you are getting a bum deal," the boys agreed. But they were not resigned to these conditions; they believed they could overcome them: "If you work hard you will succeed."

Danielle, a black female student, relayed similar experiences: "I'm gonna tell you something. I don't care if I should, but there's a whole lot of racism. My friend and I were alternates on the flag team and when they needed to replace some permanent members they got two new white girls and not my friend and I."

Kaylee, a black female student also expressed an awareness of discrimination. She said her mother told her that she had to "watch out." She might be friends with whites now, but when it came to the business world later, they would let you down.

Experience with prejudice and discrimination is not confined to black and Latino students. Tran, a junior in AVID who is Chinese, was born in Vietnam. Although he is doing well academically (carrying a 3.3 GPA), he confided to us that he is afraid of the verbal portion of the SAT because he considers it a racist test. He is also afraid that his chances of going to college will be hampered by a quota system, which limits the number of Asian students, and "there are lots of Asians smarter than me."

STRATEGIES FOR DEALING WITH DISCRIMINATION

AVID students are not only aware of these structures of discrimination, but they have developed strategies for dealing with them. When asked about what happened after the flag team incident (just described), Danielle said: "My Mom raised heck. [But] Teachers don't care. They just think they are here to teach. *You've got to get yourself through.* Except for three teachers. Mrs. Lincoln is one of them. Teachers don't say you are capable. No one really cares." Danielle believes her determination will help her deal with racism, a point she reinforced later in this same interview: "Most blacks in the community are faced with prejudice and will be held back, not me."

Teesha recognized there are barriers erected in her path and in the path of African American students generally:

> I think teachers expect more out of us [blacks]. Colleges recruit blacks because of sports but they don't get an education. That's dumb. There's lots of hurt and prejudice. People need to learn about different cultures and read about black people. They always look at us when we study about slaves as if we were slaves.

In addition to appealing for more culturally sensitive curricula, Teesha's strategy for dealing with prejudice is to "go to college. I want to be there. It's the only way to get a job."

This opinion was reinforced by David, an African American student, who said he does not have an equal opportunity to succeed because of his race: "There is more pressure because we are black and we are athletes. They are always looking to us to do the right thing and if we do anything wrong we're nobody."

Before he became involved with AVID, David believed that his athletic prowess would lead him to success. Since he has been in AVID, his strategy for dealing with the prejudice he has experienced has changed; now he plans to get good grades and not rely on athletics as his ticket to success.

Several African American males reported tales of systematic discrimination at the hands of a particular counselor. In a group interview, they reported that this counselor repeatedly tells African American males that they "won't make it to a big time college." One student reported asking for information about a 4-year college and being told, "What for? It's just a waste of your time and mine. You won't make it anyway." The counselor then gave him only information about 2-year colleges and vocational schools. Even though these students said they have protested his ill treatment, he is unwilling to help them. When one student tried to add chemistry to his schedule, this same counselor said, "You don't need that for what you are going to do after graduation. Only college-bound kids need academics." To deal with this prejudicial situation, AVID students have devised ways to avoid this counselor. Instead of going to him for advice, they rely on the AVID teacher to counsel them about college. They also talk among themselves and make it clear to new AVID students that they should avoid this counselor.

Students report other incidents that suggest they are victims of backlash from their academic teachers. It appears as though some teachers think that AVID students are only in advanced classes because they are AVID students. This "sorting privilege" can operate against AVID students. One AVID student commented that her Advanced English teacher told her on her first day that she wouldn't make it in her class. Her AVID teacher intervened on her behalf the next day, telling the English teacher that the student "would make it because [she] was getting extra help from AVID." The student finished the semester with a grade of B. When this student was asked why she felt she was able to succeed, she responded:

> I knew if I tried, I could, and I really wanted to show her I could do it. My AVID teacher told me to work with the tutor. But boy was I hurt that she [the Advanced English teacher] thought I couldn't do it. I know it was because I was a minority student. She didn't even know my ability.

Some African American males in AVID talked about their race strategically. In doing so, they sound like the "Brothers" in Mac-Leod's (1987) ethnography of urban youth. The Brothers said they thought they had more opportunity to succeed than their parents because of the influence of governmental civil rights laws. Darrien, a black male from Saratoga High School, is typical of many African American males in AVID in this respect. He believes he has a better opportunity because of his race. Colleges, especially those in California, are trying to meet affirmative action goals, so, they recruit African American males like himself. That is, in a civil rights climate, he thinks his race gives him an advantage, a fact he can use strategically.

Discrimination can cut two ways. Donald, one of the few white students in AVID, indexed what would be called reverse discrimination. He said that he doesn't have an equal opportunity because of his race: Colleges are accepting Asians over white kids. In fact, the lower college enrollment figures of white students who graduate from AVID that we reported in Chapter 2 could be used to support his argument.

Accommodating without Assimilating

AVID students recognize that academic performance is necessary for occupational success, but they have not bought the naive proposition that their individual effort will automatically breed their success. The Latino and African American students in AVID (which Ogbu would call "involuntary minorities") have also developed provocative beliefs and practices about culture contact. They affirm their cultural identities but at the same time recognize the need to develop certain cultural practices that are acceptable to the mainstream, notably achieving academically (cf. Foley, 1990, 1991). Following Gibson (1988), we talk about this aspect of their ideology as "accommodating without assimilating."

Marta Garcia represents many Latino students in AVID who affirm their cultural identity while achieving academically. Marta told us that her Latino cultural background is very important to her. In fact, when she was in third grade, she pledged to become perfectly bilingual, maintaining her native Spanish while developing acceptable English and academic skills. She has fulfilled this promise to herself, and entered the University of Ihao Americana, Tijuana, Mexico, in the fall of 1992.

When we interviewed Marta's Spanish-speaking parents, it was clear that Marta's identification with her Mexican heritage has been kept actively alive by her intense involvement with them. Spanish is the predominant language in the home; the family takes frequent trips to Mexico; religious and cultural symbols are prevalent in the home. Marta's parents respect her bicultural moves. On the one hand, they are pleased that Marta and her friends are respectful of their background. On the other hand, they encourage the academic path their children are taking. It is perhaps symbolic of the way the parents are juggling these two worlds that Marta's older brother, and also an excellent student, will be attending college with Marta.

Marta has two close friends, Serena Castro and Mercedes Duarte, both of whom are in AVID. These girls reinforce each other's love of their cultural heritage and desire to succeed. They often discuss college plans and share their concerns and excitement *in Spanish,* a sure sign of their cultural identification.

Another sign of Serena's accommodation is found in her interactions with her mother about college. Serena's mother is a widow, who speaks very little English and works as a domestic and food services worker at the University of San Diego. Serena seldom discusses academic matters with her mother, apparently. Mrs. Castro told Irene Villanueva that she provided Serena with general moral support (*apoyo moral*), but she felt ill equipped to provide the detailed technical skills Serena needed in school. Mrs. Castro always supported Serena's plans to go to college, although she didn't want her to leave the San Diego area in order to pursue this goal. She is pleased, therefore, that Serena will attend UCSD. When Irene asked Mrs. Castro about Serena's financial aid, Mrs. Castro laughed in an embarrassed way, because she was completely unaware of what Serena will be receiving, what her fees are, or how they will be paid. Serena has assumed all the responsibilities associated with college matriculation and, in the process, simultaneously maintained her family life with her mother and her school life with her friends.

Andrew, a junior at Saratoga High School, recognizes that mainstream teachers as agents of mainstream society, expect a certain style of talking and acting in school, especially from blacks. Andrew varies his speech behavior to different social situations as a strategy for dealing with this expectation; he confines his vernacular to the street and tries to talk the standard in school (cf. Matuti-Bianchi, 1986; Foley, 1990).

Managing Dual Identities

The space AVID has created is productive, because it helps AVID students foster academic identities. But this same space also created problems for AVID students, because they must deal with their friends who are academically oriented and their friends who are not academically oriented. AVID students developed a variety of strategies for balancing or managing this dilemma.

Gándara (1995) found college-bound Latino students used "denial" as a strategy to keep up their grades while still keeping up their friendships. One Latino student told her: "I didn't let on that I was studying or working hard. I mean you were cool if you didn't study."

While some AVID students submerged their academic identity entirely, most students maintained dual identities, one at school, one in the neighborhood. Because they were segregated by classes at school, it was not difficult to keep the two peer groups separate. At school, they were free to compete academically; at home in the afternoon, they would assume a different posture.

Lilia is a Latina who lives in what she described as "the ghetto":

> You don't know how awful it is there. They don't give a damn about themselves. My Mom doesn't have any education. My friends in the neighborhood think I am really stupid for staying in school. They tell me that since I have enough credits to graduate, I ought to quit school and get a job. They think the most important thing is to get married and have babies.

Lilia wants to be a lawyer and she knows the only way to achieve that goal is to "put forth the effort and go to college." But she also wants to keep her friends. Therefore, she is active in AVID during school hours and continues to date boys from her neighborhood and go to the movies with her girlfriends who live on her street.

An African American male from Monrovia said in so many words that he lives two lives. "Chris" said he really wants to go to college, and AVID provides him a place where his academic pursuits are encouraged and where he has academically oriented peers. But he has street friends, too. While he feels they are "wasting their lives" because "they are into being bad," he still hangs out with them after school and on weekends. Chris also spends some of his free time as a peer counselor for Saratoga's African American students. His counseling activities bridge the two different worlds he occupies.

The story of "Hazzard," an African American who attended Pimlico High, exemplifies a third strategy for managing dual identities. He brought his nonacademic friends with him into academic settings. Hazzard was a member of a gang when he was selected into AVID. He retained his gangbanger friends, while simultaneously developing new acquaintances in AVID. Like other AVID students, he wanted to go to college. He was, in fact, accepted at UC Berkeley, SDSU, and a local community college. Instead of enrolling at the UC campus, he said he chose to attend the college closer to his home so that he could stay with his friends. Indeed, he brought them to classes with him. Hazzard was doing what he needed to do to pass academically, while retaining his membership in his peer group.

These "border crossing" strategies (Matuti-Bianchi, 1986; Rose, 1990; Delgado-Gaitan & Trueba, 1991; Giroux, 1992) have special utility for minority students, because by the time they graduate, they will have had experience in moving between two cultures. They will have interacted with high-achieving Anglos and still be comfortable in the company of family and friends who would never leave the fields or the barrios, or go to college (cf. Gándara, 1995).

GROUP FORMATION AND THE CONSTRUCTION OF ACADEMIC IDENTITIES

The African American and Latino students who participated in the AVID untracking program for 3 years developed strategies for managing dual identities and developed new ideologies. Importantly, these ideologies were neither conformist nor assimilationist. Instead, their belief statements displayed a healthy disrespect for the romantic tenets of achievement ideology and affirmed their cultural identities while acknowledging the necessity of academic achievement for occupational success. In this section, we describe the institutional arrangements and cultural processes that contributed to the formation of academic identities and the development of a reflective achievement ideology.

Isolation of Group Members

In order to transform raw recruits into fighting men, the military isolates them from potentially conflicting social forces. Religious orders and gangs operate in a similar manner, shielding their recruits from competing interests and groups (Goffman, 1964; Jankowski, 1991).

AVID has adopted a similar principle. AVID selects promising students and isolates them in special classes, which meet once a day, every day of the school year. Once students are in these classes, AVID provides them social supports that assist them through the transition from low-track to academic-track status. These scaffolds include a special method of notetaking, test-taking strategies, procedures for filing applications, meeting deadlines for SAT tests, and requesting financial aid and scholarships. In these ways, AVID is exposing the hidden curriculum of the school, teaching explicitly in school what middle-income students learn implicitly at home.

Public Markers of Group Identity

In addition to isolating students and providing them with social supports, AVID marks their group identity in a public manner. The special class set aside for their exclusive use is one such marker. Instead of going to shop or drivers' education for their elective class period, they go to the AVID room, a classroom identified by signs and banners. Students often return to the AVID room at lunchtime or after school to do homework or socialize, actions that further mark their distinctive group membership.

AVID students are given special notebooks, emblazoned with the AVID logo, in which they are to take AVID-style class notes. These notebooks signal their membership in this special group. Some schools have designed distinctive ribbons and badges, which AVID students wear on their clothes. Others have adorned their graduation gowns or mortarboards with AVID ribbons. Still other AVID classes publish a newspaper reporting on the accomplishments of

AVID students. All of these actions further identify AVID students as members of a special group.

These markers influenced teachers as well as students. Teachers reported that when they saw students with AVID notebooks, taking notes in class and turning in neat assignments on time, it indicated to them that AVID students were serious and well intentioned, a perception that helps break down some of the stereotypes held about minority students.

Formation of Voluntary Associations

Special classrooms, badges of distinction, these are physical, material markers which define the space for AVID students to develop an academically oriented identity. Within this space, AVID students developed new academically oriented friends, or joined academic friends who were already in AVID.

Several Saratoga students told us that they did not know anyone in AVID when they joined but, after a few years, almost all of their friends were from AVID. These friendships developed because they were together in classes throughout the day and worked together in study groups. Coordinators encouraged these friendships by minimizing competition. The AVID coordinator at Monrovia High School, for example, told her students that they should think of themselves on "parallel ladders with each other. There should be no competition between students, but rather an opportunity to share notes and to help one another."

Some AVID students did join AVID to be with their friends. Cynthia, a Latina from Monrovia High School, said her friends were already in AVID, and because they were doing well, she wanted to be with them. Thomas, an African American male at Saratoga, said that he told his two good friends from elementary school that "they had to get into AVID because it would really help with their grades." He even called one of his friend's mother to convince her that AVID was good for her son. These three boys have remained good friends for their 4 AVID years and always study together.

AVID encourages the development of academically oriented associations among students through formally organized activities such as college visits. AVID coordinators take their students to such colleges as SDSU, UCSD, UCLA, and USC. Of particular note, the AVID coordinator at Pimlico High takes her AVID students on a long trip to Historically Black Colleges and Universities in Washington, D.C., and Atlanta every other year. In addition to the usual college tours, the current generation of AVID high school students meet students from San Diego who are enrolled in these schools.

Less formal activities do this work of developing academically oriented associations also. Students in AVID classrooms often talk among themselves and discuss matters relevant to their adolescence. At Golden Gate, speaking Spanish is allowed and even affirmed in the AVID classroom. Students use this period of time to bounce their values and troubles off one another, to test their principles and ideas, and to respond to others. In those schools where African American and Latino students are bussed in, the AVID classroom may be the only time minority students see each other during school hours. In those classes where older and younger AVID students mix, the younger students observe older students' behavior and how teachers interact with them.

The longer students are in the program, the more ties seem to intensify. These sentiments were articulated by a Latina who attends Monrovia. AVID provides a different environment for her. "At home they expect me to get married. Here they expect me to go to college." Because of the pressures she receives from home, Marta attributes much of her academic success to the girlfriends she has cultivated in AVID. She studies together with her two friends and they "chat a lot about college and what we want out of life. Our study group really opens up a lot of issues. Everyone is really motivated to go to college. It really helps to be around others that want to go. It makes you want it more."

Because of the treatment that "school boys" and "school girls" receive at the hands of their alienated peers (Fordham & Ogbu, 1986; Matuti-Bianchi, 1986), we thought the highly visible markers of AVID (the notebooks students are required to carry to classes, the special class periods established for them, the college visits arranged for them, the newspapers they publish) would stigmatize

AVID students in the eyes of their peers. But this marking process has had the opposite effect. AVID students reported that their friends who were not in AVID were jealous. They wanted to be in AVID for the camaraderie, to be sure, but also because they wanted to take advantage of the resources AVID made available to its students, such as information about scholarships, college entrance exams, and visits to colleges.

Many AVID students have told us that their friends who were not in AVID were jealous, and "wanted into" the program. One Latina student stated that her friends, who were mostly white, were uncomfortable with the advantages given to AVID students: "They don't like AVID because they feel racially threatened. They don't really know what it is. They are jealous and think AVID is unfair."

Another Latina student, noting that her Spanish-speaking mother is unable to help her with school work as English-speaking parents might, expressed a similar view: "Many are really jealous of the help that AVID gives me. One friend told me that it wasn't fair that Mrs. Shoemaker helped me with my composition. [But] they forget that I don't have a mother to proofread my papers like they do. I can't get any help from my parents."

A Vietnamese student suggested that this jealousy can take on overtones of reverse discrimination; his friends think that the only reason he got into USCD was because he was in AVID: "They think that AVID can get you in," he said. While these peer attitudes lead Mercedes and Tran to feel defensive about their participation in this untracking program, such attitudes also seem to fuel an increased commitment and loyalty. Pressure from outside the group creates a bond inside the group. Many students felt they were lucky to be "chosen" for the program, and know they were chosen because they need help academically.

SUMMARY: THE SOCIAL CONSEQUENCES OF UNTRACKING

The poor academic performance of poor African American and Latino youth has often been blamed on the actions they take that result from their critique of the limits of the capitalist system. The sons and daughters of the poor realize that their access to high-paying jobs is limited. As a result, they withdraw from academic pursuits. Their critique is limited and ironic, however, because their unwillingness to play the academic game insures they will stay in lowly economic positions.

Ogbu maintains that the status that African Americans, Latinos, and other involuntary immigrant groups have in relation to the power structure contributes to this condition. Whereas "voluntary" immigrants (such as the Japanese, the Koreans, the Chinese) accept achievement ideology, "involuntary minorities" tend to equate schooling with assimilation into the dominant group, an equation they detest. As a result, they do not try to achieve academically; instead, they engage in collective actions of resistance against school and societal norms. Ogbu implies that the collectivist and oppositional ideology that blacks, Latinos, and other involuntary minority groups have developed contributes to their relatively poor academic and economic success. They fail in school because they blame failure on racial discrimination and other structural forces and do not take personal responsibility for their own actions and individual initiative, a course of action that Ogbu believes is funda-mental for success in American society. Furthermore, he seems to feel that these conditions are immutable and impervious to change: "membership in a caste-like minority group is permanent and often arrives at birth" (Ogbu, 1987b: 91). Weis (1985: 132) also seems to believe that African Americans are destined to react against the system in predetermined ways:

> The fact that blacks constitute a castelike minority group in Amer-ican society means that student culture *will automatically take* a somewhat different shape and form from that of the white work-ing class. Student cultural forms is [*sic*] also affected by the nature of historic struggle for particular groups. [Our use of italics is intended to point to the determinism in this formulation.]

Relegated to an unalterable position of inferiority through exploita-tion, Weis and Ogbu predict that involuntary immigrants will con-tinuously choose acts of resistance in response to their oppression.

Ogbu's formulation is problematic because he does not explain the increasingly well documented variance in response to oppression within ethnic groups. Foley (1990, 1991) reported that a growing number of middle-class Mexicano youths no longer express the negative psychological orientation of Ogbu's involuntary minority group. Increasingly, these youths are beginning to act like youths from voluntary minority groups. In addition, the distinction in Ogbu's theory between voluntary and involuntary minorities and his typology of responses to oppression cannot account for why the African American and Latino youths who have participated in AVID feel good about being ethnic and were succeeding in school.

Ogbu's formulation is also problematic because it ignores the possibility that sociocultural processes such as school programs and teachers' interventions can alter students' perceptions of opportunities and lead them to translate these perceptions into actions. Except at Nassau High School, we did not find an oppositional ideology or pattern of resistance dominant among the black and Latino students who participated in the AVID untracking program. Instead, we found that AVID kids formed an academic identity and developed a reflective and critical ideology. Strictly speaking, their ideology was neither conformist nor assimilationist. Instead, it included a critique of many tenets of achievement ideology, an affirmation of cultural identity while acknowledging the necessity of academic achievement for occupational success.

By isolating students for significant portions of the school day, marking them as members of a special group, and providing them social supports, AVID fostered the academic identity of its students. This newly acquired academic identity posed problems for AVID students who had many nonacademic friends, however. AVID students resolved this dilemma by managing dual identities, an academic identity with academic friends at school, and a nonacademic identity with friends after school. This "border crossing" strategy is useful for minority students, because it provides them experience in moving between two cultures, a high-achieving academic culture and a supportive community culture.

AVID students face discrimination and racism, to be sure. But these antagonisms do not result in the acts of cultural inversion suggested by Willis, Matuti-Bianchi, MacLeod, and Ogbu. In fact, AVID students invite us to reexamine the typology Ogbu constructs, which designates separate and distinct ideologies for voluntary and involuntary immigrant groups. The blacks and Latinos who participate in AVID do not fit the typology proposed by Ogbu. While many African American students in AVID describe a system that is not sympathetic to students in general and discriminatory to blacks in particular, they speak of their own opportunity in terms of their individual hard work. One black male from Saratoga summarizes this argument for us: "We know that the teacher is not doing what's right. He is a real racist jerk but if you work hard you will succeed. If you get good grades, he can't hurt you."

The ethnic and linguistic minority students in this untracking project seem to have developed an ideology, a consciousness if you will, that is neither oppositional nor conformist. Instead, it combines a belief in achievement with a cultural affirmation, becoming more critical than conformist.

The ideology of AVID students, that is simultaneously culturally and academically affirming, puts a new twist on the traditional connection between academic achievement and economic success. Black and Latino AVID students sense the need to develop culturally appropriate linguistic styles, social behavior, and academic skills. And they develop these skills, but without erasing their cultural identity, which is nurtured and displayed at home and in the neighborhood.

Furthermore, these students' ideology provides an interesting counterpoint to the ideology of resistance. Here we are exposed to the circumstances in which members of ethnic and linguistic minority groups eschew oppositional ideologies in favor of the "accommodation without assimilation" belief system (Gibson, 1988) that is presumably reserved for members of "voluntary" immigrant groups (Cummins, 1986; Gibson & Ogbu, 1991; Ogbu, 1978; Suarez-Orozco, 1989).

In a sense, AVID students (who are successful by anyone's standards) have developed the ideology that Fine (1991) seems to think is reserved for the rejects of the educational system. She found that high school dropouts had developed a much more sophisticated critique of class, gender, and ethnic politics than high school graduates, who naively accepted the connection between hard work and academic success. It is important to note that AVID produces minority students who are successful in school and who have developed a critical consciousness. This means that a critical consciousness is not reserved only for the students rejected by the system. We have uncovered at least one set of social circumstances in which a critical consciousness develops among students who are academically successful.

8

PARENTS' CONTRIBUTIONS TO UNTRACKED STUDENTS' CAREERS

Yolanda Lucero is the youngest child of Raquel and Jorge Lucero. Yolanda, her sisters, and her parents live in a small house in a poor mexicano neighborhood a block away from the freeway on the San Diego–National City border. Yolanda, who graduated from Golden Gate High School with a 3.9 GPA, applied to and was accepted at UCSD, UCSC, SDSU, UC Berkeley, and the University of San Diego. She enrolled at UC Berkeley with financial support.

Mrs. Lucero said she was not actively involved in Yolanda's education. Although she volunteered to help in her daughter's elementary school classroom, she said she was never called. She concluded that it was because she didn't speak English; perhaps the teacher decided she wouldn't be able to help the children because she only spoke Spanish. A turning point in Yolanda's academic career occurred in third grade when Mrs. Lucero sent Yolanda to a school with predominantly white students in order for her to participate in the GATE program that was accepting Mexican-origin children for the first time [*Fue la primera vez que tuvieron este programa para los Mexicanos. Y por eso, tuvo la oportunidad de participar en el programa*]. Yolanda became increasingly aware of the contrasts between her and the other students when they talked about their fathers' work. Their "fathers were bank managers, worked with computers, and my dad [worked] in produce." Thus, she learned that ethnicity, language, parents' education, and occupation all contributed to her distinctiveness at school.

Our parents "always would tell us [daughters] to get an education," Yolanda said. "Basically it was up to us, whatever we wanted. [Dad] wanted us to continue our education." However, the Luceros did not know about the types of colleges that were available. Until Yolanda joined AVID, she was considering going to a local technical school or a community college. Mrs. Lucero gave Yolanda credit for learning about and taking care of the paperwork needed for college applications [*Yolanda hace todo. Yo no más firmo lo que necesito firmar* (Yolanda does everything. I just sign whatever I have to sign)].

The family is close knit. An aunt, grandmother, and other relatives live in the neighborhood or in neighboring communities. Thus, the idea that Yolanda will attend UC Berkeley was, at first, surprising. However, both Yolanda and her mother explained that a cousin in northern California recommended Berkeley and took Yolanda to visit the campus. Mrs. Lucero was less concerned that Yolanda was going away to college because her cousins live close by. If finances become a problem, she can live with them. The cultural bonds and availability of extended family close to the campus make the distance between home and college acceptable for the family.

CONTAINED IN THIS STORY ARE THE INGREDIENTS WE have found repeatedly in the Latino and African American families of AVID students: a low-income family with parents who have high aspirations for their children but who have insufficient knowledge and resources to assist their children with higher-education goals. Although AVID parents support their children's college goals, they don't know the details about required courses and tests, application forms and deadlines, scholarship possibilities and procedures. Although they understand that their children need to go to college to be successful, they express some ambivalence about them leaving home. To resolve the dilemma, they make arrangements with family and friends, which help shrink the distance, at least symbolically.

It is the purpose of this chapter to describe the relations between

AVID parents and the program in order to explore a more general issue – the contributions that parents make to their children's educational careers. We begin the chapter by placing this discussion in the context of the current concern with parent involvement in students' education. We close the chapter by recommending that prevailing approaches to parent education in which schools direct the manner and shape of parents' involvement be replaced with a dialogic relation between parents and educators.

THE "NEED" FOR PARENT INVOLVEMENT

Parent involvement has become a hot topic in American education. Statements about the need for parents to be involved in their children's education in order for them to be successful in school appear regularly in *Parents* magazine and the *Readers Digest*.

These popular sentiments are echoed in the serious research literature (Delgado-Gaitan, 1992; Comer, 1980, 1988; Epstein, 1992). Peterson (1989) and Stevenson and Baker (1987), for example, said students' academic achievement in elementary and high school improved when their parents' attended parent–teacher conferences and PTA meetings and helped their children select courses. Flaxman and Inger (1991: 3), summarizing a decade of parent involvement literature for the Department of Education, ecstatically report that parent involvement is correlated not only with academic achievement but also with heightened self-esteem and less pregnancy and crime:

> There is evidence that parent involvement leads to improved student achievement and significant long term benefits: better school attendance, reduced dropout rates, decreased delinquency and lower pregnancy rates. . . . Furthermore, these improvements occur no matter what the economic, racial or cultural background of the family. Students whose parents are actively involved with the school score higher on tests than children of similar aptitude and family background whose parents are not involved. Parents involved as partners in their children's education feel better about themselves and are often motivated to improve their own education; students' citizenship and values im-

prove and teachers find an improved working climate as the schools become safer and more conducive to learning.

Ted Sizer, reflecting on the ingredients for successfully redesigning American high schools, finds a special place for parent involvement:

> Most parents are our allies. What they want at heart, is more than a ticket for their offspring to a prestigious college. They want that, yes, but they want more; and it is by an alliance of aware and demanding teachers, parents and adolescents that a better school can be molded, a thoughtful place to teach thoughtful young citizens.

Parents of ethnically and linguistically diverse students have been chided for failing to participate in the schools in numbers comparable to majority group parents (Delgado-Gaitan, 1992; Comer, 1980). Educators complain that this lack of parental involvement contributes to the relatively poor school performance of linguistic and ethnic minority students (Schlossman, 1976; McLaughlin & Shields, 1987). U.S. Secretary of Education Richard Riley recently voiced this sentiment (quoted in Shogren, 1994: M3):

> When I talk to teachers, it has often been my observation that they don't talk to me about their pay or their long hours or the difficulty of their jobs. They talk to me about the fact that they can't get parents to help them with the education of their children. That is a real problem in American Education.

Incompetence or lack of interest have been cited as the reasons why minority parents do not participate in their children's schooling. Deutsch (1967) and Bereieter and Englemann (1966), for example, were infamous for saying that low-income, ethnic and linguistic minority families do not value education as highly as middle-income and mainstream families.

McDermott, Goldman, and Varenne (1984) show us that the concepts of match and mismatch offer a more reasonable account of differences in parental involvement than the characterization of minority parents as incompetent. As we described in Chapter 4, *students* from cultural or socioeconomic groups who are different than the mainstream often enter school and find a process discontinuous from their past experience. So too, *parents* from different cultural and socioeconomic groups can find schooling discontinuous from their past experience. Schools project "values" and "expectations" for parent involvement. If, on the one hand, parents' cultural practices match school expectations, then there is a good fit between home and school. If, on the other hand, parents' cultural practices don't map onto school expectations, then a mismatch between home and school can develop. And, by implication where sociocultural congruency exists between home and school, children have a better chance of succeeding, but where sociocultural discontinuity exists between home and school, children have a lessened chance of succeeding (Hansen, 1988; Delgado-Gaitan, 1992; Cooper et al., 1994; Goldenberg & Gallimore, 1995).

Lareau (1989), operating within the framework of Bourdieu's cultural reproduction theory, gives us an excellent description of sociocultural continuity and discontinuity in school–parent relations. She found that the schools in a white working-class neighborhood and a white upper-middle-class neighborhood both shared an ideal of family–school partnership and promoted parental involvement. Teachers in both schools saw parent involvement as a reflection of the concerns parents had for their children's academic success. Despite equivalent formal policies, the quality of parent participation varied from school to school.

The levels and quality of parent involvement were linked to the social and cultural resources available to parents in different social class positions. Working-class parents had limited time and disposable income to intervene in their children's schooling, Middle-income parents, with occupational skills and occupational prestige that matched or surpassed that of teachers, had resources to manage child care and transportation and time to meet with teachers, hire tutors, and otherwise become involved in their children's schooling.

The difference in the deployment of social resources was evident in parents' response to school policies. Teachers in both schools asked parents to get involved in their children's education (e.g., to read to their children, to help with their homework). Parents from low-income families felt that their educational skills were inadequate for this task, whereas parents from middle-income families felt comfortable helping their children in school. Teachers in both schools asked parents to share concerns with them, an action that presumes that parents see the task of educating children as divided between teachers and parents. The low-income parents were less likely to see that they had the right to raise concerns while middle-income parents had confidence in their right to monitor teachers and even criticize their behavior.

By asking low-income parents to attend school events (PTA, back-to-school night) and to help in the classroom, teachers were making demands on the time and disposable income of parents and, perhaps more important, challenging their conceptions of the teacher role and parents' relation to it. Attending afternoon parent–teacher conferences, for example, requires transportation, child care arrangements, and job flexibility. Middle-income parents had more time and disposable income than working-class parents. They defined education as a cooperative responsibility between parent and teacher. The time and income afforded by higher-class jobs coupled with an attitude that matched the policies of the school facilitated involvement in schooling by middle-income parents, whereas the absence of these resources and definition of the educational situation deflated participation by low-income parents.

Thus, social class positions and class cultures become a form of cultural capital. Although both working-class and middle-class parents want their children to succeed in school, their social location leads them to deploy different strategies to achieve that goal. The strategy deployed by working-class parents – trusting teachers to educate their children – did not promote success. The strategy deployed by middle-income parents – actively participating in supervising, monitoring, and overseeing their children's schooling – promoted success. They often challenged the school; if their children had problems, middle-income parents assumed the school was responsible. They employed the services of outside experts if the school did not respond to their satisfaction. These practices, interactional manifestations of cultural capital, appear to give middle-income students advantages over their working-class counterparts.

Lareau shows us in convincing fashion that differences in parental involvement is not a matter of parents' incompetence or lack of interest. It is the consequence of the mismatch between school and family expectations and practices. She shows that working-class and middle-class families each have a stock of knowledge, routines, rituals, and practices that are meaningful, coherent, and goal directed. But one set of social practices, those deployed by well-to-do families, maps onto school practices and is, therefore, picked up and celebrated by the school.

Although Lareau's study seems to imply that parental involvement is the key to students' academic success, we think there is a different lesson to be drawn from her work. The issue is really the match between school expectations and parental action, not parent involvement per se. In those schools which shun parental involvement (which is the case in many middle schools or junior high schools), activist parents can be seen as meddlesome. A noninterventionist school with activist parents creates as much of a mismatch as an activist school with uninvolved parents. Likewise, a school that signals it does not want parent involvement and parents who respond in kind produce a match in parent–school relations. Bhachu (1985: 83) reports that kind of relationship was productive for rural Sikhs in British schools: "This noninterventionist approach of the rural immigrants had proved just as effective within the British context in motivating children to do well in school and to pursue higher education as the more middle class urban interventionist approach."

AVID PARENTS HAVE HIGH ASPIRATIONS FOR THEIR CHILDREN

A prevalent belief in American society is that Latino and African American parents do not care about the education of their children. Research project after research project, however, dispels this myth. Latino and African American parents have the same aspirations for their children as white parents (Delgado-Gaitan, 1992; Delgado-Gaitan & Trueba, 1991: 131ff.; Goldenberg, 1987; Gonzalez et al.,

1993; Díaz, Moll, & Mehan, 1986; Hayes, 1992; Cooper et al., 1994; Goldenberg & Gallimore, 1995). For example, Azmitia et al. (1994) found that most of the Mexican American parents in their study wanted their children to go to college and become lawyers, doctors, or teachers. Parents who did not have specific educational and vocational goals for their children still had definite ideas about what they would *not* want for their children. In particular, parents hoped that their children would not have to work in the fields or the canneries as they did. As a mother of a fifth grader in Azimitia's et al.'s (1994: 18) study said: "Anything [any job] as long as it isn't in the fields. When I was very young, I started to pick strawberries and I wouldn't want him to do that."

The parents of AVID students are also like the parents of most other children. They have high aspirations for their children, which they often express in global terms. Isabel Romo, who moved from Mexico 20 years ago, said she wants her children, including her daughter Yareli, "to have a good life," which Romo defines as not worrying about bills or living from paycheck to paycheck, and being "responsible," which means not "relying on a husband for support." Yolanda, a Bay Meadows graduate told us "my Dad always would tell us to get an education." These parents want their children to do well in school, to succeed in life, and to be happy in their life choices. Irma Castro, the mother of Serena (introduced in the preceding chapter) expressed her hopes for her daughter's success this way: *Quiero lo mejor para Serena, hasta donde pueda llegar, y que termina de estudiar* (I want the best for Serena, as far as she can go, and that she complete college). Herminia Duarte, mother of Mercedes (who described herself as a homemaker, born in Guadalajara, Jalisco, Mexico, who has lived in the United States for 29 years) also commented on her aspirations for her daughter's future in general terms: "I hope [that] she doesn't have to work as hard as we do. . . . [Success means] to have a better life."

The Latino parents studied by Cooper et al. (1994) expressed the view that raising morally responsible children took priority over other aspirations. They saw schooling as only one dimension of staying on the good path (*buen camino*) and assumed that by ensuring their children's health and safety and instilling values such as responsibility, kindness, and honesty they would foster academic and vocational success. Unlike these Latino parents, the Latino and African American parents with children in AVID express a belief in the centrality of schooling, especially college, in improving the possibility of their children's success in life (cf. Goldenberg & Gallimore, 1995). Also, unlike the Latino parents studied by Cooper et al. (1994), AVID parents maintained these high aspirations as their children moved through the school system from elementary school to secondary school. Although one Latina parent has only a third-grade education and does not speak English, she told us that she had always encouraged her daughter to go to college. In fact, she feels that parents who do not have formal education themselves encourage their children more because they are painfully aware of the limited opportunities children have without education. Alma Espinosa said she wanted her children to do better than she did, and education was the only way to insure this. Myrna Salazar underlined the importance of education in her daughter's life: "It was never a question that Barbara would go to college." Salazar always told her kids that they would go.

This sentiment was reinforced by Tina Cano, a single parent of four teenage daughters, who attended secondary school in Mexico. She always talked to her daughters about the importance of going to college and cast college as the alternative to her own struggles – "how hard I've had it" [without higher education and for having married early in life]. She advised her daughters, two of whom are now attending USD, "You want a better life than what I had." She stated that she felt she had put her life "on hold because I would not put myself over my children." She told her daughters about making choices and "whatever choice you make, there will be consequences. You need to have the paper [degree] in your hand, or you won't make it in this society."

Cecilia Santos's mother, Manuelita Borges, a single parent with three married daughters for whom she provided daily care, had a 10th-grade education from Mexico. She spoke of her struggle for her children: *estoy luchando por ellos*. She said she always advised them that *la persona que no estudie se queda* (the person who doesn't study, stays behind). Kaneesha Grant's mother, an African American, agreed with these Latino parents: The only way to succeed is to "have lots of options" and the way to get them is "through education."

Salazar recalled the poverty and discrimination she had experienced growing up as a migrant worker in Crystal City, Texas. Without the benefits of intervention programs such as Headstart or ESL or counselors to guide her through the educational system, she was academically unprepared. Because of her own negative experiences in school, she wants her children to achieve more than she has. At the end of her interview, Salazar provided a vernacular version of Bourdieu's (1986) notion of cultural capital: "Going to college is the only inheritance that people like us can give."

AVID parents' general concern that their children have a "good life" forms a foundation upon which more specific, even instrumental goals, such as going to college, are built. That is, going to college and getting a good job are not set in opposition to living a moral life as Cooper et al. (1994) found. For AVID parents, the two are complementary (cf. Goldenberg & Gallimore, 1995). While AVID parents emphasized their religious sentiments, these values did not conflict with their children's education. On the contrary, their moral life supported and complemented their children's education.

Based on our research, and comparing it to the 10 years of research on Latino families conducted by Goldenberg and Gallimore (1995), it is fair to say that academic and moral goals are so intertwined for many parents that making a distinction is problematic. Parents may see morals taking precedence over academics, but only because they see morals as the foundation for academics. According to this view, academic advancement is not possible if one is not also a good person. Goldenberg and Gallimore summarize the interconnection between morality and education this way: You can be a good person (moral) and not do well in school. But it is not possible to be a good student without being a good person. Or, if a person has formal schooling but is not a good person, it hardly matters.

Cecilia Santos's family is very active in an Apostolic church, participating two evenings per week and all day Saturday and

Sunday, but her religious practices did not inhibit her from taking strong action on behalf of her daughter. One day Cecilia came home in tears – *por causa de una maestra muy racista* (because of a very racist teacher). Manuelita Borges, a parent who had not gone to the school before, spoke to other parents and students about the teacher, and demanded that the principal transfer Cecilia to another classroom. The principal approved. Borges said Cecila was very surprised that she acted on this incident, because Cecilia had never seen her mother respond so strongly before. Borges responded, *No, que por los hijos, uno no sabe que puede hacer* (when it's for your children, a mother has strength she didn't realize she had).

A stereotypical view of the low-income Latino family is that women are encouraged to adopt traditional roles. They are to stay at home, get married, raise a family. Because they adhere to these traditional values, Latino parents often make choices that impinge upon their children's academic development. Latino parents with children in AVID did not express this traditional sentiment to us. Instead, they devised strategies to facilitate their daughters' professional development while adhering to moral sentiments.

Rosario Balderrama's very small, modest home in downtown San Diego exemplified the connection between morality and education in her family's life. In the corner of their dining room was a small shrine to the Virgin de Guadalupe. Next to it was a small bookcase containing several books Eric Balderrama was very proud of. His daughter, Rosaria, said her father read all the time. The shrine and the books are tangible signs of the intertwined religious and academic dimensions of his life that are extremely important to the family. When Rosario spoke of her decision to attend UC Berkeley, her father acknowledged his approval – *Creo que está bien*. However, he added that the family will miss her and, because the distance between San Diego and Berkeley is so great, they won't be able to travel to see her – *La vamos a extrañar mucho. Es muy lejos de nosotros*. The conflict between encouraging his daughter's education and wanting to see her often was resolved by Mr. Balderrama because Rosario has an aunt in northern California. Rather than prevent Rosario from going to college out of a need to protect or shelter, or insisting that she attend a local college and live at home,

Balderrama made sure that his sister, who lives near Berkeley, would allow Rosario to stay with her if the need arose.

Amanda Summers's father is a minister at a Baptist church that serves a primarily African American population. He attributes the academic success (which he defines as going to college) of his six daughters to "the strength of our family coupled with their spirituality and faith in God." He said his family is very disciplined. He knows his daughters' friends and has always insisted on strict curfew rules. At the same time he professes his religious faith, he has extolled the virtue of higher education. He went back to college "to show his children that if he could do it, they could."

Summers wrote a poem for Amanda's graduation from Keeneland High School entitled "Why School? Why an Education?" In it he explains "excuses" for failure are not to be "scuttled for pleasure and fun." "It is not who is to blame but who will suffer." Mr. Sullivan's poem is laden with moral language: "responsibility," "hope," "discipline," "suffer." This is not a parent who has separated a moral life from an academic one. This is a parent who has consciously constructed his life and the lives of his children to incorporate both a moral life and an academic life. In these ways, these parents encouraged their daughters' academic careers, but without sacrificing traditional family values.

AVID PARENTS LACK KNOWLEDGE AND RESOURCES

While the parents of AVID students have high aspirations for their children and think that college is important for success later in life, like other low-income parents they feel they lack the skills and resources to help their children achieve their goals (Azimita et al., 1994). Some of the Latino parents we interviewed were reticent to become involved in their children's high school education because they don't speak English well and feel embarrassed about it. Instead of blaming themselves for this lack of skill, other parents we interviewed placed the responsibility on the school. Like Aida Lucero (whose story we told at the beginning of this chapter), Alma

Espinosa said she never attended any meetings at the school, AVID or otherwise, because *no hay ningun maestro que habla español* (there are not any Spanish-speaking teachers). As a result she does not know any of her daughter's teachers or anything about the AVID program. These (in)actions by parents and school can set a self-fulfilling prophecy in motion. It is out of such miscommunications that parents' beliefs about unresponsive schools and schools' beliefs about inattentive parents emerge.

Many Latino parents we interviewed said their own limited education prevented them from helping their children academically; therefore, they relied on AVID heavily for this kind of support. Serena Castro's story, which we told in the preceding chapter, is instructive in this regard. While Serena's mother said she could offer moral support (i.e., by staying up late at night to make Serena a cup of tea while she studied), she was unable to provide the detailed technical skills that Serena needed to do well in school. Mercedes' mother echoed this sentiment: "AVID was good for Mercedes because neither myself nor my husband could help her with her school work. [We] definitely couldn't help her with mathematics. AVID was able to really help her increase her grades."

Even parents with a high school education or some college also voiced limitations in being able to assist their children with homework. Myrna Salazar, a nurse who was born and educated in Texas and who attended 1 year of community college, told us about her daughter Barbara's difficulty in mathematics courses, her sense of inadequacy in higher levels of mathematics, and the availability of "help from AVID": "We can't help. Algebra is our limit. The only thing you can do is encourage them to go to after school tutoring, pick them up and take them."

Given the social location of AVID parents, these sentiments are not surprising; indeed they echo the findings of other similar studies (Azmitia et al., 1994; Cooper et al., 1994; Goldenberg & Gallimore, 1995). Some AVID parents are single parents. Most are in low-income brackets who have not had much direct experience with higher education themselves, which means they have not accrued the "cultural capital" (Bourdieu 1986) to spend on their children's future.

AVID PARENTS DEPLOY STRATEGIES
INVISIBLE TO THE SCHOOL

Despite feeling inadequate and rejected by the schools, AVID parents sometimes developed their own strategies to help their children stay on the academic track and get to college. While these strategies are effective, they are often invisible to the school. As a consequence, parents' contributions to the children's education often go unheralded.

When parents felt they were incapable of helping their children with homework, they actively sought out surrogates who could assume this role. They tapped other family members (often an older sibling, or an aunt or uncle), and sometimes a neighbor to help. One father, Juan Valdez, told us that while he was not able to help his daughter Cristina directly with her education, he had secured the assistance of a woman who lives in the apartment complex with them. This neighbor had taught for several years. After Valdez mentioned to her that they had only recently come to the United States and his high school daughter needed help with English, the neighbor volunteered to tutor her. She not only helped Cristina learn English, but also recommended readings to broaden her general education. When it came time for Cristina to take the SAT, she helped her prepare for this important college entrance exam. So, while Valdez believed "we [he and his wife] don't have the knowledge because we never got there," he devised a strategy to obtain the requisite help for his daughter from others.

Although Linda Chairez supported her daughter's goal of going to college, she repeatedly mentioned her inability to help her daughter prepare for college during her interview with us. Chairez had a third-grade education and was very concerned that she might "push [her children] in the wrong direction." Given her own limited education and work experience as a migrant farm worker, she felt inadequate and incompetent. Afraid of giving the wrong advice on educational matters, she became reticent to give any specific educational advice herself. Instead, she relied on Juanita's older brother, a medical technician in the U.S. Navy, for specific information and academic guidance.

Citizenship status on top of depressed economic conditions pose a special problem for students, and their parents devise creative strategies to deal with these circumstances. Having participated in AVID for 3 years at Keeneland High School, Cecilia Santos applied to and was accepted at 4-year universities. Cecilia was told, however, that she would have to pay nonresident tuition, a cost she could not afford. She decided to enroll in a community college, where the nonresident tuition of $200 a semester is less, but still steep for this single-parent family. Ceclia's mother has taken on extra responsibilities in order to help Cecilia transfer to the university. She paid the $200 community college tuition for her daughter from her meager savings and has organized her family so that Cecilia does not have to work while she is in school. Mrs. Santos and her older daughter both work as nurse assistants at the same convalescent hospital. They arrange to have different shifts to insure that a family member is at home to tend the three preschool-age children of Mrs. Santos's older daughters. This arrangement frees Cecilia from child care and work, enabling her to devote more time to study. To assist Cecilia achieve her goals, Mrs. Santos starts her day at 7:30 A.M. when she drives Cecilia to the community college and she attends the ESL class she is taking. She returns home after ESL to take her shift at child care from 11 A.M. until 2 P.M. while her older daughter works at the hospital. Then she works the late shift at the convalescent hospital, returning home at 11 P.M. She makes these sacrifices, and insists that her older daughters do as well, because Cecilia "has a chance." Her older daughters, like Mrs. Santos herself, "made mistakes" by getting married (and divorced) at an early age. Thus, the entire Santos family is working in order to facilitate Cecilia's college education and academic success.

Parents' involvement is also hidden from the schools because it has occurred much earlier in the students' lives. Like Lucero (whom we introduced at the outset of this chapter), many of the parents whose children are in AVID have moved them from neighborhood schools to schools they think have better reputations or better academic programs. Although (as we discussed in the previous chapter) these choices do not always turn out as hoped, this assertive action demonstrates a commitment to their children's education.

Other families moved from Tijuana to San Diego in pursuit of a better education for their children. Mary Barkley, the parent of an AVID student who graduated from Keeneland and now attends SDSU, decided to leave Mississippi because many of her son's friends were being arrested. The family of one of the few Native American students in AVID moved from its home on a reservation in New Mexico to San Diego because the student's mother, Amelia Cabo, thought it was important for her children to be "raised in the city." Native Americans "don't have this kind of experience," Cabo told us. She expects her daughter, Elena, to "get an education and make something of herself." Elena, enrolled in UC Santa Cruz, has taken the first step in fulfilling her mother's aspirations.

AVID families were extremely skillful in seeking mediators to facilitate their children's education. In fact, some families used *us* as resources to obtain information about problems pressing upon their everyday lives. During the course of a research interview, one mother explained that her son had been accepted by SDSU and a private 4-year college. However, he was not going to be able to enroll because their naturalization papers had not been processed under the provisions of the Amnesty Program. The INS had promised that the process would be completed by January 1993, which would have been in time for her son to enroll in college and receive financial aid by September 1993. Yet, when we interviewed her in July 1993, the issue had not been settled. Irene Villanueva, who had been active in the Amnesty Program, was able to intervene on her behalf, putting them in contact with immigration counselors from local Catholic Community Services and the Neighborhood House.

Another parent, Iris Santoyo, wasted no time in discussing her problems with us on the day of an interview. Her son, José, had been accepted at UCLA but had been notified that he was ineligible for financial aid. Before we had a chance to ask her our interview questions, she asked us for advice about what she could do. Because it was the summer between the end of high school and the beginning of college, the family did not have a resource person to consult, and turned to us when we arrived at the house for our interview. Mrs. Santoyo said that the family was unhappy about the decision from the university, but they did not know what to do about it. She told José "don't give up, *mi hijo,* there's gotta be a way." Neither Mrs. Santoyo nor José realized that they had information about Mr. Santoyo's lack of work and current earnings which could change this decision. We spent most of the evening providing specific directives for José so he could be reconsidered for financial aid and attend UCLA rather than the local community college.

Parents' strategies – employing mediators, changing residences, enrolling children in desegregation programs, organizing family members to support an aspiring daughter – while productive, are often invisible to the school. Further complicating the matter, their invisibility fuels stereotypes. Apparently, when schools do not have evidence to the contrary, they treat parents as unconcerned, uncommitted. At the end of this chapter, we will discuss ways to make the contributions of parents more visible to the school.

PARENTS DON'T KNOW AVID

Parents know very little about the program that has taken over so much of their children's lives. The guidelines that AVID distributes from the central office recommend that coordinators secure the permission of parents and their promise to support their children before admitting students into the program. Activities to facilitate involvement include back-to-school nights, parent advisory boards, newsletters, family study skills meetings, college awareness meetings, and potluck dinners. The "AVID Family Study Skills" series and "Destined for College" series have been translated into Spanish and are used with parents at Pimlico and Keeneland. AVID's expressed policy emphasizes parent contact, but most of the parents we interviewed said they received little information from AVID about the program and few participated in sponsored activities. Mrs. Salazar's experience was typical. She signed a paper to enable her daughter, Barbara, to join AVID, but seemed embarrassed that she knew nothing else about it. Mrs. Mendez, who identified herself as a "housekeeper" who moved from Guadalajara, Mexico, 20 years ago, said she was not familiar with AVID and had not gone to AVID events when asked this question directly in our interview with her.

But when her son, Rafael, who had been listening to the exchange reminded her that she knew the teacher, Alex Frankfurter at Golden Gate High School, her face brightened as she recalled that he helped her son with his homework after school and with nonacademic problems on many occasions (*El maestro le ayudaba, después de la escuela, con la tarea, con las clases. Era muy buen maestro. Le ayudaba con cuando tenía algún problema. En todo le ayudaba*).

The AVID parents we interviewed, whether Latino or African American, most often described AVID as a program that helps *all* students prepare for college by providing information about universities and financial aid. They did not mention or do not know about that part of AVID which emphasizes the college preparation of *underrepresented* students. Despite their lack of knowledge about and participation in the program, these parents see AVID in a positive light, as a way to fill in the gaps in their knowledge and to supply the resources they lack. The parents we interviewed were virtually unanimous in detailing the benefits of AVID, recognizing that this program helped their children improve their grades and to learn about financial aid, scholarships, and all important SAT and college application deadlines. Looked at from the point of view of a school that values active parents (Lareau, 1989), these parents have turned over their academic responsibilities to the program. That handoff makes AVID a surrogate parent in situations where families feel they lack the resources to assist their children's education.

On the one hand, this is a successful maneuver. Since AVID is willing to provide support, students are not discredited for having parents who are not involved. The college preparation process is so complex that even the most educated parents have difficulty navigating that maze. This point is made clear by Mrs. Marquez's experiences in getting past the gatekeepers at her daughter's school. A college graduate and an elementary school teacher, Mrs. Marquez is very familiar with the inner workings of the school system. When her daughter, Esperanza, began having trouble with honors biology and chemistry, Mrs. Marquez found that she was unable to help her daughter change classes. The school administrators refused even to listen to her as a parent, but when the AVID coordinator got involved, the situation changed. The AVID coordinator was able to transfer Esperanza out of advanced chemistry, saving this more difficult course for the summer. With this reduced course load, Esperanza was able to finish the school year successfully, and graduated from high school with a 3.8 GPA. The AVID coordinator was able to resolve a situation that even a willing and knowledgeable parent could not.

Mr. Ramirez gave credit to AVID for reinforcing parental positions. He knew "AVID would make his son [Tomás] realize how important it is to stay in school, get good grades, and stay in college." He explained that parents sometimes have trouble getting these messages across to their own children:

> AVID reinforces what you want them to hear. It's not just a father and mother talking, but they hear from a professional, someone who is learned, a really excellent person, someone who has a reputation, somebody they can relate to and someone who tells them what is good for them.

In these instances, program and parents are in a complimentary relationship. Both share high aspirations for the children and a belief in higher education. Parents provide highly motivated children; they trust and believe in schooling. AVID provides the students with a college prep curriculum, study skills, and knowledge about the intricacies of the college application and financial aid process – that is, the cultural capital that the AVID parents do not have the resources to supply. This complimentarity is the positive side of the AVID–parent relationship.

There is a potential downside to this program–parent relationship, however. Program coordinators at the eight school sites we studied and parents reported that there is less contact between program and parents once parents have agreed to enroll their children in AVID. Back-to-school nights and other social functions have low attendance, and ongoing communication and coordination concerning program operation are limited.

Not all AVID parents have adopted a stance of distance. Roma Gutierrez is the most extreme exception to this noninvolvement pattern. Her first experience with her daughter's school came when she attended a PTA meeting, but "couldn't understand a thing" because the meeting was conducted entirely in English. In response, she joined an educational program to help Latino parents learn to become more involved with their children and their schooling. She taught other Bay Meadows parents how to communicate better with their own children and provided them information about drugs, peer relationships, and gangs.

The existing gaps between parents and program suggest that paternalism is a potential danger in this otherwise successful untracking program. As it stands, the program is acting on behalf of parents, performing services for students in the place of parents. Parents are not involved as active participants in their children's education.

TOWARD A REDEFINITION OF PARENT INVOLVEMENT

AVID parents, who have limited formal education, income, and English skills and who are typically thought to devalue education because they do not volunteer in classrooms or attend PTA meetings, are, in fact, involved in their children's education. While their involvement often does not take traditional forms, these parents are encouraging, supportive, and consciously involved in the lives of their children.

Misconceptions about the beliefs and practices of low-income, ethnic and linguistic minority parents have resulted in conclusions that serve to further disadvantage those children who are already underserved by our educational system. Our findings reinforce the idea that the prevailing approach to parent–school relations needs revision and a different approach might assist the education of students from underrepresented groups.

What Parent Education Has Been

When educators and researchers talk about "parent involvement," they often mean two things: (1) parents participating in academic activities and (2) parents participating in school events (Comer,

1980; Epstein, 1986; Delgado-Gaitan, 1991). In the first case, parents are said to take an "active role" in their children's education when they reinforce at home what the schools teach their students at school. Parents assisting their kids with homework is the quintessential example of parental involvement in educational activities at home. In the second case, parents are said to take an active role in education when they participate in the classroom as an aide or when they help with plays, sports, fund raisers, cafeteria duty, library, media center (Comer, 1980; Epstein, 1984; Delgado-Gaitan, 1991). In both versions, parents' involvement has been defined and directed by the school. School officials and teachers tell parents what they want them to do. They typically define the content, the structure and the scheduling of parent-involvement activities on the school's terms (McLaughlin & Shields, 1987: 157).

So-called parent education often has this school-centered focus. For example, Flaxman and Inger (1991: 3–5) present a catalog of ways in which the Department of Education says parents can be involved in their children's education. They encourage parents to take a more active role in choosing schools, sit on school site councils, and participate in "parent effectiveness workshops."

Note that the thrust of these proposals is one-directional. They direct parents to participate in activities defined for them by the school. The DOE proposals do not start with the parents' lives or inquire about parents' interests and concerns. And they do not incorporate parents' knowledge and resources in educational activities.

Particularly questionable are those parent effectiveness training programs that propose to teach low-income and minority parents to interact with their children in the ways middle-income parents presumably do. Training programs such as PET and STEP propose to teach "active listening," "encouragement," "win-win conflict resolution strategies," "communication skills," "self discipline," and "achievement orientation" to low-income and minority parents, presumably because these strategies have been beneficial for middle-income parents (Flaxman & Inger, 1991: 4). This perspective runs the risk of interpreting differences between families and schools as deficits in either families or schools, which in turn may provoke mutual blaming between parents and teachers (Azmitia, et al., 1994: 4).

Another danger in one-directional parent effectiveness training programs is that they do not take the complexities of low-income, ethnic and linguistic minority families seriously. Therefore, they may overlook the resources for student learning that are available in the home and the community. As we have shown in this chapter, low-income parents live incredibly complex lives, often in challenging circumstances. Because of their humble material conditions, they often find it difficult to respond to school requests for involvement. Despite their limited material resources, however, they have a deep reservoir of cultural knowledge. Even though they lack the resources to mimic middle-income strategies, they deploy strategies that are productive for traversing everyday life.

If reading books and being read to are vital educational activities, does it really matter if the mother or a big sister does the reading – especially when parents are not literate? If support with homework is important, does it really matter if the parents or a neighbor provides the assistance – especially when the parents have not gone past third grade? If parents hold down two jobs, is it reasonable to expect them to volunteer in the classroom or attend school site council meetings or chaperone field trips? If parents do not speak the language of the school, is it reasonable to expect them to attend PTA meetings when the schools do not provide personnel who can speak to them?

Just because parents are not visible in school, it does not mean they are not involved in their children's education. So-called parent education programs have to be sensitive to the social conditions and cultural arrangements of low-income and minority parents; otherwise they will fall into the trap of usurping the parental role.

What Parent Education Could Be

Our findings suggest a different form of interaction between parents and educators. Taking a lead from Freire (1973), we call for dialogic interaction between educators and parents. Freire conceives of the learning process as one in which teachers and students participate together, learning from each other. Applied to parent education, a dialogic process prompts teachers to learn from parents while parents learn from teachers, instead of the school dictating courses of action to parents.

Parent education programs should really be renamed "parent–school education programs" or "school and family partnerships" (Epstein, 1992; Azmitia et al., 1994) to emphasize the two-way interaction between parents and teachers. Programs that emphasize two-way interaction have a greater potential to enable parents to take action on behalf of their children and are less susceptible to cultural deprivation thinking and acting. Parent–school education programs that are sensitive to social and economic realities and cultural nuances can facilitate the achievement of families' goals by working in a complimentary, not a compensatory, relationship.

An interactional school–parent education program would start with a dialogue centered on parents' concerns and interests. When we ask parents what they want from the school, they speak personally, in terms of their own children, not abstractly in terms of children generally (cf. Epstein, 1992; Lewis & Nakagawa, 1994). They have a general concern for educational equity, to be sure, but the equity they seek is specific; they want their children to have access to a quality education. They have a concern for power to be sure, but the control they seek is over the information they need to insure that their children will do well in school with this teacher, with this subject matter, this year. Parents seem to want more interaction and communication with particular teachers and principals and are less interested in exerting more power and authority over the general school bureaucracy (Lewis & Nakagawa, 1994).

One could argue that if parents are only concerned about their own children's interests, then they will not build a community perspective on their collective needs and interests. Without this collective sense, they will not be empowered in the political process. That may be, but parents express a concern with improving the education of their children, and with these political and educational expressions, the dialogue must begin. To achieve a collective, shared sense of purpose would mean starting with and then building on parents' local concerns in the way Delgado-Gaitan (1991), Fine

(1993), Epstein (1992), and Azmitia et al., (1994) have done so effectively. This political dimension of parent–school education might include discussions about the ways schools work (e.g., the hidden curriculum and implicit culture we have discussed in this book), their rights and responsibilities as parents (e.g., their right to request schools and teachers, their right to special services, special education, gifted and talented programs), how to increase communication with teachers and principals, how to take action on behalf of their children, the way high school preparation fits with future career goals (e.g., college, employment, citizenship).

Our conception of parent–school education does not stop when parents learn about ways to assist their children, the organization of schooling, or political strategies, however. The dialogue would continue, focusing educators' attention on the organization of their parents' family life. School personnel need to understand people's work and living arrangements so that the requests they make of families will not be an imposition and can be carried out in a reasonable manner.

McDermott et al., (1984: 397) realized the importance of this idea a decade ago as a result of their study of the social organization of homework. They revealed two different patterns of parent–child interaction surrounding homework within two similar working-class families. One family, which met the formal requirements of homework recommended by most parent education plans, set up a special time and place for homework. By focusing more on procedural and timing matters than the homework task, however, this family succeeded only in reproducing its child's incompetence. The other family, which blended homework assignments into the flow of family life, accomplished homework tasks smoothly. Before legislating the structure and form of a seemingly benign parent involvement activity such as homework, McDermott et al. (1984) instruct us to learn what such activities mean to the participants, how they are organized at home and school, and what they do to the persons relating to each other around them.

When sensitive dialogue between home and school occurs, educators will learn about the "funds of knowledge" (Gonzalez et al., 1993) that exist in the community so that the richness of people's lives can be incorporated into educational activities. Moll, Gonzalez, and their colleagues (Gonzalez et al., 1993; Moll, Vélez-Ibáñez, & Greenberg, 1988, 1989; Moll & Díaz 1987; Díaz et al., 1986) have used Latino students' lives as educational resources by tapping into the domains in which students and their families are experts. Employing a collaborative approach to research, the teachers and researchers with the Gonzalez-Moll group first work together to learn about the demographic and economic patterns, the social networks and the social knowledge that exist in households and neighborhoods, within the local community. Then teachers mobilize the information they acquire for instructional purposes.

Moll et al. (1989) relate a provocative example in which a sixth-grade teacher incorporated information about construction gleaned from the local *barrio* to enliven literacy instruction. After students were sent to the library in the usual fashion to gather and read books on constructing houses and other buildings, the teacher invited members of the local community (some of whom were the parents of the students) to share their knowledge about building. A mason told the students about how to mix mortar, measure straight lines, and stack bricks neatly and strongly. A carpenter told about the relative strength of brick and wood, and sawing and nailing techniques. Students applied this knowledge to a model they built in their classroom. Analysis of the students' writing during and after the model building showed that the students' incidentally acquired new vocabulary (joists, ridge hangers, waffle boards, etc.), wrote eloquently about the skill involved in the building trades, and, perhaps most important, developed an appreciation for their parents' "funds of knowledge." The students were surprised and pleased that the school would validate their parents' skills and experience, even though they did not have formal education.

These projects suggest that teachers adopt the perspective of researchers in order to learn about the culture of their students and community. Two teachers in San Diego County, Natalie Weston and Betsy Eck, followed this recommendation in designing curriculum projects in language arts and math respectively. They developed a variety of activities through which their students became researchers of their own culture. In both of these projects, students and teachers set out to learn about the families, their cultural practices, oral histories, and how this information could be utilized in the curriculum. Through this dialogic process, families were comfortable about their participation and the information they could provide to their children about themselves. They believed they had something to contribute and they were acknowledged as experts.

Weston (1992) created and implemented a language arts curriculum for bilingual Spanish and English students and their families. Families participated in several activities, including tape-recording interviews conducted by the students, and responding in writing to students' questions on particular themes. The products of these activities became resources and class books for the Home-School Library. Thus, students, families, and the teacher participated in learning about the families' sociocultural experiences, values, interests, and skills. Their texts were related to and read by peers and other families as they circulated through the Home-School Library.

Eck (1993) followed a similar strategy of including family interaction in her work with students and families in developing a math curriculum. The similarity in the two projects is seen in the approach of obtaining information from the home for incorporation in the classroom rather than in presenting curriculum that may be unrelated and irrelevant to the lives of the students. In Eck's math curriculum, students became investigators and experts, focusing on learning about math as a practical tool in the world around them by locating the various ways in which their families utilized math in their daily lives. The students became aware of the value of money, time, schedules, and measurement through recording the real-life experiences of their families. Through photographs, writing, and audiotape recordings, the cultural aspects of both curriculum projects became apparent as students related the diverse stories of their families in rural and urban settings, and their educational and sociohistorical experiences in the United States and other countries.

These studies have wider implications. It helps redefine the African American and Latino family for educators, researchers, and the public. Educational activities that bring the home culture into the school demonstrate that the households and neighborhoods of even the poorest families are full of knowledge and are well organized. Economically poor conditions do not create culturally poor conditions. Rural and urban poor families are connected to extensive social networks that provide different forms of economic assistance and labor cooperation, which help families avoid the cost of plumbers, car mechanics, even physicians. These social networks also provide emotional and service support in the form of child care, job information, and social networks.

While educators are correct when they say they are strapped for material resources in the classroom, they can learn from Gonzalez, Eck, Moll, and Weston that even the poorest neighborhood is rich in cultural resources that can connect the classroom to the world. And they can make this connection without denigrating local cultural practices or demanding that low-income and minority parents replace their indigenous parenting practices with mainstream ones.

9
IMPLICATIONS FOR EDUCATIONAL PRACTICE

STUDENTS FROM LINGUISTIC AND ETHNIC MINORITY backgrounds are expected to compose an increasing percentage of the U.S. population just when jobs that require higher education are expected to increase in number. Students from linguistic and ethnic minority backgrounds, however, are neither performing in high school well enough nor enrolling in college in sufficient numbers to qualify for the increasing number of jobs that will require baccalaureate degrees.

Historically, educators in the United States have responded to differences among individuals and groups by altering the content of the curriculum to which they are exposed while delivering it in essentially the same way to all. Under this "compensatory education" strategy, low-achieving students (most of whom are from low-income, ethnic and linguistic minority backgrounds) are placed in special programs or "tracks" where the curriculum is reduced in scope, content, and pace. The hope is that underachieving students will develop basic skills, then be promoted to "regular education" or even college-bound programs.

Despite their commendable goals of attempting to compensate for deficiencies in education through remedial instruction, tracking systems that segregate underachieving students in special programs have been criticized for contributing to the very problems they were to solve. On the one hand, those students who are comfortable in the intersection between the academic curriculum and the unvarying mode by which public schools are organized have gotten a good education. On the other hand, students placed in remedial tracks seldom catch up to their peers, seldom receive equivalent curriculum or instruction, but they often have suffered the stigmatizing consequences of negative labeling. As Graham (1989) puts it, "education is a vintage wine, one that is damaged by adulterations."

We have examined the educational and social consequences of "untracking," an alternative to tracking underachieving high school students, especially those from ethnic and linguistic minority backgrounds. Untracking is the educational practice of placing low-achieving and high-achieving students in the same rigorous academic program. In the San Diego area, this approach operates under the auspices of the "Advancement Via Individual Determination" (AVID) program.

Our objective has been to see whether untracking helps students. More specifically, we want to know whether previously low-achieving students from low-income ethnic and linguistic minority backgrounds who are placed in college-bound courses with high-achieving students benefit academically and socially by the experience.

THE ACADEMIC CONSEQUENCES OF UNTRACKING

From 1990 to 1992, 1,053 students who had participated in the AVID untracking experiment for 3 years graduated from 14 high schools in the San Diego City Schools (SDCS) system. In those same years an additional 288 students started the program but left after completing 1 year or less. We interviewed 248 of the 3-year AVID students and 146 of the 1-year AVID students.

Of the 248 students who "graduated" from AVID, 120 (48%) reported attending 4-year colleges, 99 (40%) reported attending 2-year or junior colleges, and the remaining 29 students (12%) said they are working or doing other things. The 48% 4-year college enrollment rate for students who have been "untracked" compares favorably with the San Diego City Schools' average of 37% and the national average of 39%. It also compares favorably with the college enrollment rate of students who started, but did not complete the untracking program; 34% of them enrolled in 4-year colleges within a year of graduating from high school.

Furthermore, the untracking experiment assists the academic achievement of students who are from low-income families and the two major ethnic groups that are underrepresented in college. African Americans and Latinos from AVID enroll in college in numbers that exceed local and national averages. Of the Latino students who have participated in AVID for 3 years, 43% enroll in 4-year colleges. This figure compares favorably to the San Diego City Schools average of 25% and the national average of 29%. African American students who participate in AVID for 3 years also enroll in college at rates higher than the local and national averages; 55% of black students from AVID enroll in 4-year colleges, compared with 35% from the SDCS and the national average of 33%.

AVID students who come from the lowest income strata (parents' median income below $19,999) enroll in 4-year colleges in equal or higher proportion to students who come from higher income strata (parents' median income between $20,000 and $65,000). AVID students who come from families in which their parents have less than a college education enroll in 4-year colleges more than students who come from families who have a college education.

The longer students stay in the untracking program, the better their college enrollment record. This relationship holds regardless of the students' family income level, a finding that gives us a further indication that the program, and not the students' socioeconomic background or previous academic record, is influential. Students who completed 3 years of AVID enrolled in college in greater proportion than students who completed 1 year or less of AVID regardless of their family's income level: 57% of 3-year AVID students from families who earned less than $20,000 enrolled in college, compared with 31% of 1-year AVID students whose families were in this income bracket; 46% of 3-year AVID students from families in the $20,000–$39,000 income range enrolled in college versus 35% of 1-year AVID students whose families were in this range; 49% of 3-year AVID students whose families were in the $40,000–$59,000 range and 37% of the 1-year AVID students whose families were in this income range enrolled in college.

THE SOCIAL CONSEQUENCES OF UNTRACKING

In addition to these educational consequences, there are social consequences of this untracking effort as well. The African American and Latino students in AVID developed a reflective system of beliefs, a critical consciousness, about the limits and possibilities of the actions they take and the limitations and constraints they face in life.

While acknowledging the importance of academic achievement for success later in life, AVID students did not subscribe to a romantic version of the achievement ideology. Having experienced the pain of prejudice and discrimination, Latinos and African Americans in AVID realized that their individual effort and hard work will not inevitably lead to success. Furthermore, the African American and Latino students in AVID recognized that they must develop linguistic styles, social behavior, and academic skills that are acceptable to the mainstream. And they did develop these skills, but without sacrificing their cultural identity, which they nurtured at home and displayed in the neighborhood.

AVID students come from friendship groups that are not always academically oriented. In order to manage the tension created by their participation in academics during school with their participation in life with friends after school, AVID students adopted a number of strategies. Some hid their academic activities entirely, both at school and with their local friends; but most worked to manage two identities. They engaged in academic pursuits with their AVID friends at school, and engaged in recreational pursuits with their neighborhood friends after school and on weekends. These "border crossing strategies" seem to be effective for the Latino and African American students in AVID, just as they have been effective for recent immigrants to the United States.

In recent ethnographies of schooling (e.g., Apple & Weis, 1983; Foley, 1991; MacLeod, 1987; Weis, 1985, 1990; Fine, 1991; Willis, 1977), students who have been discarded by the system or drop out from it have been characterized as having a sophisticated critique of the power relations in society, while the students who have been successful have been characterized as naively accepting the tenets of achievement ideology. We found an ideology among Latino and African American students from low-income families that was more critical than conformist, more accommodationist than assimilationist. This means that a critical consciousness is not reserved for those pushed out of the educational and social system. We have uncovered at least one set of circumstances in which a critical consciousness develops among students who are academically successful.

The critical consciousness and accommodationist strategies deployed by AVID students enable us to reflect on the presumed relationship between immigrant status and adaptive strategies. The academically successful students in AVID come from "involuntary minority" backgrounds, groups that have been condemned for deploying oppositional and resistant strategies that produce school failure (Ogbu, 1978, 1987a, 1987b 1991; Chavez, 1991; Anderson, 1991). The border-crossing strategies deployed by Latino and African American students suggest accommodationist strategies are not reserved for members of voluntary immigrant groups. Given the appropriate social and institutional supports, students from many different ethnic groups can be coached to adopt social behavior that is productive in school without sacrificing national or ethnic identity at home.

This study, even though preliminary, then, points to the power of academically oriented programs for the educational improvement and social development of previously underachieving students. The college enrollment record and critical consciousness of students who have participated in AVID's untracking program gives us reason to believe that rigorous academic programs serve the educational and social needs of low-achieving students better than remedial, compensatory education programs.

THE FACTORS CONTRIBUTING TO THE SUCCESS OF UNTRACKING

We reviewed the academic curriculum, the classroom and school practices, and the relations among AVID students and their peers as well as program–parent relations in order to determine the reasons for the success of the San Diego untracking experiment. AVID's academic placement practices are vital to its success. Students placed in college prep classes are given access to the academic track that leads to college. Unless those academic placements are made, the rest of the program is irrelevant. The program emphasizes the writing process, the inquiry method, collaborative learning groups, and intensive staff development. The most striking writing activity in the AVID elective classes involved seniors in their preparation for college entry. Seniors were coached on how to complete college application forms, and financial aid forms, write college essays and personal statements. To be sure, students in AVID classrooms worked in small, collaborative groups, but tutors assigned to the AVID classrooms were much more likely to assist with homework than engage students in inquiry. AVID students did not complain about the way in which their tutors were used, however. In fact, they liked the opportunity that the elective class period gave them for organized homework time, and appreciated the help tutors gave them with homework and the time it gave them to interact with like-minded classmates.

While it is necessary to place students in college prep classes to make them eligible for college, academic placement in and of itself is not sufficient. Social scaffolds must be in place in order to insure that students who have not had experience with academically oriented classes succeed in them. AVID isolates its students in special classrooms and marks their academic identity. Among the most visible supports within the special classrooms are instruction in note-taking, test-taking, and study strategies. By dispensing these academic techniques, AVID gives its students explicit instruction in the implicit or hidden curriculum of the school. In Bourdieu's (1986) terms, AVID gives low-income students some of the *cultural* capital at school that is similar to the cultural capital that more economically advantaged parents give to their children at home.

Institutional support of students augments this explicit socialization process. The academic life of AVID students in high school is supported by dedicated teachers who mediate between them and their high schools and build bridges between high school and the college system. AVID coordinators help remove impediments to students' academic achievement by intervening on their behalf with other teachers, administrators, and college admissions officers. In Bourdieu's (1986) terms, AVID connects its students to social networks – that is, provides its students with the *social* capital at school that is similar to the social capital that more economically advantaged parents are able to provide to their students through their family connections. One way that working-class and minority youth can enjoy the same advantages as their more privileged peers, then, is for schools and their agents to act collectively in a deliberate, intensive, and explicit fashion to generate a socialization process that produces the same sorts of strategies and resources deployed in privileged homes and institutions.

Peer group relations also support untracking. AVID selects promising students and places them together in special classes that meet daily throughout the school year. AVID marks their group identity publicly. Their notebooks clearly display the AVID logo, as does the AVID classroom that is used for lunch and social gatherings as well as academic instruction. Within the social space demarcated for them, AVID students form new academically oriented friendships and develop academic identities. The time that students spend together on field trips to colleges, in collaborative study groups, and informal discussions with college tutors and guest speakers from local colleges and businesses facilitates this process.

The parents and the program are in a complimentary relationship. The parents of AVID students have high expectations and aspirations for their children, but reported to us that they lack the knowledge to propel their children toward their goals. The program gives AVID students access to the resources that parents feel they lack. Paternalism is a potential danger in this arrangement, however. As it stands, the program is acting on behalf of parents and performing services for students without much consultation. To achieve a more balanced relationship, the program needs to engage parents about their concerns and interests in their children's education.

In sum, the social scaffolds, institutional supports, and academically oriented peers and parents constitute the possibility of the academic success of AVID students. Although the academic and curricular dimensions of the untracking effort are vital, they can not exist without institutional supports. In fact, removing any of the components supporting academic placement – exposing the hidden curriculum, bridging, advocacy – can derail the career of the untracked student.

AVID's practice reverses prevailing practice. Schools have long been faced with students with different experiences. Heretofore, the tendency has been to separate them into different groups and provide them with different curricula. Instead of that curriculum differentiation, AVID is providing students who have different academic backgrounds with similar academic experiences while providing different amounts of social supports.

IMPLICATIONS FOR EDUCATIONAL REFORM

Although the field work supporting this study is limited, our ethnographic data do yield some suggestions for educational improvement. We make our modest suggestions against the backdrop of this conviction: Educational reform cannot be viewed as a substitute for more fundamental political, economic, and social change in the attempt to solve the problem of the transmission of inequality from generation to generation.

In this decade of educational reform, we have been advised that better schools will improve the equality of opportunity in the United States. If only poor and minority children could be given equal access to a higher-quality education, either through a revised curriculum (that stresses heterogeneous grouping, cooperative learning, higher-order thinking), through improved parent involvement, or through improved neighborhood schools, magnet schools, restructured schools, or (more recently) voucher-plan or charter schools, then the opportunity for individual mobility would be equalized and the gap between rich and poor would be substantially reduced.

There is a major problem with this approach: Educational reform, in and of itself, is incapable of effecting change in the structure of inequality in the United States. The real problem is in the organization of work and the culture of our society, not in the organization of schools. Those issues are not touched by the variety of school reform efforts that have been proposed since the publication of *A Nation At Risk* in 1983.

Traditionally, the metaphor for the American occupational system has been a ladder; workers are represented as starting at the bottom of this ladder in unskilled or semiskilled work, gaining skills, and moving up the ladder, handhold by handhold. This metaphor has always hidden a contradiction in the organization of work in capitalist society: The occupational structure is more like a pyramid than a ladder, which means there is never enough room at the top. Exacerbating this condition are trends in postindustrial capitalism. The movement of jobs offshore, the deskilling of work, the shift to a small core of permanent workers surrounded by rings and rings of part-time employees make the ladder metaphor even more problematic. The ladder of social mobility is less accessible to all, there are gaping holes between the rungs, and the bottom rungs are not as easy to grasp as they once were.

Deep-seated cultural beliefs support tracking practices. Tracking is a structural manifestation of a meaning system deeply rooted in the culture of schooling and the wider society. Therefore, tinkering with a few sorting techniques will not promote equality of opportunity. We must also address cultural beliefs about such matters as human capacities, individual and group differences, fairness, individualism, competition, and the goals of public education today.

Although wrapped in a cloak of scientific competence, Herrnstein and Murray (1994) recently captured some of the popular conceptions of intelligence, human capacity, and group differences that pervade American society. Intelligence is fixed and inherited, Herrnstein and Murray tell us. Therefore, it can be accurately measured by IQ tests. Members of the working class or those on welfare ("the cognitive underclass") have less intelligence to pass on to their sons and daughters. Therefore, their place at the bottom of the status hierarchy is relatively permanent. Although their position there is regrettable, it is understandable.

Recent research in cognitive development suggests a radically different conception of human capacity. All normally functioning humans have the capacity to reason sufficiently well to finish schooling and enter the work force (Cicourel & Mehan, 1983; Bruner, 1986; Laboratory of Comparative Human Cognition, 1983). Furthermore, standardized tests only measure a limited range of human abilities and reward only a narrow knowledge base. They do not measure students' higher-order thinking skills, how well they solve new and complex problems, how well they transfer knowledge gained in one situation to another situation, how well they communicate ideas. Furthermore, business and educational leaders tell us these skills are needed in our highly technical and information-based economy.

The American system of public education was designed to promote the common good and to prepare children to participate in a democratic society. Increasingly, however, this democratic function has been overpowered by the credentialing function of schooling (Collins, 1979). The cultural belief that the purpose of schooling is to enable people to accrue wealth, power, and status redefines schooling. A good education becomes a scarce commodity, available only to the few people who win the contest for upward mobility.

Because these cultural beliefs are so deep-seated but often unarticulated, we should not be surprised to learn that efforts to untrack schools have met with an uneven response. On the one hand, efforts to dismantle the tracking system are celebrated by civil rights and desegregation advocates such as the NAACP Legal Defense Fund, the American Civil Liberties Union, the Children's Legal Defense Fund, and the Mexican American Legal Defense Fund. Cooperative learning is especially appreciated by the parents and educators of low-income, ethnic and linguistic minority students because their academic achievement is enhanced.

On the other hand, other interest groups are more wary of these reform efforts. You will recall that vocational education teachers told us they fear they will lose their clientele. Teachers of mainstream students told us they resented the "special privileges" bestowed on untracked students. The parents of high-achieving students worry that their children will suffer in heterogeneously grouped classrooms because minority-student enrollments will lead to lower educational standards. These parents truly believe that their children will receive a better education in a homogeneous classroom. Their beliefs in these matters are certainly bolstered by the research evidence we have reviewed that shows students in high tracks receive a better education than students in low tracks.

Parents of students in high-track classes are clearly advantaged by the present arrangement. They have the better teachers, the better educational opportunities, and the higher status. Because the current educational system offers only a small number of students access to high-track classes, it is understandable why parents work so hard to place their children in these demonstrably superior environments and resist the entry of other students into them.

Well-to-do parents who want their children enrolled in the best classes exert a tremendous political pressure on schools. In most communities, it is the well-to-do white parents who better understand the differentials in a school's offerings and know how to pressure a school into responding positively to their children (Lareau, 1989). Under the current system, white and wealthy parents often lobby to enroll their children in more ethnically and socioeconomically homogeneous gifted and talented programs or honors classes within desegregated schools.

School administrators fear that dismantling tracking will drive the parents of high-achieving students, who tend to come from white middle-income backgrounds, away from their schools. This fear has been fueled by advocates of high-achieving students, especially those in programs for the gifted and talented. They perceive the critiques of tracking that we reviewed here as a threat to the high-quality education their constituents enjoy under the current system.

Public schools are caught in the middle of competing agendas. On the one hand, educators are entreated to educate all students to the best of their abilities. On the other hand, educators are entreated to provide an equitable education for all students. In order to meet the demands of the excellence and the equity agendas simultaneously, as we saw at Nassau High School, school administrators in desegregated schools often make uneasy accommodations. They detrack the majority of their classes to encourage minority students and their parents while simultaneously they allow some tracking (e.g., separate college prep and advanced placement programs) in order to keep more advantaged parents involved in their schools.

The pressure from more affluent and better educated parents to keep schools tracked and to have their children placed in the highest-level courses certainly reflects a competitive and individualistic attitude toward the function of schooling. But in ethnically and racially mixed schools, this view can take on another meaning. Because the race and social class of students correlates with track placement, untracking means ethnic and racial intergation in classes where no mixing existed before. A parent's request for a high-quality class, then, can mask a request for a segregated educational program.

These deep-seated cultural beliefs must be addressed head on if untracking is going to be widely accepted in our society. Parents and advocates of academically successful students must be convinced that spending class time among those who are socioeconomically and academically less well off does not, in and of itself, reduce competitive advantage. If it is going to be successful, all parents must come to believe that untracking neither reduces the probability that their children can attain the career of their choice nor hinders their intellectual development. Achieving educational equity, then, will require fundamental changes in the organization of work and the culture of the society, as well as technical modifications of the sorting practices of the school.

Based on this study, we can not propose a comprehensive alternative educational philosophy for our postindustrial society. But sifting through our ethnographic notes, we do find some material that might inform educational policy until there is a major overhaul in the social, political, and economic system. Our suggestions deal with the importance of providing social scaffolds to students when elevating their educational curriculum, the possibility of appropriating students' knowledge and expertise for classroom instruction, and the dangers of trying to duplicate or copy the features of this untracking effort.

The Importance of Aspirations and Academic Rigor, the Necessity of Social Supports

Students' aspirations and teachers' expectations are often touted as the reasons previously low-achieving students start performing well in school. Our findings suggest, however, that neither elevated academic placements nor high aspirations and expectations can do the job in the absence of institutionalized systems of support. Juxtaposing our findings with those of MacLeod (1987) and Weis (1990) is instructive for understanding the relationship between students' aspirations, teachers' expectations, demanding curricula, and institutionalized systems of social support for increasing the possibility of improving the educational opportunities of low-achieving students.

MacLeod (1987) depicted a compelling group of high school students, the Brothers, who did not succumb to the ideology and practice of resisting school culture and societal norms of achievement. Citing the ameliorating effects of the Civil Rights era, they expressed a belief in the power of their own agency to succeed in school and in the world of work. Unfortunately, their lofty aspirations did not translate into lofty results. Despite their beliefs, the Brothers did poorly in school and got the same kind of low-paying jobs as their nonacademically oriented contemporaries.

Weis (1990) tells a similar story about the sons and daughters of the white working class in the city of "Freeway." In response to a question Weis asked about what students wanted to do after they complete high school, "Bob" (an advanced student at "Freeway High") told her:

> Well, I want to go to college. I don't know what for yet. I was thinking of something like biology, something like that. Probably [City Community College] or [Suburban Community College]. Probably transfer [to a four-year school].
>
> My mother wants me to [go to college]. So does my father. My mother has post-education [at a local hospital]. She was a worker there. But my father quit school in the middle of the twelfth grade. (Weis, 1990: 22)

Weis says this statement (which is typical of the students from the northeastern city she studied) shows that kids from the working class have different attitudes and aspirations than a decade before. Unlike the lads in Willis's (1977) study of working-class youth in the 1970s, working-class high school students in the 1980s do not celebrate working-class jobs. They no longer want to follow their fathers to the shop floor; they want up and out. In fact, 40% of the high school boys Weis interviewed said they wanted to go to college.

Although Weis found that the students in this working-class high school expressed some affirmation of school culture and knowledge, they did not necessarily act on this affirmation in any meaningful fashion. On the one hand, they tend to attend school and not drop out, and most express a desire to continue their education. On the other hand, only 33% of juniors took the PSAT and 27% of seniors took the SAT. This lack of action is striking in light of expressed desires, because the SAT is mandatory for entrance into college.

Weis interprets this disparity between words and deeds in terms of the shift in the macrostructures of capitalism. During the high period of U.S. industrialization, labor accepted the logic of profitability and markets as the guiding principle of resource allocation in return for an assurance that minimal living standards, trade union rights and liberal democracy rights would be protected. As a result of deindustrialization, this labor–management accord has eroded. Previous studies of the white working class (e.g., Willis, 1977) showed that students' behavior within the school reflected their accurate perception that they were being routed toward a life on the shop floor. The antiacademic posture adopted by Willis's lads shows they recognized that upward mobility was not possible for them. Their perceptions and actions, words and deeds, were consistent. Now, Weis says, as a result of deindustrialization, there are fewer working-class jobs for workers to be slotted into. The white working-class students at Freeway High perceive this fact about job possibilities, Weis says, but they do not act completely upon it. They participate in the form of schooling – going to classes, turning in assignments – but they do not participate in the process of learning. They try to get through assignments with the least effort and not to master the material.

The inconsistency between words and deeds that is developing among the white working class moves it closer to the pattern that has been apparent in the black underclass for some time (Weis, 1990: 37). Weis (1985) had previously reported that black students in community college actively affirmed the value of school-based knowledge but criticized teachers for being too impersonal and for not working hard enough to help them. Furthermore, their actions were not consistent with their affirmation of schooling. They exerted little effort, often came to class late, used drugs on campus, or withdrew entirely from school.

Without denying the importance of students' perceptions of the operation of distal macrostructures, we offer an account of this paradoxical, simultaneous affirmation and rejection of schooling, one that emphasizes local practice. The gap between students' expressed desires for further education and their limited actions to attain this goal reflects the absence of social supports within the limits of cultural knowledge. Students are not completely knowledgeable about the intricacies of the college application process. Unless they come from middle-income (i.e., college-attending) families, they may not know about the importance of the SAT and the value of practicing on the PSAT. Students in the high schools we studied who were not in AVID expressed frustration at not knowing about the intricacies of the college application process, and awe at the information that AVID provided. Therefore, we think that the gap between words and deeds, high aspirations and lowly actions, can be accounted for in terms of the differential distribution of cultural capital – more specifically, the absence of social supports for students who are interested in attending college, but who are not plugged into the complex institutional processes that are involved.

The work of MacLeod and Weis shows that it is vitally important that students have goals and aspirations for life after high school, but our work shows that unless students are instructed in the mechanisms, the processes by which to get to college or good jobs, they do not make it. Students' lofty aspirations, like teachers' high expectations, are essential ingredients for school success, but unless those cognitive processes are accompanied by social support systems, even the highest goals may go unrealized.

Heterogeneous grouping and cooperative learning are being touted as the newest panacea for students' achievement problems. For example, a recent report from the U.S. Department of Education (Knapp & Turnbull, 1990) recommends that teachers of "disadvantaged students" emphasize higher-order tasks, meaning and understanding in academic tasks, a combination of teacher-directed and learner-directed instruction, and more flexibility in grouping arrangements. Similar exhortations appear in Sizer's (1984, 1992) plans to redesign America's high schools and Levin's (1987) appeals for accelerated schools.

Although these are commendable recommendations, and stand in stark contrast to the conventional wisdom we have referred to throughout this book, the advocates of cooperative learning often devote scant attention to the "transportation problem" – how to get students from here (compensatory and remedial instruction) to there (rigorous academic instruction). In order to insure that previously low-achieving students achieve in demanding courses, we must pay an equal amount of attention to the hidden curriculum of the school and provide the social support systems that will assist students adapt to these new, rigorous academic arrangements.

If students do not succeed in these new arrangements, then skeptics will have a new round of ammunition to fire at the ability of low-income and underrepresented students to succeed in academic programs. To blunt that criticism, it appears necessary to treat the academic success of low-achieving students as a schoolwide issue, because researchers who have studied educational reform (Sarason, 1982; Cuban, 1986; Oakes & Wells, in preparation) have shown that educational innovations have the greatest chance of success when significant portions of the school culture are mobilized.

To Assist More Students, Build Stronger Scaffolds

When we have presented preliminary versions of our findings, a criticism that has been frequently raised concerns the kinds of students served by this untracking effort. Critics have suggested that this untracking scheme is a feeble effort or, worse, a cynical one, selecting and preparing students with excellent academic records, students who would succeed without this program.

As we showed in Chapter 4, the high school academic record and the college enrollment record of AVID students does vary according to their past academic record. The higher the students' entering GPA and test scores, the higher their college enrollment rate.

This relationship can be used as evidence to support the claim that the AVID untracking program is simply creaming the top students. According to this logic, the African American and Latino students that AVID selects would do well in school even without this untracking program. This line of questioning has long plagued affirmative action programs, which have been criticized in recent years for assisting members of the middle and professional classes but not bolstering the opportunities of the truly disadvantaged (Wilson, 1987).

While acknowledging the relationship between academic background and subsequent academic performance, we propose an alternative interpretation of the social and educational work AVID is doing with the students it selects, one that addresses the role played by social support systems. At the present time, AVID selects students with high potential and midrange grades and then enrolls students for 2 or 3 high school years. Students are placed in college prep classes starting in 9th or 10th grade. The existing system of social supports surrounding AVID students is 180 hours of an elective class in which tutoring is supposed to take place at a 1:7 tutor–student ratio. These academic practices are supported by social scaffolds, notably exposing the hidden curriculum, teacher advocacy, and institutional sponsorship.

This academic arrangement with its accompanying social support system is apparently adequate to elevate students with average to high GPAs and CTBS scores to college eligibility. This arrangement is apparently *not* adequate to elevate students with average to low GPAs and test scores to this status. In order to enhance the opportunities of students with average-to-low academic records, the academic and social program would have to be deepened and broadened.

The academic program would need to be deepened so that students would spend more time in academic subjects. Instead of the current practice of spending 3 to 5 hours per week on laboratory sciences, 3 to 5 hours in trig, or geometry or algebra, perhaps two or three times that amount of time would need to be spent with students who enter the program with weak academic records. This could be accomplished by extending the school day, the school year, or a combination of both. This recommendation is in line with Sizer's (1992) idea to lengthen the school calendar from 36 to 42 weeks, and the school day by an hour or two.

Imagine an arrangement in which AVID students participate in regular lab or math courses along with their peers during the school day and then participate in their AVID elective class, as is the procedure now. Imagine a second or third session of academic courses that met after school, the purpose of which would be to deepen the students' knowledge of the work they had in their regular courses. In addition, imagine extending the school year so that students who did not grasp the material within the current system of 180 class meetings, had an extra 30 or 40 class meetings to gain mastery.

The social support system accompanying this academic activity would have to be broadened so that students would receive more preparation in test taking, study skills, essay writing, and the like. Students who enter the program with low grades and low test scores would need more than 180 hours per year of mentoring and tutoring. Perhaps twice that amount would be required. Basically, we are proposing a sliding scale of academic enrichment and social support. Students who begin AVID with a high academic record will need less support within AVID than students who have a weak academic record at the start of the program (see Figure 13).

We cannot underestimate the beneficial effects of increasing the quantity of instructional time for students with weak academic records. Even before we consider modifying or improving the quality of classroom practices, we need to increase the amount of time previously low-achieving students spend on math, science, literature, and history. In effect, this is the approach that the highly celebrated Garfield High School teacher, Jaime Escalante, took with his previously low-achieving Latino calculus students. Although he was rightfully applauded for his charismatic motivational efforts,

less social support   more social support

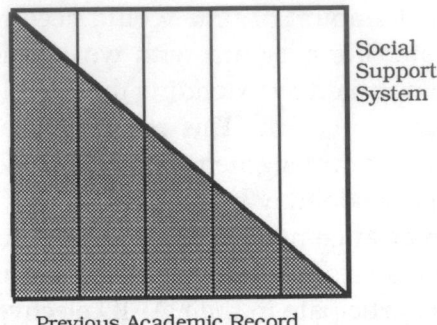

Social
Support
System

Previous Academic Record

high academic record   low academic record

Figure 13. Dynamic Support of Academic Development

Escalante really increased exponentially the number of hours, days, and weeks that his students spent in the classroom. Instead of spending 180 hours in business or consumer math in one academic year, his students spent three times that amount each year in algebra, trig, or calculus courses (Escalante & Dirmann, 1990).

Of course, there must be a qualitative dimension as well as a quantitative dimension to transform an untracking experiment to a full-scale detracking activity. It would do little good to increase the amount of instructional time if that instructional time is not well spent. Fortunately, there are a number of promising proposals before us for improving the quality of classroom instructional practices.

Cooperative learning, the classroom practice of grouping students heterogeneously for the purpose of accomplishing tasks collaboratively, is one such promising proposal. This practice seems to help low-achieving students improve their classroom performance while helping high-achieving students maintain their classroom performance. Furthermore, cooperative learning seems to work as well for students from linguistic and ethnic minority backgrounds as it does for "majority" students (Kagan, 1986; Slavin et al., 1989).

The proposals to build instruction on inquiry, solving authentic problems in natural science, math, and social science, reading genuine texts, and writing for meaningful purpose that are contained in the current round of the California frameworks for instruction are other provocative possibilities. And, as we will describe in the following section, employing students' expertise as a resource also holds promise for making school a meaningful experience once again for disaffected youth.

Expanding and deepening an untracking program like AVID would accomplish two goals. One, AVID would serve better the students it already accepts. Those students AVID accepts now with low GPAs and test scores would be given a bigger boost toward academic success. Two, AVID would change from its present status as a program that assists a small number of select students to move to the top track (while leaving the tracking system intact) to a program that provides assistance to the broader base of the school population while dismantling the tracking system itself.

Appropriating Students' Knowledge and Expertise for Classroom Instruction

MacLeod (1987: 152) insists that achievement ideology "must go" because the claim that America is an open society, a land of opportunity in which any child can grow up to be president, is a myth. His ethnography, like those of Weis, Ogbu, Foley, Willis, and others, shows students at the bottom of the class structure so trapped in their subordinate positions that they do not even aspire to move upward. MacLeod says the refrain "behave yourself, study hard, earn good grades, graduate with your class, go to college, get a good job, and make a lot of money" doesn't map on to the experiences of working-class youth. As a result, it reinforces the feelings of personal failure and inadequacy of working-class students. Their personal experience contradicts achievement ideology. Because it shrouds class, race, and gender barriers to success, students often reject it. The equality-of-opportunity line of reasoning may work in middle-class schools, but its utility in urban schools serving low-income neighborhoods is diminished greatly.

Although we agree with MacLeod that achievement ideology is not working for low students from low-income families, we can not simply drop it. Because ideology is so important as an organizing principle in people's lives, we must substitute a more productive belief system, not simply discard belief systems all together.

If students like Rose's voc ed students, MacLeod's "Brothers," and Matuti-Bianchi's and Foley's *"vatos,"* who are the students AVID is trying to prepare for college, are to be motivated to achieve in school, it must not be at the expense of their self-esteem. Mac-Leod (1987: 153) says, "Schools serving low-income neighborhoods must help students build positive identities as working-class black and white young men and women. Rather than denying the existence of barriers to success, schools should acknowledge them explicitly." We certainly agree with this sentiment. The process of building students' positive academic identities seems to involve connecting (or in the cases of alienated youth, *re*connecting) classroom instruction with the everyday lives of students. But that platitude has been with us since the days of Dewey. Finding specific strategies to use students' experiences, knowledge, and expertise as instructional resources is a much more difficult task. While heeding Giroux and Simon's (1989: 249) warning about the problem of exploiting students' everyday culture, we are offered some suggestions in recent research with teachers who have been successful in reaching ethnic minority and working-class students by bringing aspects of their linguistic and cultural patterns into the classroom.

Heath (1982) found that the mode of language use and language socialization that was prevalent in the homes of middle-income families was not as apparent in the homes of low-income students in "Trackton." Low-income adults only seldom addressed questions to their children at home, and even less often to preverbal children. Where Trackton teachers would use questions, Trackton parents would use statements or imperatives. And when questions were asked of Trackton children by their parents, they were much different than the types of questions asked by teachers. Questions at home called for nonspecific comparisons or analogies as answers. They were not the known information or information-seeking questions associated with the classroom. Heath concludes that the language used in Trackton homes did not prepare children to cope with the major characteristics of the language used in classrooms: utterances that were interrogative in form but directive in pragmatic function, known information questions, and questions that asked for information from books.

In order to increase Trackton students' verbal skills in naming objects, identifying their characteristics, providing descriptions out of context, and responding to known information questions, Heath (1982) worked with the Trackton teachers on ways to adapt to the community's ways of asking questions. After reviewing audiotapes of community speech patterns with researchers, teachers began social studies lessons with questions that ask for personal experiences and analogic responses – for example, "What's happening there?" "Have you ever been there?" "What's this like?" These questions were similar to the questions that parents asked their children at home. The use of these questions in early stages of instruction were productive in generating active responses from previously passive and "nonverbal" Trackton students. Once the teachers increased the students' participation in lessons using home questioning styles, they were able to move them through a zone of learning toward school-based questioning styles.

In an analogous fashion, teachers teaching native Hawaiian students spontaneously introduced narratives jointly produced by the children into the beginning of reading lessons, a fact later observed by researchers associated with the project (Au, 1980; Au & Jordan, 1981; Tharp & Gallimore, 1988). In addition, they shifted the focus of instruction from decoding to comprehension, implemented small-group instruction to encourage cooperation, and included the native children's experiences as part of the discussion of reading materials. All of these modifications were consistent with Hawaiian cultural norms and had important consequences. Student participation in lessons increased and their scores on standardized tests increased. Both of these effects were important because of their antidote to the notoriously low school performance of Native Hawaiians.

By modifying classroom discourse to emphasize inquiry and information-seeking questions, McCarty, Lynch, and Benally (1991) help dispel the myth of the nonverbal Indian student, and in the process challenge the concept of learning styles. For decades, Native American students have been portrayed in the literature as quiet, passive, nonresponsive (John, 1972; More, 1989). They have been said to learn by observing and doing, not through listening and saying (Tharp, 1988; More, 1989). Often in the name of cultural compatibility, educators have emphasized nonverbal means of instruction and cue–response scripted drills, as a way to reach passive Indian students. McCarty et al. (1991) say that these erstwhile attempts have had an unfortunate side effect. Indian students are not taught with higher-order questioning and inquiry methods.

Working with the Navajo-staffed Native American Materials Development Center, staff members of the Rough Rock Indian reservation school implemented an inquiry-based bilingual social studies program. In the first lesson, the teacher-demonstrator showed students local scenes and asked them to identify things needed in their community. After accumulating a long list, students were asked to group like items and justify their choices. Eventually they reached a consensus, identifying things needed and things they'd like to have. That consensus led to the lesson generalization: "Rough Rock is a community because people work together to meet their needs and solve mutual problems."

The lessons in "Navajo Humanities" suggest that Navajo students will indeed respond, eagerly and enthusiastically, to inquiry-based questioning. What made these lessons work? McCarty and her associates suggest that this curriculum was effective because it encouraged students to draw upon their prior knowledge to solve new problems. The materials presented familiar scenes and the teachers' questions tapped students' knowledge and experience. When the classroom environment was changed, Navajo children became verbal, assertive, spoke up in class, made innovative generalizations.

In addition to illustrating that Native American children will respond to inquiry-based instruction when it is grounded in the experiences of their everyday life, this study shows us the limitations of the cognitive styles concept. Native American and other minority children may in fact appear to be nonverbal when classroom discourse patterns limit their expression, but if the expression of students' ideas is sought and if aspects of students' lives are meaningfully incorporated into curricular content, and if students are encouraged to use their cultural and linguistic knowledge to solve new problems, then Native American students respond eagerly and verbally to questioning. This validates the observation made by Scribner and Cole (1974) many years ago: Cognitive differences reside more in the situations in which particular cognitive processes are applied than in the existence of a process in a cultural group and its absence in another.

Organizing classroom discourse around the idea that scientific understanding is shaped by a community through scientific argument rather than received from authority has produced similar results with Haitian students (Roseberry, Warren, and Conant, 1992). The "Water Taste Test" was designed to investigate the "truth" of a belief held by most junior high school students that the water from the fountain on the third floor was superior to the water from the other fountains in the school (in part, because "all the little kids slobber" in the first-floor fountain). First, they designed and then took a blind taste test of water from several fountains. They were surprised when two-thirds chose the water from the first-floor fountain even though they said they preferred the third-floor fountain. Next, they extended their study to include a wider sample of students from other classes. They discussed methodological issues of sampling, masking the identity of the water, and ways to overcome bias in voting. When the students analyzed their data, they found 88% of the junior high school students thought they preferred water from the third-floor fountain, but 55% actually chose water from the first floor. In order to interpret their findings, the students analyzed the school's water. They found that the water from the first-floor fountain was 20 degrees colder than the other fountains (and theorized that the water was cooled by underground pipes, and was warmed as it flowed to the third floor). Therefore, they concluded that temperature was probably a deciding factor in students' preferences.

This sense-making approach to science with linguistic minority students is a radical departure from the textbook memorizing or even experimental demonstrations found in most classrooms. In the sense-making approach, we see students constructing scientific understandings through an iterative process of theory building, hypothesis testing, and data collection. These students posed their own questions, generated their own hypotheses, and analyzed their own data. This activity facilitated students' appreciation of responses that were different than their own, which Vygotskyeans and Piagetians alike agree is important in learning to take the perspective of the other. Like scientists in real-life laboratories, these students challenged one another's thoughts, negotiated conflicts about evidence and conclusions, and shared their knowledge in order to achieve an understanding that looks just like scientific understanding. Like scientists in real-life laboratories, these students were working in a community of practice in which the exploration of individual participants was guided and supported by the whole group.

The research discussed in this section reinforces a more general point made by Erickson and Schultz (1992): The engagement of students in learning activities results from a connection between social participation structure (form) and academic curriculum (content). On the one hand, if the social participation structure is familiar to students, then performing with new academic content is less alienating (viz., the KEEP reading lessons). On the other hand, if the academic content is familiar or engaging, then students may be willing to try out new ways of interacting and using language (viz., the Rough Rock lessons). The issue underlying both cases is safety – not having to risk looking clumsy or stupid in front of others. Lesson content and form, taken together or separately, can reduce the risk of embarrassment, which, in turn, triggers resistance – the withholding of assent to learn and to participate in learning activities.

Furthermore, the strategies these teachers have explored seem to make students feel as if they belong in school so "they need not choose between rendering themselves naked and vulnerable by stripping off their street identities or aggressively asserting their street culture in disruptive rebellion" (MacLeod, 1987: 153). Importantly, in achieving their effectiveness, these strategies do not attempt to duplicate street culture or import it undiluted into the classroom. Students' expertise is celebrated to be sure, but it is used as a vehicle to achieve worthwhile educational goals – developing literacy, engaging in scientific inquiry. Using students' expertise as a resource in the classroom, then, is one way to help students achieve the two interrelated goals we have found to be important in their academic achievement: maintaining their street identity while developing their academic identity.

Employing curriculum that appropriates students' expertise does not just eliminate achievement ideology with its built-in assumption of assimilation, as MacLeod implores us to do. It replaces it with a different ideology, one that we have called, following Gibson, "accommodation without assimilation."

Export Principles, Don't Duplicate Programs

The success of the San Diego experiment in untracking raises issues about the feasibility of duplicating it in other districts and with other groups of students. In this section, we reflect on the implications of our findings for implementing similar untracking efforts in other locations.

AVID is an unusual innovation in education for many reasons, but not the least of which is its origins. Unlike most innovations in education in the past 30 years (e.g., professionalizing teaching, imposing national standards, establishing a core curriculum, restructuring and decentralizing schools), it emerged from the bottom up. It was not imposed from the top down.

The grass-roots impetus for AVID was the impact that court-ordered desegregation in the San Diego Unified School District had on Clairemont High School in 1980. Clairemont had been providing a traditional enriched curriculum to a homogeneous middle-class student population. When a new high school drew away many affluent students and replaced them with low-income Latino and African American students, the Clairemont faculty responded by integrating them in the academic track and developing AVID instead of segregating them into separate, compensatory tracks.

Thus, AVID was a local response to practical circumstances. It was not a policy decision mandated at a high level of the school system or government. Likewise, the program's elements – its curriculum, its social supports, its institutional sponsorship – were built up over time. They were not the immediate result of a preset group of theoretical principles. When the program initially spread throughout San Diego County, it moved from school site to school site often when an AVID coordinator transferred to a new school. Dedicated teachers, who implemented the program at the school-site level, were the driving forces then, not central office authorities.

Now that the program has demonstrated success, there is pressure for it to be duplicated and disseminated. Although the impulse to replicate successful educational innovations is certainly understandable, we are fearful that AVID may fall victim to its own success in the process.

Our fear is that when a large school district or an entire state wants to copy AVID, it will become distorted, because the driving force will shift from a voluntary, grass-roots effort, to a mandated, top-down program. It is not clear that the same type of dedicated, charismatic teachers who are so essential for the success of this untracking effort will be involved if a program committed to enriching the academic life of linguistic and ethnic minority youth is mandated from the top down.

In complex social environments like schools, there are no photocopies. At best, general principles can be adopted to local circumstances. Therefore, an alternative to the "replication and dissemination" approach to implementation involves modeling, a kind of "show-and-tell effort." Here we have in mind identifying a handful of school sites in the San Diego area that exemplify the AVID approach to untracking. School officials who are considering restructuring their schools would be invited to watch the program in action. They would observe classes, talk to teachers, students, and parents, and perhaps view videotapes illustrating significant program components.

On returning to their schools, their purpose would be to adopt the principles to their local circumstances, not to copy an existing program. That is, they would attempt to create an educationally challenging activity with a system of social supports, but modified to meet local circumstances. Of necessity, this arrangement would require a system of accountability to AVID Center in order to insure that program standards are met. But, equally necessary, responding to local needs would create educational environments that are different than those which exist currently.

10

IMPLICATIONS FOR THEORIES EXPLAINING EDUCATIONAL INEQUALITY

THE REASONS FOR THE INEQUALITY IN EDUCATIONAL outcomes, which break out along ethnic, gender, racial, and class lines in American society, has been a matter of intense debate. Some explanations blame genetically transmitted deficiencies between racial and ethnic groups (Jensen, 1969; Herrnstein, 1974; Herrnstein & Murray, 1994), others attribute differences to the failure of hard work and effort (Parsons, 1959; Davis & Moore, 1945). More recent and controversial theories blame government-sponsored welfare systems for poverty and inequality (Murray, 1984), while others blame the stratifying effects of such school sorting practices as tracking, testing, poor counseling, and ability grouping (Rosenbaum, 1976; Erickson & Schultz, 1982; Oakes, 1985; Oakes et al., 1992).

One of the most persuasive arguments in the debate about inequality is "reproduction theory," which suggests that inequality is the consequence of capitalist structures and forces that constrain the mobility of lower-class youth (Bowles & Gintis, 1976; Bourdieu & Passeron, 1977a, 1977b). Our research, although conducted on a relatively small number of students and in a relatively small number of schools in one school district, invites us to reconsider some of the basic principles of reproduction theory and its explanation of the causes of inequality.

THE POTENTIAL MALLEABILITY OF CULTURAL AND SOCIAL CAPITAL

Two concepts that are central to reproduction theory are Bourdieu's notions of cultural capital and social capital. Our materials suggest some modifications in both of those ideas are in order.

Bourdieu starts with an idea of cultural knowledge that is reminiscent of Alfred Schutz's (1966) formulation: Groups in society possess and inherit distinctive skills and abilities. These are distributed socially; that is, different groups possess different types of knowledge. Bourdieu departs from Schutz by pointing out the stratified nature of cultural knowledge. Distinctive cultural knowledge is transmitted by the families of each social class; as a consequence, children of upper-class origin inherit substantially different skills, manners, norms, dress, style of interaction, and linguistic facility than do the sons and daughters of lower-class origin.

Furthermore, the sons and daughters of elite families benefit from their families' connections to important and productive social relationships, or what Bourdieu (1986) has called "social capital" (cf. Bourdieu & Passeron, 1977a, 1977b). Social capital is understood by analogy to economic capital. In the same way that money can be exchanged for valued outcomes, such as goods and services, a social relationship can be converted into valued outcomes, such as getting into college or acquiring employment. Thus, social capital, like economic capital, can produce profits or benefits in the social world, can be converted into other forms of capital, can accumulate, and can reproduce itself in identical or in expanded form (Bourdieu, 1986).

Schools and other symbolic institutions enter the picture at this point. They contribute to the reproduction of inequality by devising a curriculum that rewards the "cultural capital" of the dominant classes and systematically devalues that of the lower classes. Upper-class students, by virtue of a certain linguistic and cultural competence acquired through family socialization, are provided with the means of appropriating success in school. Children who read books, visit museums, attend concerts, and go to the theater and movies acquire a familiarity with the dominant culture that the educational system implicitly requires of its students for academic attainment. Participation in these cultural activities also connects elite parents and their sons and daughters with each other, which, in turn, strengthens their ties to privileged social networks.

The lack of success experienced by members of the working class in the occupational structure occurs not just because they lack financial resources; they also do not have the appropriate cultural capital and social connections to climb the occupational ladder. Knowledge and familiarity with dominant uses of language, types of writing, and cultural and literary allusion transmitted through the family are required to gain and maintain access to and mastery of the curriculum. Without the right kind of cultural capital, students are limited in their chances to learn from educational material and interact profitably with teachers.

In order for students to progress through the educational system and exercise control over their lives and their futures, they need to gain access to social capital, namely, social networks. Within these networks are institutionally well placed adults who either directly or indirectly provide institutional resources and opportunities. These "institutional agents" (Stanton-Salazar, Vasquez, & Mehan, 1996) are usually located within formal bureaucratic contexts (e.g., schools, government agencies, federally sponsored programs, colleges and universities, churches), but they also appear in voluntary civic and political associations, and small-scale institutions in the neighborhood. Due to their privileged positions in social networks, institutional agents have the power to give or withhold knowledge about resources and opportunities under the control of their own institution or under the control of neighboring institutions (Stanton-Salazar et al., 1996). Thus, the power of institutional agents is derived from their ability to situate youth within resource-rich social networks by actively manipulating the social and institutional forces that determine who shall "make it" and who shall not. From the point of view of the student then, gaining access to educational opportunities and life choices essentially entails gaining acess to social networks.

Although Bourdieu says the school is a vital mechanism in the reproduction of inequality, Bourdieu does not provide us with the detailed ethnographic information we need in order to determine just how the school devalues the cultural capital of the lower classes while valorizing the cultural capital of the upper classes (Lareau, 1989; Mehan, 1992). Instead of looking at the locally managed practices of schooling that reproduce inequality, Bourdieu concentrates on the attitudes, beliefs, experiences of those inhabiting children's social world – what he calls "the habitus" (Bourdieu & Passeron, 1977a). The habitus provides the basis for developing deeply internalized values that define an individual's orientation toward the world. For low-status people, it engenders conduct that keeps them in low-income positions. Lower-class children grow up in an environment where success is rare; they rarely see their brothers and sisters, friends and neighbors secure good jobs. The experiences and attitudes of those close to lower-class children infiltrate their systems of belief. Responding to the attitudes and experiences of those around them, lower-income children lose interest in school and resign themselves to low-level jobs, thereby contributing to the reproduction of existing status relations.

Especially by contrast to that of Bowles and Gintis (1976), Bourdieu's cultural model of reproduction is not a mechanical transmission belt. Schools work in a more subtle way for Bourdieu and Passeron than they do for Bowles and Gintis. They do not simply mirror the social relations of production; relatively autonomous institutions, they are only indirectly influenced by economic considerations. Rather than imposing docility and repression, schools are depicted as reproducing existing power relations subtly via the production and distribution of a dominant culture that conforms to what it means to be educated (Giroux, 1983: 87).

Despite this more nuanced view of the reproduction of inequality, however, there is a darkly pessimistic view of the possibility of social change in Bourdieu's analysis. For Bourdieu, social action is largely determined by social structure and power relations. He leaves little room for variation, creativity, alternatives, or changes at the interpersonal level. This dark view is shared by other reproduction theorists:

> Although individuals can interpret and respond to constraint in
> different ways, they must still face the effects of institutionalized

forms of class domination. As Giroux reminds us, "while school cultures may take complex and heterogeneous forms, the principle that remains constant is that they are situated within a network of power relations *from which they cannot escape.*" (MacLeod, 1987: 149; emphasis added)

Social change is difficult, if not impossible within Bourdieu's framework because he says that the tastes and manners of the upper class are *natural* (natural in the sense that they are given in class structure). Because they flow with ease, on fluid movements and gestures, relaxed utterances and phrases, the nuances of social and cultural capital are not easily acquired.

The strategies for dealing with complex circumstances that AVID students develop and the actions that AVID coordinators take seem to present counterexamples to Bourdieu's immutable formulation. Here we have students, most of whom are from low-income families and African American and Latino backgrounds, who seem to be acquiring some of the cultural capital, a commodity Bourdieu says is natural and is reserved for the sons and daughters of the elite. Here we have AVID teachers and coordinators operating as institutional agents, making essential connections between important formal institutions – high schools and colleges. They are serving in a role that Bourdieu says is especially reserved for elite families.

Furthermore, AVID students are gaining cultural and social capital from a nonhabitus source, indeed a state-sponsored source. It is in the school, not in the family, that they are learning the value of timeliness, orderliness, neatness, answering out-of-context questions, responding to known information questions. It is in the school, not in the family, that they are acquiring some of the academic skills that seem to be so essential to academic success: test-taking strategies (when to guess, how to read back to the questions from the multiple-choice answers given, how to eliminate distracting answers), essay-writing strategies, note-taking strategies, how to get information from teachers, or how to challenge questionable grades, policies, or decisions. They have learned how to talk to teachers in school, while confining street talk and behavior to the street.

AVID coordinators lead their students through the murky maze of the college application and financial aid process. They play the role usually played by parents of elite students – intervening on their behalf with administrators or teachers who resist their academic plans or desires. They play the role usually played by private counselors or admissions officers at elite schools – advocating on their behalf with admissions officers or financial aid officers at colleges or universities.

If the sons and daughters of low-status students can *learn* the skills, manners, norms presumably *inherited* by elite students, then this raises questions about the immutability of cultural capital. If teachers and coordinators can embed their low-status students in productive social networks, then this raises questions about the unique privilege of social capital. Both of these activities raise the possibility of social change in Bourdieu's formulation. Without doubt, the possibilities open to AVID students, as lower-class teenagers and ethnic minority students, are limited objectively. We know from the outset that they will not make a great leap forward from the lower to the upper classes, but our data suggest they will move up one or two rungs on the ladder of mobility. Because we have circumstances in which students are increasing the probabilities for their social advancement, we must make the concepts of social and cultural capital more subtle. Cultural capital must be flexible enough to include the prospect of its acquisition by less fortunate members of society. It is necessary to consider the possibility that social capital will be exchanged by agencies not connected to elite families.

If the sons and daughters of low-status families are acquiring cultural capital from their teachers, and if the teachers of low-status students are activating social networks, then reproduction theorists must also modify the rigid way in which they think about schools. Schools are not always and necessarily reproductive systems. We have described circumstances in which schools, or at least segments within schools, can be transformed to increase the possibility of social mobility by passing on cultural capital and constructing social networks.

Before we celebrate the transformation of the schools from settings for the reproduction of social inequality into instruments of social equity, we must, of course, determine if the actions we have observed are substantial, long-term institutional changes. For, if we have only revealed changes on the margin, then we do not have genuine mobility patterns, but a cynical affordance – a process of allowing a precious few members of the underclass through the gates so as to legitimate achievement ideology, while the great masses are kept down.

TOWARD A REFLEXIVE RELATIONSHIP BETWEEN STRUCTURAL CONSTRAINTS, CULTURE, AND SOCIAL AGENCY

The representation of the cause of inequality contained in reproduction theory, while powerful, suffers from an overly deterministic world view. It emphasizes structural constraints while virtually ignoring the social organization of school practices, cultural arrangements, and individuals' actions. As a result, we second the motion made by Giroux (1983: 119) and MacLeod (1987) who call for a reflexive relationship between social agency, culture, and structural constraints. A first step in building this reflexive relationship is to establish a more comprehensive sense of social agency.

Toward a Comprehensive Sense of Social Agency

A series of articulate ethnographies has begun to establish a balance between structural determinants and social agency in explaining inequality. While acknowledging that structural constraints inhibit mobility and school practices contribute to inequality, they focus on students' own contributions to their difficulties.

Willis's (1977) study of disaffected white working-class males in a British secondary school is the hallmark study in this so-called resistance tradition. He found the "lads," a group of high school dropouts who rejected achievement ideology, subverted teacher and administrator authority, and disrupted classes. Willis says that the lads' rejection of the school is partly the result of their deep insights into the economic condition of their social class under capitalism. But their cultural outlook limited their options; equating manual labor with success and mental labor with failure prevented them from seeing their actions led to dead-end, lower-paying jobs. Blind to the connection between schooling and mobility, they *chose* to join their brothers and fathers on the shop floor, a choice apparently made happily and freely from coercion. Thus, what begins as a potential insight into the social relations of production is transformed into a surprisingly uncritical affirmation of class domination. This identification of manual labor with masculinity ensures the lads' acceptance of their subordinate economic fate and the successful reproduction of the class structure.

Apple and Weis (1983) continue in this tradition, saying U.S. working-class students see schooling as tacitly teaching middle-class norms, values, and dispositions through institutional expectations and the routines of day-to-day school life. Working-class subcultures oppose the rigid rules, the respect for external rewards, the orderly work habits, and the demand for subordination.

Solomon (1992) reports a similar pattern among West Indian children in a major Canadian city. These newly arrived immigrants come to school with beliefs and actions that work against their academic success. These attitudes lead them to respond to their treatment by the school in a manner that compounds their problem: They form separatist groups, do not follow school rules, and play sports rather than do school work. Solomon, like Willis and Weis before him, gives student subcultures some political savvy: They oppose school culture and achievement ideology because of the school's hidden curriculum and because they see limited economic opportunities ahead of them. The net result is these newly arrived immigrant students fail, in spite of their expressed desire to succeed in school.

What distinguishes these ethnographic accounts from the theorizing of either Bowles and Gintis or Bourdieu and Passeron is the agency attributed to the students. Unlike the students in Bowles and Gintis's rendition who passively internalize mainstream values of individual achievement or the students in Bourdieu and Passeron's theory who simply carry cultural capital on their backs or in their heads, these working-class and ethnic minority students make real choices in their everyday lives. While at first glance, the working-class students' rebellious behavior, their low academic achievement and high dropout rate seem to stem from lack of self-discipline, dullness, laziness, or inability to project themselves into the future, their actual causes are quite different. Their unwillingness to participate comes from their assessment of the costs and benefits of playing the game. It is not that schooling will not propel them up the ladder of success; it is that chances are too slim to warrant the attempt. Given this logic, the oppositional behavior of the Hallway Hangers, the *vatos*, the lads, and the rest is a form of resistance to an institution that cannot deliver on its promise of upward mobility for all students.

Adding the notion of "resistance" to the lexicon employed to understand inequality in schools, then, reveals the contributions social actors make to their own plight. As Ogbu (1992) phrases it, this line of research shows how "victims contribute to their own victimization."

While ethnographies in the resistance tradition are important because they show that people actively make choices in life rather than respond passively to socioeconomic pressures bearing down on them, the sense of agency that resistance theorists attribute to social actors is limited. We are told actors subvert and reject the expectations of schools and society, a conception that leads to at least three problems: It tends to romanticize people's nonconformity, to support tacitly the existing system of power relations, and to present a restricted repertoire of students' actions. If reproduction theory is to provide us with a helpful account of social inequality, then we must broaden its sense of social agency to make it more comprehensive.

The sense of agency found in educational reproduction theory has its roots in recent postmodern analyses of popular culture (deCerteau, 1984; Fiske, 1988). Fiske (1988) claims that popular culture is in a symbiotic, albeit hierarchical, relationship with mainstream culture. In an industrial society, there is no authentic folk culture because the dominant culture has pushed local productions far off stage. As a result, subordinates are forced to make their own culture from the resources and commodities provided by the culture that dominates them. This hierarchical view of culture limits subordinates to remaking the culture of the elites; it leaves no room for "the folk" to make their own culture.

Depicting popular culture within capitalist economies as a struggle, deCerteau (1984) uses military metaphors to express this struggle: The privileged "deploy their huge, well organized forces," which are met by "the fleeting tactics" of the weak. The tactics of the subordinated involve spotting the weak points in the forces of the powerful and raiding them as guerrilla fighters constantly harry and attack an invading army. They never challenge the powerful in open warfare for that challenge would invite defeat. Being weak, the powerless use guerrilla tactics against the strategies of the powerful – making poaching raids on their texts or structures, playing tricks on the system, winning small fleeting victories, keeping the enemy on alert.

The powerful construct *places* where they can exercise their power – cities, shopping malls, schools, workplaces, houses, prisons, hospitals. The weak make *spaces* within those places; they occupy them as long as they can or have to: "A place is where strategy operates" whereas "space is practice's place" (deCerteau, 1984: 32–33). While the powerful attempt to control the places and the commodities that constitute the parameters of everyday life, the weak, once in those buildings, transform the space, making it over into their own space.

"The everyday practices of the weak" – particularly the "browsers" who windowshop, hang out, use public facilities (water fountains, rest areas, bathrooms, mirrors), try on clothes or taste samples of ice cream with no intent to buy, go home and fashion up a cheaper version of a high fashion outfit – deCerteau celebrates as "using what is imposed" for new meanings that resist the system. Shoplifting (especially when the shopper returns the stolen goods for a refund) and "proletarian shopping" – bringing home pens, pencils, papers from work for kids, using company copiers or computers for personal mail and video games and the like – are other examples of the weak "expropriating" (Fiske, 1988) the oppressing system.

Erickson (1984) and Ogbu (1992) address the first problem within resistance theory – its romanticization of nonconformity. They correctly remind us that not every instance of student misbehavior, including crumpling homework, raiding the mall, browsing and shoplifting, can be interpreted as evidence of resistance. The executive who lets her kid play video games on the office computer may be simply exercising an implicit entitlement to company perks, not resisting the system. All actions are ambiguous. Subject to multiple interpretations from multiple perspectives, it is not always clear when an action is resistance, deviance, or conformance to an alternative code of conduct. Acts of resistance are distinguished from acts of deviance because they are presumably based on a critique, implicit or explicit, of societally constructed ideologies (Giroux, 1983; Weiler, 1985; Holland & Eisenhart, 1990). We have to be able to specify, based on careful analyses of social situations, just when ditching school, raiding the mall, and proletarian shopping stem from an articulate critique of relations of domination, or are simply acts of bored or rebellious youth.

While it is clear that deCerteau delights in the small victories, the adaptations, the ways of bending imposed systems that the weak employ, it is not as clear what he thinks about these actions. Are these actors moralists or are they tricksters? Is deCerteau attributing to the underdog a superior ethic than the oppressors of the elite class? Or is he more like Goffman (1964), who treats people as con artists and thieves, engaging in acts of deviance to fill an otherwise boring existence with some modicum of pleasure?

Although Fiske and deCerteau celebrate the resistance of the weak against the hegemonic forces of the powerful, they don't present very many compelling instances of resistance. Teenagers who rip the jeans made by capitalist conglomerates, or shoppers who browse without intending to buy, or youth who redirect the meanings of everyday words by scrawling graffiti on walls are not very threatening to the powerful. They disrupt, but they do not transform power relations. Because it has adopted a version of the guerrilla warfare conception of resistance, reproduction theory faces its second problem. By asserting that subordinates only maintain their opposition within the social order dominated by the powerful, the guerrilla warfare conception of popular culture contained within reproduction theory tacitly rationalizes and legitimates existing status distinctions and inequalities.

Our research on high-achieving, low-status students addresses the third and final problem with resistance theory: its limited portrayal of students' actions. "Resisting" and "opposing" are not the only actions that African American and Latino students take. As we have documented throughout this study, students from relatively weak and powerless backgrounds have engaged in a wide range of behaviors, ones that go far beyond opposition and resistance.

By participating in college prep classes and applying for and enrolling in college, Latino and African American AVID students are clearly engaged in academic pursuits, not in their rejection. Furthermore, they work on their academic identities without sacrificing their ethnic identities by employing elaborate border-crossing strategies, which include segregating their academic friends from their neighborhood friends and using socially acceptable expressive speech styles at school and street styles in the neighborhood.

Many managed the complex practicalities of family life; they translated the many forms and literature that came into the home from public agencies and businesses; they ran interference between their parents and their schools concerning a wide range of educational matters; they balanced family checkbooks and paid family bills.

Many parents were reticent about the prospect of their children leaving home to attend college. Some parents openly resisted the idea and rebuffed AVID's entreaties to participate in the college application and selection process. These parental positions left many AVID students in a delicate situation; they wanted to show respect for their parents and their wishes, while at the same time they wanted to pursue the opportunity to attend college. The AVID students caught in these binds employed sophisticated strategies to achieve both goals simultaneously. Some chose to attend college in the local area so they could live at home; others waited until they had scholarship offers which met their parents' fears about the cost of college; others agreed to attend college in cities where relatives from the extended family lived nearby.

Many parents admitted they did not know much about the college-going process, even though they supported the higher-education goals of their children. This absence of parental resources forced many AVID students to become extremely enterprising, acquiring the knowledge and information about colleges, applications, and financial aid on their own or with the help of their AVID coordinator.

The impression we want to leave through this summary of students' actions is that the expressive and behavioral repertoire of Latino and African American students is much more extensive than that portrayed by resistance theory and its parent, reproduction theory. Students' actions are not limited to opposing or resisting structures of constraints; they take positive courses of action to achieve socially accepted goals and attempt to break down constraining barriers. The students in our study did not passively respond to structural forces; rather they defined and shaped actions against those forces in creative ways.

Circumscribing students' actions as only negative or oppositional produces a puny depiction of their social agency. Having witnessed a wide and diverse range of students' actions, it is clear to us that we need a more subtle and inclusive conception of social agency in order to understand how the inequality between rich and poor, "majority" and "minority" is sustained generation after generation. This more comprehensive sense of agency to which we have alluded in this study attempts to capture the processes by which people give meaning to their lives through complex cultural and political processes while appreciating the power of the constraints under which they labor (cf. Giroux & Simon, 1989; Rose, 1990).

Cultural Processes Mediating Structural Constraints and Social Outcomes

A second step in building a reflexive theory of social inequality involves the incorporation of cultural processes that mediate the relationship between structural constraints and social agency. Holland and Eisenhart (1990) describe the power of one such cultural process, the college peer group, in the construction of the traditional female identity that suppresses the school identity offered by college.

Holland and Eisenhart (1990) found that talented women at "Bradford" and "Southern University" scaled back their aspirations for business and professional careers even though they have expressed high aspirations throughout their lives. Holland and Eisenhart say that the intervening mechanism of the college peer group, a cultural meaning system arranged around romantic love, was responsible for these changes. It "pulls down" academically oriented girls and reinforces those who see college only in instrumental terms, as a way to get a job.

This "culture of romance" begins its work early in life. Adolescent girls see a grim world composed of class and gender systems. With the help of television shows, romantic novels, and news stories, they socially construct and occupy a fantasy world that excludes these grim details. The culture of romance operated at "Bradford" and "Southern University" as an exchange system in which attractiveness and eventually sex were bartered for status and heterosexual relationships. Women students presented themselves in sexually attractive ways. Men responded to women's sexual presentations with personal attention and gifts. Women then showed their appreciation by allowing intimacy, in increments. Experiencing the world through this cultural meaning system, the young women who enrolled in college are content to come out with lower credentials and lower career skills and are happy to enter into dating relations, eventually marriage (Holland & Eisenhart, 1990: 94ff.).

The culture of romance is an escape with sad consequences. While women utilize sexual attractiveness to escape dreary lives and to avoid bumping up against the glass ceiling, they did not acquire the credentials that college has to offer. Therefore, such women wind up untrained for any good job and assured of economic dependence on men. Ironically, then, women's immersion in romance embeds them more deeply in the culture of male domination and female submission and in doubled work: waged and unwaged (Holland & Eisenhart, 1990: 50).

MacLeod's (1987) comparison of the responses of two groups of teenage boys who live in similar socioeconomic circumstances shows the diversity in responses among subcultural groups to structural constraints. One group that MacLeod studied, "the Hallway Hangers," reacted in ways reminiscent of the lads in Willis's account: cutting classes, acting out in the few they attended, dropping out, smoking, drinking, using drugs, committing crimes. In short, they took every opportunity to oppose the regimen of the school and resist its achievement ideology. By contrast, "the Brothers" tried to fulfill societally approved roles: attending classes, conforming to rules, studying hard, rejecting drugs, playing basketball, cultivating girlfriends.

MacLeod says cultural factors shaped the differential responses of the two groups of students. The Brothers think that racial inequality has been curbed and that educational opportunity has been improved in the past 20 years because of the Civil Rights movement. Family life also mediates. The parents of the Brothers want their children to have professional careers. Toward that goal, they exercised control over their sons, setting a relatively early curfew, expecting them to perform to a certain level at school; violations of academic expectations were punished by restrictions and the punishments stuck. The parents of the Hallway Hangers did not act in this manner. They gave their sons free rein and did not monitor schoolwork. Thus, ethnicity, beliefs, and family life, each of which are cultural processes, serve as mediators between structural constraints and attainment.

The fact that two different groups of students reacted differently to objectively similar socioeconomic circumstances reveals that some reproduction theories are overly deterministic and underplay the role of cultural processes. The reaction of the Hallway Hangers vindicates Bourdieu's theory. Confronting a closed opportunity structure, they lowered their aspirations, openly resisted the educational institution and its achievement ideology. But neither Bowles and Gintis nor Bourdieu and Passeron do as well with the Brothers. The Brothers experienced the same habitus and were exposed to the same hidden curriculum of the school as were the Hallway Hangers, but the Brothers responded to it by eagerly adopting achievement ideology and maintaining high aspirations for success.

Holland and Eisenhart's and MacLeod's work forcefully informs us that externally constraining forces, such as those in the theories of Bowles and Gintis and Bourdieu and Passeron, do not account adequately for the actions of people. Culturally grounded resources help people interpret patriarchal and socioeconomic constraints. Furthermore, comparing the actions of the Hallway Hangers and the Brothers, or males and females, demonstrates quite clearly that individuals and groups respond to structures of domination in diverse and unpredictable ways.

The women studied by Holland and Eisenhart do not fit the pattern of collective resistance offered by Willis's lads and Mac-Leod's Hallway Hangers. The girls' response is more a matter of individual accommodation to existing social conditions than a collective rejection of school culture (Weiler, 1985). While girls may have negative attitudes about school, they do not act out their criticisms in antisocial ways. Even though the female students at "Bradford" and "Southern University" were aware and critical of the racism and sexism in society, they worked in college with the promise to exchange schoolwork for a credential and a credential for a better job. They did not act out the model of an academically oriented student to be sure, but they did do the work to obtain a credential. That pragmatic accommodation implies they filtered the ideological messages of the school and produced their own meaning systems to interpret the world in which they live.

We have described an institutionally based educational process that mediates structural constraints and educational outcomes. The San Diego untracking program places students in college prep classes in order to make them eligible for college. These untracked students are not left to sink or swim in this new academic environment, however. The untracking program builds social scaffolds in order to insure that the untracked students have a better chance to succeed in them. To support the untracked students, AVID isolates them in special classrooms. Among the most visible supports untracked students receive in these special classrooms is instruction in the college application process, and in note-taking, test-taking, and study strategies.

In addition to providing its students with explicit instruction in the implicit curriculum of the school, AVID teachers mediate between the untracked students and their high schools in other ways. AVID coordinators intervene on the behalf of their students with other high school teachers, counselors, and administrators. AVID coordinators also build bridges between the high school and the college system by forming special relationships with college admissions officers.

Unlike the culture of romance and the culture of the shop floor, the culture that this mediating system creates has had a positive benefit on the educational achievement of previously underachieving students. Working-class and minority youth have derived some of the same advantages as their more privileged peers when schools and their agents collectively act deliberately and explicitly to mediate the relations between the influential institutions impacting educational achievement.

CONCLUSIONS: CONSTITUTIVE PROCESSES PRODUCING SOCIAL INEQUALITY AND SOCIAL EQUALITY

We have suggested that theories attempting to understand inequality in U.S. society can be improved by an expanded view of cultural and social capital, by incorporating a more dynamic sense of human agency, and by including the cultural processes that mediate social constraints and social or educational outcomes. If our thinking is to be rescued from deterministic tendencies, then we must especially insure that the cultural processes that *produce* inequality are included in our theorizing. Willis, MacLeod, Foley, and Holland and Eisenhart have used the concept of cultural production effectively to portray the way students actively confront the ideological and material conditions presented by schooling and often, ironically, contribute to their own lowly status.

As we conclude our analysis, we want to emphasize that the interaction between educators and students is another vital cultural process that produces inequality. The actions that educators take everyday in school settings constitute students' educational careers, indeed their identities. Depending on the vector of their actions, the prospects for more equitable education is increased or prevailing inequities are reinforced.

Teachers, testers, assistant principals, counselors constantly interpret students' skills and abilities, their presentations of self and appearance, and judge whether tokens of their behavior count as instances of certain educational categories. This constitutive process unfolds in the flow of classroom lessons when teachers judge the correctness and appropriateness of students' answers (McDermott, Godspodinoff, & Aron, 1978; Mehan, 1979; Michaels, 1981; Eder, 1981; Wilcox, 1982; Collins, 1986). The accumulation of such judgments often results in the placement of students in ability groups or different educational tracks, including special education or gifted programs. When counselors meet with students to make curricular choices or design curricular programs, the possibility of entire educational career options is created or negated (Cicourel & Kitsuse, 1963; Rosenbaum, 1976; Erickson & Schultz, 1982).

A particularly influential version of this constitutive work appears in educational testing sessions when a psychologist decides whether a student's answer is correct or incorrect and tabulates a sum of such answers to count as the student's intelligence (Mehan, 1978; Mehan et al., 1985: 88–108; Marlaire & Maynard, 1990; Poole, 1994). The social organization of tester–student interaction influences students' test results. Depending on which behaviors are treated as answers, a student's test score can vary by as much as 25% (Mehan, 1978). That variation in test scores is sufficient to change a student's identity from "learning disabled" to "normal," or from "normal" to "gifted."

When we examine the day-to-day educational practices operating in educational settings such as lessons, tests, and counseling sessions, we learn that students are constructed in different ways, and their ascribed characteristics, such as gender, race, ethnicity, and social class influence the resulting representations. Students' intelligence, their access to educational curriculum, their scholastic achievement, and options later in life are assembled from such practice.

By calling attention to the practices and routines of educators as they engage in the work of teaching, testing, and sorting students, we have tried to demonstrate the situated relevance of social structures in the practical work activities performed by people in social interaction. Educators carry out the routine work of conducting lessons, assigning students to ability groups or tracks, administering tests, and attending meetings. The notion of *work* stresses the constructive aspect of institutional practice. Educators' work is repetitive and routine. Its mundane character should not overshadow the drama of its importance, however, because steps on students' career ladders are assembled from such practice. The enactment of routine bureaucratic practices construct students' educational careers by opening or closing their access to particular educational opportunities.

This line of thinking invites us to recast our representation of schooling. Schools are not innocent sites of cultural transmission or places where consensual values are inculcated or meritocratic springboards for mobility. Nor are they automatic reproduction machines, exacerbating or perpetuating social inequalities in mechanical ways. A more realistic conception recognizes that public schools are caught in the middle of competing agendas. On the one hand, schools are asked to insure that all students achieve to the best of their ability. On the other hand, schools are asked to insure that all students gain access to the same educational opportunities. Traditionally, schools have established separate ability groups and tracks in order to meet the often competing demands of these "excellence" and "equity" agendas. This solution, unfortunately, has created its own problems: segregation, curriculum differentiation, unequal access.

The sorting practices of the school constitute the very identities of the students they touch. *It is not that dumb kids are placed in slow groups or low tracks; it is that kids are made dumb by being placed into slow groups or low tracks.* And as we have seen in this study, students can be made smart by being placed in challenging courses when they have a system of social scaffolding supporting them.

There are more general lessons to be learned from the constructivist approach that motivates this thinking. The structural aspects of society are not pale reflections of large-scale institutional and historical forces; they are contingent outcomes of people's practical activity. Therefore, they must be conceptualized as constantly constituted rather than constantly reproduced (Connell 1987: 44). Likewise, culture must be conceptualized as a process, as something that is continually produced, even as it may be reproduced – not as a bounded, static, and unchanging entity. If we are to understand the structure of inequality, then we must continue to examine the interactional mechanisms by which that structure is generated. And, if we are to find ways to defeat reproductive mechanisms, then we must institutionalize practices that increase the possibility of equality.

REFERENCES

Allington, Richard L. 1980. Teacher Interruption Behaviors during Primary Grade Oral Reading. *Journal of Educational Society, 72* (3): 371–374.

Anderson, Elijah. 1991. *Streetwise: Race, Class and Change in an Urban Community.* Chicago: University of Chicago Press.

Apple, Michael W. 1982. *Education and Power.* Boston: Routledge & Kegan Paul.

Apple, Michael W., & Lois Weis. 1983. *Ideology and Practice in Education: A Political and Conceptual Introduction.* Philadelphia: Temple University Press.

Au, Kathy. 1980. Participation Structures in a Reading Lesson with Hawaiian Children. *Anthropology and Education Quarterly, 11* (2): 91–115.

Au, Kathy, & Cathy Jordan. 1981. Teaching Reading to Hawaiian Children: Finding a Culturally Appropriate Solution. In H. Trueba, G. P. Guthrie, & K. H. Au (Eds.), *Culture and the Bilingual Classroom* (pp. 139–152). Rowley, MA: Newberry House.

Austin, J. L. 1962. *Philosophical Papers.* London: Oxford University Press.

Azmitia, Margarita, Catherine R. Cooper, Eugene E. Garcia, Angela Ittel, Bonnie Johanson, Edward Lopez, Rebeca Martinez-Chavez, & Lourdes Rivera. 1994. *Links between Home and School among Low-Income Mexican American and European-American Families.* Educational Practice Report No. 9. Santa Cruz: National Center for Research on Cultural Diversity and Second Language Learning.

Behar, Ruth. 1991. *Translated Woman: Crossing the Border with Esperanza's Story.* Boston: Beacon.

Bell, Peter. 1993. *Graduate Follow-up Study: San Diego Unified School Districts' Class of 1991: The First Year after Graduation.* San Diego: San Diego City Schools, School Services Division, Planning, Research and Accountability Team.

Bellah, Robert N., Richard Madsen, William M. Sullivan, Ann Swidler, & Steven M. Tipton. 1985. *Habits of the Heart.* Berkeley: University of California Press.

Bereiter, Karl, & Siegfried Englemann. 1966. *Teaching the Disadvantaged Child in the Preschool.* Englewood Cliffs, NJ: Prentice-Hall.

Bernstein, Basil. 1973. *Class, Codes and Control: Vol. 3. Toward a Theory of Educational Transmissions*. London: Routledge & Kegan Paul.

Bhachu, Parminder K. 1985. *Twice Migrants: East African Sikh Settlers in Britain*. London: Tavistock.

Bixler, Paul. 1991. *A Mathematical and Computer Simulation Approach to Robotics in Senior High School*. Unpublished Master's thesis, University of California, San Diego.

Bourdieu, Pierre. 1977. *Outline of a Theory of Practice*. Cambridge: Cambridge University Press.

Bourdieu, Pierre. 1986. The Forms of Capital. In John G. Richardson (Ed.), *Handbook of Theory and Research for the Sociology of Education* (pp. 241–258). New York: Greenwood Press.

Bourdieu, Pierre. 1989. Social Space and Symbolic Power. *Sociological Theory, 7* (1): 14–25.

Bourdieu, Pierre, & Claude Passeron. 1977a. *Reproduction in Education, Society and Culture*. London: Sage.

Bourdieu, Pierre, & Claude Passeron. 1977b. Cultural Reproduction and Social Reproduction. In J. Karabel & E. H. Halsey (Eds.), *Power and Ideology in Education* (pp. 487–510). Oxford: Oxford University Press.

Bowles, Samuel, & Herbert I. Gintis. 1976. *Schooling in Capitalist America*. New York: Basic Books.

Bruner, Jerome. 1986. *Actual Minds, Possible Worlds*. Cambridge, MA: Harvard University Press.

Carnegie Council on Adolescent Development. 1989. *Turning Points. Preparing American Youth for the 21st Century*. Rochester, NY: Carnegie.

Carter, Deborah J., & Reginald Wilson. 1991. *Minorities in Higher Education: Ninth Annual Status Report*. Washington, DC: American Council on Education.

Cazden, Courtney B. 1986. Classroom Discourse. In M. Wittrock (Ed.), *Handbook of Research on Teaching* (pp. 432–463). New York: Macmillan.

Cazden, Courtney B., & Hugh Mehan. 1989. Principles from Sociology and Anthropology. In M. C. Reynolds (Ed.), *Knowledge Base for the Beginning Teacher* (pp. 47–57). Oxford: Pergamon Press.

Center for Education Statistics. 1986. *The Condition of Education: A Statistical Report*. Washington, DC: U.S. Department of Education.

Chavez, Linda. 1991. *Out of the Barrio: Toward a New Politics of Hispanic Assimilation*. New York: Basic Books.

Cicourel, Aaron V., & John I. Kitsuse. 1963. *The Educational Decision Makers*. Indianapolis: Bobbs-Merrill.

Cicourel, Aaron V., & Hugh Mehan. 1983. Universal Development, Stratifying Practices and Status Attainment. *Research in Social Stratification and Mobility, 4:* 3–27.

Clark, Burton R. 1960. The Cooling Out Function in Higher Education. *American Journal of Sociology, 65:* 569–576.

Cole, Michael, & Peg Griffin. 1987. *Contextual Factors in Education.* Madison: Wisconsin Center for Education Research.

Coleman, James S., E. Q. Campbell, C. J. Hobson, J. McPartland, A. M. Mood, F. D. Weinfeld, & R. L. York. 1966. *Equality of Educational Opportunity.* Washington, DC: U.S. Office of Education.

Collins, James. 1986. Differential Instruction in Reading Groups. In J. Cook-Gumperz (Ed.), *The Social Construction of Literacy* (pp. 117–137). Cambridge: Cambridge University Press.

Collins, Randall. 1971. Functional and Conflict Theories of Educational Stratification. *American Sociological Review, 36:* 1002–1019.

Collins, Randall. 1979. *The Credential Society.* New York: Academic Press.

Comer, James P. 1980. *School Power.* New York: Free Press.

Comer, James P. 1988. Educating Poor Minority Children. *Scientific American, 259* (5): 42–48.

Commission on the Skills of the American Workforce. 1990. *America's Choice: High Skills or Low Wages.* Washington, DC: National Center for Education and the Economy.

Connell, R. W. 1987. *Gender and Power: Society, the Person and Sexual Politics.* Stanford, CA: Stanford University Press.

Cookson, Peter W., Jr., & Caroline Hodges Persell. 1985. *Preparing for Power: America's Elite Boarding Schools.* New York: Basic Books.

Cooper, Catherine R., Margarita Azmitia, Eugene E. Garcia, Angela Ittel, Edward Lopez, Lourdes Rivera, Rebecca Martinez-Chavez. 1994. "I Would Like Her to Go to College, But Well, the Way Things Are Now, Who Knows?" *New Directions for Child Development, 63:* 65–81.

Cuban, Larry. 1986. *Teachers and Machines: The Classroom Use of Technology since 1920.* New York: Columbia Teachers College Press.

Cuban, Larry. 1992. What Happens to Reforms That Last? The Case of the Junior High School. *American Educational Research Journal, 29* (2): 227–251.

Cummins, Jim. 1986. Empowering Minority Students: A Framework for Intervention. *Harvard Educational Review, 56* (1): 18–36.

Davis, Kingsley, & Wilbert E. Moore. 1945. Some Principles of Stratification. *American Sociological Review, 10:* 242–249.

deCerteau, Michel. 1984. *The Practice of Everyday Life.* Berkeley: University of California Press.

Delgado-Gaitan, Concha. 1987. Traditions and Transitions in the Learning Process of Mexican American Children. In George Spindler & Louise Spindler (Eds.), *Interpretive Ethnography of Education* (pp. 333–362). Norwood, NJ: Erlbaum.

Delgado-Gaitan, Concha. 1991. Involving Parents in Schools: A Process of Empowerment. *American Journal of Education, 100* (1): 20–46.

Delgado-Gaitan, Concha. 1992. School Matters in the Mexican-American Home: Socializing Children to Education. *American Educational Research Journal, 29:* 495–513.

Delgado-Gaitan, Concha, & Henry Trueba. 1991. *Crossing Cultural Borders: Education for Immigrant Families in America.* New York: Falmer.

DeMott, Benjamin. 1990. *The Imperial Middle: Why Americans Can't Think Straight about Class.* New York: Morrow.

DeNora, Tia, & Hugh Mehan. 1994. The Social Construction of Genius. In Theodore Sarbin & John I. Kitsuse (Eds.), *Constructing the Social* (pp. 157–173). Los Angeles: Sage.

Deutsch, Martin. 1967. *Disadvantaged Children.* New York: Basic Books.

Díaz, Steven, Luis C. Moll, & Hugh Mehan. 1986. Sociocultural Resources in Instruction: A Context Specific Approach. In *Beyond Language* (pp. 187–230). Los Angeles: California State University Evaluation, Dissemination, and Assessment Center.

Dreeben, Robert. 1968. *On What Is Learned in School.* Reading, MA: Addison-Wesley.

Drevlow, Sue. 1990. *Total UCSD Undergraduate Enrollment by Ethnicity, 1985 and 1990.* La Jolla: UCSD Student Research and Information Office.

Eck, Elizabeth. 1992. *Math To Go: A K–6 Curriculum Linking Home and School.* Unpublished Master's thesis, University of California, San Diego.

Eder, Donna. 1981. Ability Grouping as a Self Fulfilling Prophecy: A Microanalysis of Teacher – Student Interaction. *Sociology of Education, 54:* 151–161.

Epstein, Joyce L. 1986. Parents' Reactions to Teacher Practices of Parent Involvement. *Elementary School Journal, 86* (3): 277–294.

Epstein, Joyce L. 1992. School and Family Partnerships. In *Encyclopedia of Educational Research* (6th ed., pp. 1139–1151). New York: Macmillan.

Erickson, Frederick. 1984. School Literacy, Reasoning and Civility: An Anthropologist's Perspective. *Review of Educational Research, 54* (4): 525–546.

Erickson, Frederick. 1987. Transformation and School Success: The Politics of Culture and Educational Achievement. *Anthropology and Education Quarterly, 18* (4): 335–356.

Erickson, Frederick, & Gerry Mohatt. 1982. Participant Structures in Two Communities. In George D. Spindler (Ed.), *Doing the Ethnography of Schooling* (pp.132–175). New York: Holt, Rinehart & Winston.

Erickson, Frederick, & Jeffrey Schultz. 1982. *The Counselor as Gatekeeper.* New York: Academic Press.

Erickson, Frederick, & Jeffrey Schultz. 1992. Student Experience and the Curriculum. In *The Handbook of Curriculum.* New York: Macmillan.

Escalante, Jaime, & Jack Dirmann. 1990. *The Jaime Escalante Math Program.* Washington, DC: National Education Association.

Feldman, David. 1986. *Nature's Gambit: Child Prodiges and the Development of Human Potential.* New York: Basic Books.

Fine, Michelle. 1991. *Framing Dropouts: Notes on the Politics of an Urban Public High School.* Albany, NY: SUNY Press.

Fine, Michelle. 1993. [Ap]parent Involvement: Reflections on Parents, Power and Urban Public Schools. *Teachers College Record, 94* (4): 682–710.

Finn, Chester. 1991. *We Must Take Charge.* New York: Basic Books.

Fiske, John. 1988. *Understanding Popular Culture.* Sydney: Unwin Hyman.

Flaxman, Erwin, & Morton Inger. 1991. Parents and Schooling in the 1990s. *ERIC Review, 1* (1): 2–6.

Foley, Douglas E. 1990. *Learning Capitalist Culture: Deep in the Heart of Tejas.* Philadelphia: University of Pennsylvania Press.

Foley, Douglas E. 1991. Reconsidering Anthropological Explanations of Ethnic School Failure. *Anthropology and Education Quarterly, 22* (1): 60–86.

Fordham S., & John U. Ogbu. 1986. Black Students' School Success: Coping with the Burden of Acting White. *Urban Review, 18:* 176–206.

Foster, Michelle. 1989. "It's Cookin' Now": A Performance Analysis of the Speech Events in an Urban Community College. *Language in Society, 18:* 1–29.

Freire, Paolo. 1973. *Pedagogy of the Oppressed.* Boston: Herder & Herder.

Gamaron, Adam. 1987. The Stratification of High School Learning Opportunities. *Sociology of Education, 60:* 135–155.

Gándara, Patricia. 1995. *Over the Ivy Walls: The Educational Mobility of Low-Income Chicanos.* Albany, NY: SUNY Press.

Garcia, Eugene E. 1992. "Hispanic" Children: Theoretical, Empirical and Related Policy Issues. *Educational Psychology Review, 4* (1): 69–93.

Gibson, Margaret. 1988. *Accommodation without Assimilation: Sikh Immigrants in an American High School*. Ithaca, NY: Cornell University Press.

Gibson, Margaret, & John U. Ogbu. 1991. *Minority Status and Schooling: A Comparative Study of Immigrant and Involuntary Minorities*. New York: Garland.

Giroux, Henry. 1983. *Theory and Resistance in Education*. London: Heinemann Education Books.

Giroux, Henry. 1992. *Border Crossing: Cultural Workers and the Politics of Education*. London: Routledge & Kegan Paul.

Giroux, Henry, & Peter McLaren (Eds.). 1989. *Critical Pedagogy: The State and Cultural Struggle*. Albany NY: SUNY Press.

Giroux, Henry, & Roger Simon. 1989. Popular Culture and Critical Pedagogy. In Henry Giroux & Peter McLaren (Eds.), *Critical Pedagogy: The State and Cultural Struggle* (pp. 236–252). Albany NY: SUNY Press.

Goffman, Erving. 1959. *The Presentation of Self in Everyday Life*. New York: Doubleday.

Goffman, Erving. 1964. *Asylums*. New York: Doubleday.

Goldenberg, Claude N. 1987. Low Income Hispanic Parents' Contributions to Their First Grade Children's Word-Recognition Skills. *Anthropology and Education Quarterly, 18:* 149–179.

Goldenberg, Claude, & Ronald Gallimore. 1995. Immigrant Latino Parents' Values and Beliefs about Their Children's Education: Continuities and Discontinuities across Cultures and Generations. In P. Pintrich & M. Maehr (Eds.), *Advancement in Achievement Motivation*.

Gonzalez, Norma, Luis C. Moll, Martha Floyd-Tenery, Anna Rivera, Patricia Rendon, Raquel Gonzales, & Cathy Amanti. 1993. *Teacher Research on Funds of Knowledge: Learning from Households*. Educational Practice Report No. 6. Santa Cruz: National Center for Research on Cultural Diversity and Second Language Learning.

Goodlad, John. 1983. *A Place Called School*. New York: McGraw-Hill.

Graham, Patricia. 1989. Revolution in Pedagogy. In *Preparing Schools for the 1990s: An Essay Collection*. New York: Metropolitan Life.

Haycock, Kati, & Susanne Navarro. 1988. *Unfinished Business*. Oakland, CA: Achievement Council.

Hayes, Katherine G. 1992. Attitudes toward Education: Voluntary and Involuntary Immigrants from the Same Families. *Anthropology and Education Quarterly, 23:* 250–267.

Heath, Shirley Brice. 1982. Questioning at Home and at School: A Comparative Study. In George Spindler (Ed.), *Doing the Ethnography of Schooling* (pp. 96–101). New York: Holt, Rinehart & Winston.

Heath, Shirley Brice. 1986. Sociocultural Contexts of Language Development. In *Beyond Language* (pp. 143–86). Los Angeles: California State University Evaluation, Dissemination, and Assessment Center.

Herrnstein, Richard J. 1974. *IQ in the Meritocracy.* Boston: Little Brown.

Herrnstein, Richard J., & Charles Murray. 1994. *The Bell Curve.* New York: Free Press.

Holland, Dorothy, & Margaret A. Eisenhart. 1990. *Educated in Romance: Women, Achievement and College Culture.* Chicago: University of Chicago Press.

Ima, Kenji, & Eugene M. Labovitz. 1991. *Changing Ethnic/Racial Student Composition and Test Performances: Taking Account of Increasing Student Diversity.* Paper Presented at the Pacific Sociological Association Meetings.

Jankowski, Martín Sánchez. 1991. *Islands in the Street: Gangs and American Urban Society.* Berkeley: University of California Press.

Jencks, Christopher, S. Bartlett, M. Corcoran, J. Crouse, D. Eaglesfield, G. Jackson, R. McClelland, P. Mueser, M. Olneck, J. Swartz, S. Ward, & J. Williams. 1972. *Inequality.* New York: Basic Books.

Jensen, Arthur R. 1969. How Much Can We Boost IQ and Scholastic Achievement. *Harvard Educational Review, 39* (1): 1–123.

John, Vera K. 1972. Styles of Learning – Styles of Teaching: Reflections on the Education of Navajo Children. In Courtney B. Cazden, Dell H. Hymes, & Vera K. John (Eds.), *Functions of Language in the Classroom* (pp. 331–343). New York: Columbia Teachers College Press.

Jules-Rosette, Bennetta, & Hugh Mehan. 1978. Schools and Social Structure: An Interactionist Perspective. In Michael J. Lerner (Ed.), *Advancing the Art of Inquiry in School Desegregation Research* (pp. 205–228). New York: Plenum.

Kagan, Spencer. 1986. Cooperative Learning and Sociocultural Factors in Schooling. In *Beyond Language* (pp. 231–298). Los Angeles: California State University Evaluation, Dissemination and Assessment Center.

Karabel, Jerome. 1972. Community Colleges and Social Stratification. *Harvard Educational Review, 42:* 521–562.

Knapp, Michael S., & Brenda J. Turnbull. 1990. *Better Schooling for the Children of Poverty: Alternatives to Conventional Wisdom.* Washington, DC: U.S. Department of Education.

Laboratory of Comparative Human Cognition [LCHC]. 1983. Culture and Cognitive Development. In William Kessen (Ed.), *Mussen's Handbook of*

Child Psychology: Vol. 1. History, Theory and Method (4th ed., pp. 295–356). New York: Wiley.

Labov, William. 1982. Competing Value Systems in the Inner City Schools. In Perry Gilmore & Alan Glathorn (Eds.), *Children In and Out of School: Ethnography and Education* (pp. 148–171). Washington, DC: Center for Applied Linguistics.

Lamont, Michelle, & Annette Lareau. 1988. Cultural Capital: Allusions, Gaps and Glissandos in Recent Theoretical Developments. *Theoretical Sociology, 6* (2): 153–168.

Lareau, Annette. 1989. *Home Advantage: Social Class and Parental Intervention in Elementary Education*. New York: Falmer.

Lather, Patti. 1991. *Getting Smart: Feminist Research and Pedagogy with/in the Postmodern*. Boston: Routledge & Kegan Paul.

LeCompte Margaret, & Anthony Dworkin. 1991. *Giving Up on School: Student Dropouts and Teacher Burnouts*. Newberry Park, CA: Corwin Press.

Levin, Henry M. 1986. *Educational Reform for Disadvantaged Students: An Emerging Crisis*. West Haven, CT: NEA Professional Library.

Levin, Henry M. 1987. Accelerated Schools for Disadvantaged Students. *Educational Leadership, 44* (6): 19–21.

Lewis, Dan A., & Kathryn Nakagawa. 1994. *Race and Educational Reform in the American Metropolis: A Study of School Decentralization*. Albany, NY: SUNY Press.

MacLeod, Jay. 1987. *Ain't No Makin It: Leveled Aspirations in a Low-Income Neighborhood*. Boulder, CO: Westview Press.

Marlaire, C. L., & Maynard, D. E. 1990. Standardized Testing as an Interactional Phenomenon. *Sociology of Education, 63*: 83–101.

Matuti-Bianchi, Maria Eugenia. 1986. Ethnic Identity and Patterns of School Success and Failure among Mexican-descent and Japanese American Students in a California High School: An Ethnographic Analysis. *American Journal of Education, 95*: 233–257.

McCarty, T. L., Stephen Wallace, Regina Hadley Lynch, & AnCita Benally. 1991. Classroom Inquiry and Navajo Learning Styles: A Call for Reassessment. *Anthropology and Education Quarterly, 22*: 42–59.

McDermott, R. P., Kenneth Godspodinoff, & Jeffrey Aron. 1978. Criteria for an Ethnographically Adequate Description of Concerted Activities and Their Contexts. *Semiotica, 24* (3 – 4): 245–275.

McDermott, R. P., Shelley V. Goldman, & Herve Varenne. 1984. When School Goes Home: Some Problems in the Organization of Homework. *Teachers College Record, 85* (3): 391–410.

McDonough, Patricia M. 1994. Buying and Selling Higher Education. *Journal of Higher Education, 65* (4): 427–447.

McLaren, Peter. 1989. *Life in Schools*. New York: Longman.

McLaughlin, Milbray W., & Patrick M. Shields. 1987. Involving Low Income Parents in the Schools: A Role for Policy? *Phi Delta Kappan, 69:* 156–160.

Mehan, Hugh. 1978. Structuring School Structure. *Harvard Educational Review, 45* (1): 311–338.

Mehan, Hugh. 1979. *Learning Lessons: The Social Organization of Classroom Instruction.* Cambridge, MA: Harvard University Press.

Mehan, Hugh. 1992. Understanding Inequality in Schools: The Contribution of Interpretive Studies. *Sociology of Education, 65* (1): 1–20.

Mehan, Hugh, Alma J. Hertweck, & J. Lee Meihls. 1985. *Handicapping the Handicapped: Decision Making in Students' Careers.* Stanford, CA: Stanford University Press.

Mehan, Hugh, & Houston Wood. 1975. *The Reality of Ethnomethodology.* New York: Wiley Interscience.

Mehan, Hugh, Jane R. Mercer, & Robert Rueda. In press. Special Education. In *Encyclopedia of Sociology and Education.* New York: Garland.

Mercer, Jane. 1974. *Labeling the Mentally Retarded.* Berkeley: University of California Press.

Michaels, Sarah. 1981. Sharing Time: Children's Narrative Styles and Differential Access to Literacy. *Language in Society, 10:* 423–442.

Michels, Robert. 1949. *Political Parties.* Glencoe, IL: Free Fress.

Moll, Luis C., & Stephen Díaz. 1987. Change as the Goal of Educational Research. *Anthropology and Education Quarterly, 18:* 300–311.

Moll, L. C., C. Vélez-Ibáñez, & J. Greenberg. 1988. *Project Implementation Plan: Community Knowledge and Classroom Practice: Combining Resources for Literacy Instruction.* Tucson: University of Arizona.

Moll, L. C., C. Vélez-Ibáñez, & J. Greenberg. 1989. *Fieldwork Summary: Community Knowledge and Classroom Practice: Combining Resources for Literacy Instruction.* Tucson: University of Arizona.

Moll, L. C., C. Amanti, D. Neff, & N. Gonzalez. 1992. Funds of Knowledge: Using a Qualitative Approach to Connect Homes and Classrooms. *Theory into Practice, 31* (2): 132–141.

More, A. J. 1989. Native Indian Learning Styles: A Review for Researchers and Teachers. *Journal of American Indian Education, 3:* 15–28.

Morrell, Darlene. 1990. *Research Note: First Quarter Performance of First Time Freshmen.* San Diego: University of California Student Research and Information Office.

Murray, Charles. 1984. *Losing Ground: American Social Policy, 1950–1980*. New York: Basic Books.

Ninio, A., & J. Bruner. 1978. The Achievement and Antecedents of Labeling. *Journal of Child Language, 5:* 5–15.

Oakes, Jeannie. 1985. *Keeping Track: How Schools Structure Inequality*. New Haven, CT: Yale University Press.

Oakes, Jeannie, Adam Gamoran, & Reba N. Page. 1992. Curriculum Differentiation: Opportunities, Outcomes and Meanings. In Philip Jackson (Ed.), *Handbook of Research on Curriculum* (pp. 570–608). New York: Macmillan.

Oakes, Jeannie, & Amy Wells. In preparation. *Beyond Sorting and Stratification: Creating Alternatives to Tracking in Racially Mixed Secondary Schools*.

Ogbu, John. 1978. *Minority Education and Caste: The American System in Cross-Cultural Perspective*. New York: Academic Press.

Ogbu, John U. 1987a. Variability in Minority School Performance: A Problem in Search of an Explanation. *Anthropology and Education Quarterly, 18* (4): 312–334.

Ogbu, John U. 1987b. Variability in Minority Responses to Schooling: Nonimmigrants vs. Immigrants. In George Spindler & Louise Spindler (Eds.), *Interpretive Ethnography at Home and Abroad* (pp. 225–280). Hillsdale NJ.: Erlbaum.

Ogbu, John U. 1991. Immigrant and Involuntary Minorities in Comparative Perspective. In M. Gibson & J. Ogbu (Eds.), *Minority Status and Schooling*. New York: Garland.

Ogbu, John U. 1992. Understanding Cultural Diversity and Learning. *Educational Researcher, 22:* 5–14, 24.

Ogbu, John U., & Maria Eugenia Matuti-Bianchi. 1986. Understanding Sociocultural Factors: Knowledge, Identity and School Adjustment. In *Beyond Language* (pp. 73–142). Los Angeles: California State University Evaluation, Dissemination and Assessment Center.

Page, Reba N., & Linda Valli. 1990. *Curriculum Differentiation*. Albany NY: SUNY Press.

Parsons, Talcott. 1959. The School Classroom as a Social System. *Harvard Educational Review, 29:* 297–318.

Pelavin, Sol H., & Michael Kane. 1990. *Changing the Odds: Factors Increasing Access to College*. New York: College Entrance Examination Board.

Peterson, D. 1989. *Parent Involvement in the Educational Process*. Urbana, IL: ERIC Clearinghouse on Educational Management.

Piestrup, Ann. 1973. *Black Dialect Interference and Accommodation of Reading*

Instruction in the First Grade. Monograph No. 4. Berkeley: University of California, Language Behavior Research Lab.

Philips, Susan U. 1982. *The Invisible Culture: Communication in Classroom and Community on the Warmsprings Indian Reservation.* New York: Longman.

Pollner, Melvin. 1987. *Mundane Reason.* Cambridge: Cambridge University Press.

Poole, Deborah. 1994. Differentiation as an Interactional Consequence of Routine Classroom Testing. *Qualitative Studies in Education,* 7 (1): 1–17.

Rose, Mike. 1990. *Lives on the Boundary.* New York: Free Press.

Roseberry, Ann S., Beth Warren, & Faith R. Conant. 1992. Appropriating Scientific Discourse: Findings from Language Minority Classrooms. *Journal of the Learning Sciences,* 2 (10): 61–94.

Rosenbaum, James M. 1976. *Making Inequality.* New York: Wiley.

Rothman, David. 1980. *Conscience and Convenience.* Boston: Little Brown.

Rumbaut, Ruben, & Kenji Ima. 1988. *The Adaptation of Southeast Asian Refugee Youth: A Comparative Study.* San Diego: San Diego State University.

Sarason, Seymour B. 1982. *The Culture of the School and the Problem of Change.* Boston: Allyn & Bacon.

Sarason, Seymour B. 1991. *The Predictable Failure of Educational Reform.* San Francisco: Jossey-Bass.

Schlossman, Steven. 1976. *Before Home-Start: Notes toward a Theory of Parent Education in America, 1897–1929.* Unpublished manuscript.

Schutz, Alfred. 1966. *Collected Papers.* The Hague: Nijhoff.

Scribner, Sylvia, & Michael Cole. 1974. *Culture and Cognition.* New York: Wiley Interscience.

Selznick, Phillip. 1949. *TVA and the Grassroots.* Berkeley: University of California Press.

Sewell, W. H., & R. M. Hauser. 1975. Education, Occupation: Achievement in the Early Career. New York: Academic Press.

Shogren, Elizabeth. 1994. Richard Riley: Rebuilding the Nation's Public Education System. *Los Angeles Times,* February 13, M3.

Sizer, Theodore R. 1984. *Horace's Compromise: The Dilemma of the American High School.* Boston: Houghton Mifflin.

Sizer, Theodore R. 1992. *Horace's School: Redesigning the American High School.* New York: Houghton Mifflin.

Slavin, Robert E. 1990. Achievement Effects of Ability Grouping in Secondary Schools: A Best Evidence Synthesis. *Review of Educational Research,* 60 (3): 471–499.

Slavin, Robert E., Nancy L. Karweit, & Nancy A. Madden. 1989. *Effective Programs for Students at Risk.*. Boston: Allyn & Bacon.

Solomon, R. Patrick. 1992. *Black Resistance in School: Forging a Separatist Culture.* Albany: SUNY Press.

Stanton-Salazar, Ricardo, Olga Vasquez, & Hugh Mehan. 1996. Engineering Success with Institutional Support. In Aida Hurtado (Ed.), *Latino Eligibility Task Force Report.* Santa Cruz, CA: Regents of the University of California.

Stevenson, D., & D. Baker. 1987. The Family–School Relation and the Child's School Performance. *Child Development, 58:* 1348–1357.

Suarez-Orosco, Marcelo. 1989. *Central-American Refugees and US High Schools: A Psychosocial Study of Motivation and Achievement.* Stanford, CA: Stanford University Press.

Swanson, Mary Catherine. No date. *AVID: A College Prepatory Program for Underrepresented Students.* San Diego: San Diego County Office of Education.

Tharp, R. G. 1989. Culturally Compatible Education: A Formula for Designing Effective Classrooms. In Henry T. Trueba, George Spindler, & Louise Spindler (Eds.), *What do Anthropologists Have to Say about Dropouts?* (pp 51–66). New York: Falmer.

Tharp, Roland, & Ronald Gallimore. 1988. *Rousing Minds to Life: Teaching, Learning and Schooling in Social Context.* Cambridge: Cambridge University Press.

Trueba, Henry T. 1988. Culturally Based Explanations of Minority Students' Academic Achievement. *Anthropology and Education Quarterly, 19* (3): 270–287.

Turner, Ralph H. 1960. Sponsored and Contest Mobility and the School System. *American Sociological Review, 25:* 855–867.

U.S. Department of Labor's Secretary's Commission on Achieving Necessary Skills. 1992. *Learning a Living: What Work Requires of Schools.* Washington, DC: U.S. Government Printing Office.

Villanueva, Irene. 1990. *Cultural Practices and Language Use: Three Generations of Change.* Unpublished doctoral dissertation, University of California, San Diego.

Vogt, L. A., C. Jordan, & R. Tharp. 1987. Explaining School Failure, Producing School Success: Two Cases. *Anthropology and Education Quarterly, 18* (4): 276–288.

Vygotsky, L. S. 1978. *Mind in Society: The Development of Higher Psychological Processes.* Michael Cole, Vera John-Steiner, Sylvia Scribner, & E. Souberman (Eds.). Cambridge, MA: Harvard University Press.

243

Wagner, Jon. 1990. Sprucewood High's First Year: A Report to the STL Foundation. Davis: University of California CRESS Center.

Wehlage, Gary G., Robert A. Rutter, Gregory A. Smith, Nancy Lesko, & Ricardo R. Fernandez. 1989. *Reducing the Risk: Schools as Communities of Support.* Philadelphia: Falmer.

Weiler, Kathleen. 1985. *Women Teaching for Change: Gender, Class and Power.* New York: Bergin & Garvey.

Weis, Lois. 1985. *Between Two Worlds: Black Students in an Urban Community College.* New York: Routledge & Kegan Paul.

Weis, Lois. 1990. *Working Class without Work: High School Students in a De-Industralizing Economy.* New York: Routledge & Kegan Paul.

Weston, Natalie D. 1992. *The Home-School Library: Improving the Educational Success of Students through Family Involvement.* Unpublished Master's Thesis. La Jolla, University of California, San Diego.

Wheelock, Anne. 1992. *Crossing the Tracks: How "Untracking" Can Save America's Schools.* New York: New Press.

Wilcox, Kathleen. 1982. Differential Socialization in the Classroom: Implications for Educational Opportunity. In George Spindler & Louise Spindler (Eds.), *Doing the Ethnography of Schooling* (pp. 268–309). New York: Harcourt, Brace, World.

Willis, Paul. 1977. *Learning to Labor: How Working Class Kids Get Working Class Jobs.* Westmead, England: Saxon House.

Wilson, William Julius. 1987. *The Truly Disadvantaged.* Chicago: University of Chicago Press.

Wood, D., J. S. Bruner, & G. Ross. 1976. The Role of Tutoring in Problem Solving. *Journal of Child Psychology and Psychiatry, 17:* 89–100.

Young, M. F. K. 1971. *Knowledge and Control.* London: Routledge & Kegan Paul.

Zald, Mayer, & Patricia Denton. 1963. From Evangelicism to General Service: The Transformation of the YMCA. *Administrative Science Quarterly, 8:* 214–234.

INDEX